LIVING
HERALDRY

LIVING HERALDRY

THE ANCIENT ART AND ITS
MODERN APPLICATIONS

STEPHEN SLATER

southwater

THIS BOOK IS DEDICATED TO MA, THE DOGS,
ALAN AND THE GANG OF FOUR

This edition is published by Southwater

Southwater is an imprint of Anness Publishing Ltd
Hermes House, 88–89 Blackfriars Road, London SE1 8HA
tel. 020 7401 2077; fax 020 7633 9499
www.southwaterbooks.com; info@anness.com

© Anness Publishing Ltd 2004

UK agent: The Manning Partnership Ltd
6 The Old Dairy, Melcombe Road, Bath BA2 3LR
tel. 01225 478444; fax 01225 478440
sales@manning-partnership.co.uk

UK distributor: Grantham Book Services Ltd
Isaac Newton Way, Alma Park Industrial Estate,
Grantham, Lincs NG31 9SD
tel. 01476 541080; fax 01476 541061
orders@gbs.tbs-ltd.co.uk

North American agent/distributor: National Book Network
4501 Forbes Boulevard, Suite 200, Lanham, MD 20706
tel. 301 459 3366; fax 301 429 5746
www.nbnbooks.com

Australian agent/distributor: Pan Macmillan Australia
Level 18, St Martins Tower, 31 Market St, Sydney, NSW 2000
tel. 1300 135 113; fax 1300 135 103
customer.service@macmillan.com.au

New Zealand agent/distributor: David Bateman Ltd
30 Tarndale Grove, Off Bush Road, Albany, Auckland
tel. (09) 415 7664; fax (09) 415 8892

A CIP catalogue record for this book is available
from the British Library.

Previously published as part of a larger volume,
The Complete Book of Heraldry

Publisher: Joanna Lorenz
Senior Editor: Joanne Rippin
Project Editor: Elizabeth Woodland
Editor: Beverley Jollands
Illustrators: Antony Duke, Marco Foppoli,
and Alfred Znamierowski (for details see page 157)
Designer: Nigel Partridge
Production Controller: Darren Price

1 3 5 7 9 10 8 6 4 2

CONTENTS

INTRODUCTION

A product of the medieval battlefield and tournament, heraldry has been called both the "shorthand of history" and "the noble science". It is best defined as a hereditary system of colours and symbols used for personal identification.

No one knows exactly where or when heraldry was born, but its origins are usually attributed to an area of northern Europe, around the Low Countries and northern France, in the mid-12th century. At this time Europe was in an almost constant state of conflict arising from dynastic and territorial disputes. The armoured formation needed for battle was provided by the knights, skilled horsemen who raised troops of fighting men from the lands they were granted by their monarchs in return for military support. Medieval warfare consisted largely of hand-to-hand fighting with swords, axes and maces, and armour gave the knight some protection. However, it also made him unrecognizable to his own forces, and the first heraldic devices – simple geometric patterns painted on the knights' shields – may have been intended to aid identification in the confusion of battle.

By the second half of the 12th century, the nobles of Europe were starting to place upon their shields devices – known as "charges" – such as chevrons and lions, which then became associated with their families. As the marrying of shield and symbol became hereditary, what we now recognize as heraldry was born. Over the next two centuries it grew in sophistication and spread to every part of the knight's accoutrements, decorating not just his shield but the extravagant crest on his helmet and the embroidered surcoat he wore over his armour. Even his horse would be decorated with his coat of arms. Meanwhile, a knight's or lord's followers wore his personal livery and badge to proclaim their allegiance and impress his power upon his enemies and rivals.

Fighting men needed to be trained, and this was the purpose of the tournament, a series of contests that reflected the modes of contemporary warfare. The noblest event was the joust, in which two mounted knights bearing lances rode against each other. This prestigious sport was an excellent opportunity for the ruling class to show off their armorial bearings, and the display of finery soon gained the notice of the officials who helped marshal the tournament: the heralds. In due course they became the acknowledged experts on the subject, and the whole study of matters armorial became known as heraldry. The heralds compiled detailed "rolls of arms" that identified all who bore them, and as heraldry developed into an organized science they were empowered to regulate its use and display.

Though new methods of fighting and changing fashions in armour meant that heraldry had lost its original function on the battlefield by 1500, it continued to be used by noble families as an indicator of bloodlines and status. The "quartering" of shields recorded alliances through marriage, and arms could also show a family's history by including charges derived from royal rewards or notable exploits.

The art of heraldic display embraced not just the shield but all the other symbolic elements that go to make up an "achievement of arms": the helmet with its mantling and wreath, the splendid crest that surmounts it, the motto and the supporters. It delivered a graphic message of dignity and power, and the noble families of Europe used it none too subtly to stamp their authority over their lands and tenants. For the same reason it was eagerly adopted by institutions. The personal arms of sovereigns became national symbols, while civic authorities used heraldry to establish their standing and sometimes to assert their independence. The Church was quick to adopt the symbolism of heraldry, and the religious chivalric orders that grew up at the time of the Crusades acquired arms and insignia heavy with religious imagery. Military forces everywhere have preserved the heraldic traditions of their medieval forebears, but unwarlike professions such as medicine, law and education are equally keen to appropriate coats of arms for their learned societies and institutions.

Heraldry has been adapted to serve the customs and art forms of successive ages, and continues to do so today. This book surveys the many different uses that have been found for it, by individuals and institutions all over the world. It has long excited the imagination and can still inspire admiration, jealousy or derision. Some see heraldry as a quaint pleasantry, others as a snobbish anachronism, but it is certainly a survivor, and still has the power to evoke a noble past.

FEAR · GOD · HONOUR · THE · KING

THE LANGUAGE OF HERALDRY

Many people are baffled by the language used by heraldists in the English-speaking world. In many countries it relies heavily on Norman French, the language of William the Conqueror, which was spoken by the nobility in much of Europe during the period when heraldry was evolving. To take one example, "Vert three estoiles Or" would be the correct way to describe a green shield upon which were three gold stars with wavy rays, yet none of the descriptive words are English. In other nations, such as Germany, heraldic language is much nearer to modern-day usage.

The language of heraldry is known in the English-speaking world as "blazonry", from the old German word *blasen,* meaning to blow a horn. At a tournament, it was the duty of the medieval herald to call out the names, titles, genealogy and arms of the participating knights, accompanied by a flourish of trumpets, and the word thus also came to mean a public proclamation.

◀ *The unusual crest of the Davenport family of Capesthorne, England – showing an anonymous felon on his way to execution.*

COLOURS, METALS AND FUR

Heraldic language – no less vivid than the contrasting colours and bright metals of heraldry itself – paints a word picture of the luxurious accoutrements of medieval nobles. The terms suggest exotic and costly goods imported from the far corners of the known world, such as sable – the sleek, black fur of the marten, brought by merchants from far-off Muscovy – or gules, the rose-red dye produced in Persia and Turkey. The general term used to define all colours and textures on a shield of arms is equally picturesque and evocative: colours, metals and furs are together known as "tinctures", a word that at one time meant a dye or tint.

COLOURS AND METALS

To begin the "blazoning", or description in heraldic terms, of any shield of arms, it is necessary to deal with colour, since the very first word used in the description refers to the colour of the background or "field"

▲ *Two good examples of the reason behind the rule against colour on colour. From a distance identification would be very difficult.*

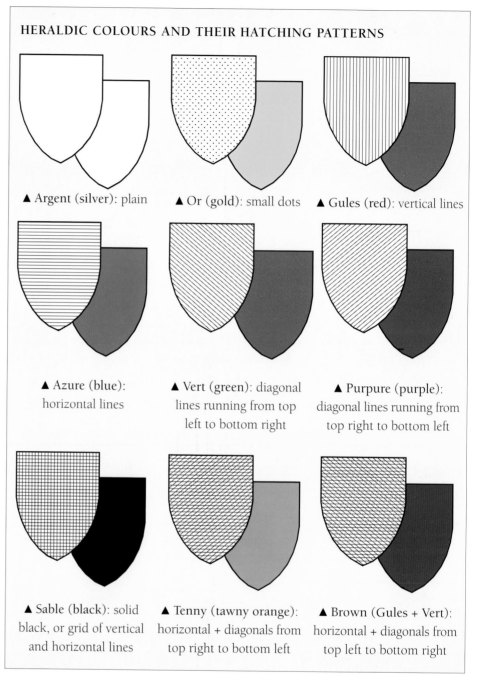

HERALDIC COLOURS AND THEIR HATCHING PATTERNS

▲ Argent (silver): plain

▲ Or (gold): small dots

▲ Gules (red): vertical lines

▲ Azure (blue): horizontal lines

▲ Vert (green): diagonal lines running from top left to bottom right

▲ Purpure (purple): diagonal lines running from top right to bottom left

▲ Sable (black): solid black, or grid of vertical and horizontal lines

▲ Tenny (tawny orange): horizontal + diagonals from top right to bottom left

▲ Brown (Gules + Vert): horizontal + diagonals from top left to bottom right

of the shield. There are five main colours in heraldry (although this differs slightly from nation to nation): red, blue, black, green and purple. Some mixed colours, known as stains, are also sometimes used. The two metals – gold and silver – are usually depicted as yellow and white. In British heraldry Norman French names are used for colours and metals, though gold and silver are also sometimes used in blazonry instead of "Or" and "Argent".

The colour green has intrigued heraldic writers for centuries. Some suggest that it

was actually unknown in early heraldry, yet one of the earliest compilations of arms, illustrating the *Historia Anglorum* (written between 1250–59 by an English cleric, Matthew Paris), clearly shows the shield of one of chivalry's greatest names, William Marshal, with a field of gold and green.

THE RULE OF TINCTURES

An important heraldic principle governs the use of colours and metals: "Never place a colour on a colour or a metal on a metal". It is a very sensible rule, remembering that the original purpose of heraldry was quick and ready identification on the battlefield. Life could depend on it. A blue charge on a black field, for example, or gold on silver, would be difficult to distinguish in the melée of medieval warfare. However, as long as the charge lies partly on an opposite – such as a red lion on a field of gold and blue – this does not constitute a breaking of the rule.

The rule is not strictly observed in some countries, and Archbishop Bruno Heim in his book *Or and Argent* (1994) gives many examples of gold charges on a white field, the most famous being the arms of Jerusalem. Some heraldic writers have suggested, however, that the gold crosses on this shield were originally red, but that medieval painting methods and materials caused the red to oxidize, causing later heraldists to mistake the original colour.

HERALDIC FURS

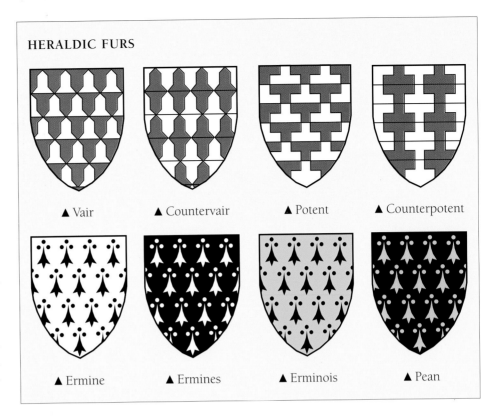

▲ Vair   ▲ Countervair   ▲ Potent   ▲ Counterpotent

▲ Ermine   ▲ Ermines   ▲ Erminois   ▲ Pean

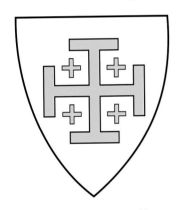

▲ *The arms of Jerusalem, possibly an exception to the rule against metal on metal, allowed because of the holiness of the city.*

FURS

In addition to the colours and metals, heraldry makes use of "furs" – patterns that suggest the costly furs worn by the medieval nobility. The two main furs are "ermine" and "vair", and each has several derivatives. Fur, just like a coloured field, can have any variety of charges placed upon it, and can take the place of either metal or colour.

Ermine is the highly prized winter fur of the common stoat. The animal's coat changes colour from chestnut brown to white except for the tip of its tail, which remains black. In heraldry, ermine is shown as a white field strewn with little black tail-tips, usually accompanied by

three black dots, which represent the fastenings by which the pelts were sewn into a robe. Ermine by itself constitutes the arms of the dukes of Brittany and makes a simple but splendid appearance in *The Book of Tourneys* of King René of Anjou.

Vair is indicated by a white and blue pattern said to represent the pelts of a species of squirrel, the blue-grey fur from its back arranged alternately with the paler fur from its underbelly. Vair was the arms of the Beauchamp family of Somerset, England and is often included in the quarterings of Henry VIII's wife, Jane Seymour.

▲ *A real piece of vair, the fur made from the back and fronts of squirrel pelts sewn into a warm and handsome covering, from which the heraldic fur is derived.*

HATCHING AND TRICKING

It is, of course, not always possible to use colour in depictions of arms, and various methods of identifying heraldic colours in black and white have been used. The two most common are known as "hatching" and "tricking". Silvestro de Petra Sancta, a 17th-century Jesuit writer, devised the method of showing colours represented by lines and dots, which was later named hatching, and which has been universally used.

A simple description of a shield of arms can also be made by tricking: this involves a sketch of the arms being annotated with abbreviations for each colour, as in the example below. In this system azure becomes az, gules gu and so on.

▲ *An example of the tricking of a crest, where each colour is denoted by the letters of the heraldic tincture.*

THE DIVISION OF THE FIELD

The entire surface of the heraldic shield is known as the field, and its tincture is always described first in blazonry. It is said that the simplest arms are the best, and indeed there have been cases where an ancient family has borne for its arms a shield of just a single plain colour. The most famous example is probably the noble French family of d'Albret, which bore a shield simply Gules, while the English knight Sir Thomas Holland (1320–60) abandoned his ancient family arms in favour of a plain shield Sable.

Of course, to allow for the numerous variations needed to ensure that every shield is unique, a more elaborate scheme is usually required. Any number of motifs, known as charges, may be placed on the field, from basic geometric shapes to representations of any object, animate or inanimate. Whether or not charges appear, the field may be divided into sections of different colours.

DESCRIBING THE DIVISIONS

When the shield is divided, or "parted", into various simple divisions or blocks, this is signalled by the words "party per" (divided by), or more simply "per", followed by the particular nature of the division, such as "party per chevron" (divided by a chevron) or "party per pale" (divided in half vertically). The descriptions of the

▼ *The field of the Fisher family of Lancashire is diapered with little fishes.*

▲ *The later version of the d'Albret family arms, the 2nd and 3rd quarters are the original arms – here hatched to represent gules – the 1st and 4th quarters were augmented by the King of France.*

divisions utilize the names given to the corresponding "ordinaries" – the fundamental geometric charges (see opposite). Where the shield is parted in an even number of small divisions the number of divisions is then specified, such as "bendy of six"; "paly of eight"; "barry of ten". Any parted field can bear another charge or charges of either a metal or a colour, without breaking the metal-on-metal, colour-on-colour rule.

In spite of their simplicity, it is quite possible for one of these basic divisions of the shield to comprise a family arms. For at least 650 years, the ancient English family of Waldegrave has used a shield that is simply Per pale Argent and Gules (a shield divided in half, one half silver, one half red). The Scottish dukes of Argyll, Chiefs of the Clan Campbell, bear Gyronny of eight Or and Sable; the Campbells of London bear Gyronny of eight ermine and Gules, and the Swedish family of Natt och Dag ("night and day") derived its name from its simple shield Per fess Or and Azure (divided in two horizontally, one half blue for night and one half gold for day).

DIAPERING

Where a shield has a large expanse of field, the artist often adds textural interest with a faint overall pattern. This technique is called "diapering", and can lead to the most beautiful of heraldic art forms as long as the pattern is not mistaken for part of the heraldic design.

SHIELD DIVISIONS

The simplest way of creating arms that are distinct from any other, is to divide the surface of the shield into two parts by a line, one part a metal – gold or silver – the other a colour. Further variations can be made by subdividing the shield with more lines, and varying the edges of the lines in many ways. The option of adding furs to the variations makes the possibilities for new but simple geometric designs almost endless.

▲ (Party) per pale

▲ (Party) per fess

▲ (Party) per bend

▲ (Party) per bend sinister

▲ (Party) per chevron

▲ (Party) per saltire

▲ Tierced per pale

▲ Tierced per fess

▲ Quarterly

▲ Gyronny

▲ Barry (six)

▲ Bendy (six)

▲ Bendy sinister

▲ Paly

▲ Chevronny

▲ Chequy

▲ Lozengy

▲ Barry bendy

▲ Paly bendy

▲ Gyronny of twelve

▲ Pily

Pily bendy

▲ Pily bendy sinister

THE HONOURABLE ORDINARIES

The most simple charges, or devices, found on the heraldic shield are geometric patterns called the ordinaries. These charges have long been considered to hold a special place in heraldry, hence the appellation "honourable". The ordinary normally occupies about one-third of the area of the shield, and can be borne alone or in conjunction with other charges. It can also itself bear further charges. In blazonry, the ordinary is always mentioned directly after the field.

Various theories about the origins of the ordinaries have been put forward, including the fanciful suggestion that the chevron, for example, is a charge suitable for the head of a family who gives shelter to other family members. An interesting but unexplained visual clue lies in a Roman mosaic representing the amphitheatre of Lyons in France (and now in the city's museum). The mosaic shows a wooden palisade around the arena that contains many of the ordinaries and subordinaries found in heraldry. Whether there is a link between a Roman geometrical conceit and heraldry, or if it is just a curious coincidence is still debated.

VARIATIONS ON THE ORDINARIES

Some of the ordinaries, such as the bands, can also be borne in smaller forms in pairs or more. These diminutive ordinaries have names that reflect their nature, so that chevrons give rise to chevronels, pales to pallets and two or more bends are described as bendlets. Any ordinary can be "voided" by having its centre removed to reveal the field or another tincture; it can also be "fimbriated", that is, edged with a narrow band of another tincture.

THE CROSS

The heraldic cross is formed by a combination of the "fess" (horizontal band) and the "pale" (vertical band). In its simple form it is set centrally on the shield, with each limb extending to one edge. The cross has bred more variants than any other

THE ORDINARIES
Although various writers quibble about the exact number of ordinaries, the following selection, with their diminutives behind them, is generally considered to be a complete list:

▲ The chief ▲ The pale and pallets

▲ Fess ▲ 2 bars ▲ A barrulet ▲ Bend ▲ 3 bendlets ▲ A riband

▲ Bend sinister ▲ 2 bendlets sinister ▲ Chevron ▲ 3 chevronels ▲ Saltire ▲ A fillet saltire

▲ Pall ▲ A fillet pall ▲ Cross ▲ A fillet cross ▲ Pile ▲ 3 piles in point

charge: some writers say there are over 30 variants, others over 50, while one 19th-century writer listed 450. Apart from the simple cross the most commonly met with are the "cross" patty (or "formy") where the four limbs are wide at their heads but narrow towards the central join, and the Maltese or eight-pointed cross, which is similar to the former except that the heads

of the limbs are notched at their centres. If the bottom limb of the cross narrows to a point it is said to be "fitched". Crosses patty and "crosslet" can often be found with this variant, and are then described as a "cross patty fitchy" or a "cross crosslet fitchy".

▶ A Flemish armorial c1560 showing ordinaries and divisions of the field.

VARIATIONS ON THE CROSS

▲ Cross potent:
T-shaped limbs,
resembling crutches.

▲ Cross patonce:
Concave, tapered
limbs, with each head
divided into three.

▲ Cross fleury or
flory: the accentuated
points end in the form
of a fleur de lis.

▲ Cross crosslet: The
heads of each limb are
themselves crossed.

▲ Cross bottony:
Straight limbs, each
headed with three
roundels or buttons.

▲ Formy (Patty)

▲ Maltese

▲ Moline

▲ Pommée

▲ Fleuretty

THE SUB-ORDINARIES

The lesser geometric charges are known as the "sub-ordinaries"; they can be borne singly or in groups according to their nature. The sub-ordinaries are deemed the less common of the geometric patterns found on shields of arms, but like many of the honourable ordinaries, most of them owe their origins to the construction of the medieval shield.

The most non-controversial sub-ordinaries are the "canton" (and its larger cousin, the quarter), the "bordure", the "inescutcheon", the "orle" and the "tressure". The last four are probably reminders of metal reinforcements that were part of the structure of the medieval shield. Other writers have also included further charges in the list of the sub-ordinaries, including the "lozenge" and its derivatives, the "rustre", "mascle", and "fusil", the "gyron", the "pairle", the "billet" and "flanches".

The bordure, or border, is simply that: a border around the edge of the shield. In Scottish heraldry the bordure is often used as a means of identifying junior branches of the family, the bordure bearing charges taken from the arms of the mother. A similar practice is found in Spanish and Portuguese heraldry, where the bordure may even include small shields of arms of near relatives.

The inescutcheon is a small shield borne as a charge. It may be plain or may bear other charges and may be in any number, not just single. The arms of Burrell, Baron Gwydir, make use of this and another sub-ordinary, blazoned Vert on each of three escutcheons Argent a bordure engrailed Or, while the family of Hay, Earl of Erroll, High Constable of Scotland, are blazoned Argent three escutcheons Gules.

The orle appears as an inner border set between the middle and edge of the shield. French heraldists also call it a faux, or false, escutcheon, or inescutcheon voided.

The tressure is really little more than a narrow orle and often appears in pairs in Scottish heraldry where, garnished with fleurs de lis, it is usually associated with the royal arms of Scotland and other families allied to the Scottish monarchy through marriage.

The canton is a square or rectangle in the dexter chief corner of the shield, smaller than the less-common quarter. The canton often bears other charges and in the heraldry of some nations can be used to denote certain relationships.

Flanches are always borne in pairs, and are formed by arcs on each side of the shield extending from the upper corner to a point slightly to the side of the base.

The lozenge is a diamond-shaped charge that has several variants, the most common of which is the mascle – a lozenge with its centre removed to show the field. A rustre is a lozenge pierced with a circular opening, and a fusil is an elongated lozenge. A field patterned overall with lozenges is called "lozengy"; with squares it is "chequy".

A billet is a small elongated rectangular

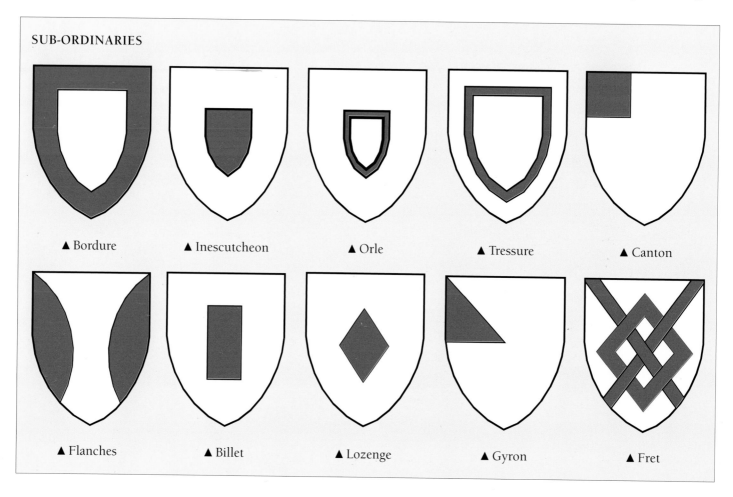

SUB-ORDINARIES

▲ Bordure ▲ Inescutcheon ▲ Orle ▲ Tressure ▲ Canton

▲ Flanches ▲ Billet ▲ Lozenge ▲ Gyron ▲ Fret

figure. Numerous billets are often strewn across the field, described as "billety".

The gyron is a triangular charge that seldom appears singly. Usually the shield is divided into a number of gyrons, arranged like the sails of a windmill, and the field is described as "gyronny of [the number of pieces]". The most famous example of a gyronny coat is that of the Scottish family of Campbell, who bear Gyronny of eight Or and Sable. Branches of the family often charge the gyrons with other charges or vary their edges and colours.

The "fret" is formed of interlaced bendlets and bendlets sinister. It can be encountered in the singular but is more often repeated to cover the whole field in an interlacing pattern, which resembles a garden trellis; this is then described as "fretty".

OVERALL PATTERNS

Generally, if charges are repeated on a shield, their number tends to be less than ten, and is specified in the blazon. Furthermore, they are usually placed within the perimeter of the shield so that they appear in their entirety. Sometimes, however, small charges – which may be of any kind – are strewn in a plentiful degree all over the shield. This effect is described as "semy".

There are special terms for the strewing of certain charges. For example, a shield strewn with billets is billety and one strewn with fleur de lis is semy de lis. Any object, no matter how humble or curious, can be strewn across the shield – such as semy of coffee beans in the arms of the district of Haut Ogooué in Gabon.

ROUNDELS

Plain round charges called "roundels" are depicted in heraldic colours and metals. Whereas in most heraldics the roundel is described simply in its true colour, English blazonry has a distinct name for each roundel. The "bezant", or gold roundel, is said to be named after the gold coin of Byzantium, while the "torteau", or red roundel, resembles a tartlet. A blue roundel is a "hurt", which may refer either to a bruise or to a hurtleberry (blueberry). Droplets are a variation of the roundel, and look something like tadpoles. They are known as "gouttés". Once again, in English heraldry Norman French is utilized: red droplets are goutté de sang – drops of blood – gold droplets are goutté d'or. A roundel bearing blue and white wavy bars is often used to denote water: this is termed the "fountain". It is seen in the arms of the Sykes family, since a "syke" is a spring or fountain.

The English family of Stourton makes use of fountains and a bend to tell the story of their ancient estate. Six springs rise at Stourhead, forming the source of the River Stour: three were originally inside the estate boundary, the other three outside. The Stourton arms, Sable a bend Or between six fountains, neatly describes the geography and history of the estate.

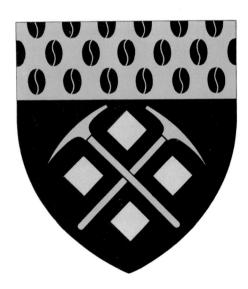

▲ The nine billets, and fiddle, on the arms of the family of Winter of Bohlanden.

▲ A novel use of semy – the chief in the shield of the Gabonaise region of Haut Ogooué is semy of coffee beans.

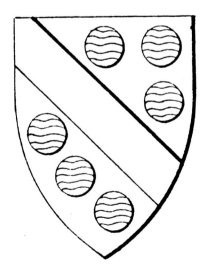

▲ The six fountains and bend in the arms of the Stourton family reflect the position on the family property of six springs. A sketched map above explains the pattern.

LINES OF PARTITION

Heraldry is nothing if not inventive and over the centuries its regulators have come up with every possible method to ensure that each shield of arms can be unique. This is especially true of the many ways that a shield can be divided. To increase the number of possible variations, the edges of the divisions and the ordinaries, which are known as "lines of partition", can be drawn in many different styles.

Partition lines make the fullest use of the edges of the ordinaries and they are considered sufficiently distinctive for unrelated families to have a coat of arms that is identical in colour and ordinary, but with different edges. For example, a green cross with straight edges on a white shield may belong to a family unrelated to one whose white shield bears a green cross with wavy edges. In fact, lines are included in the blazon only if they are not straight.

Apart from the styles shown here, in recent years new lines of partition have been evolved by the heraldic artists of Scandinavia, South Africa and Canada.

COUNTERCHANGING

One of the most enjoyable stratagems in blazon is a partitioned shield that is counterchanged. Counterchanging is the

▲ *Counterchanging in practice on the shield of a community in Greenland. The shield here is divided per fess.*

COMMON LINES OF PARTITION

The following shields show a selection of the many ways in which the heraldic division can be varied.

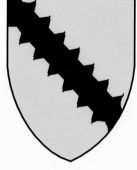

▲ Engrailed: scalloped, points facing outwards.

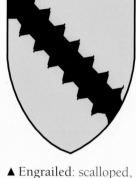

▲ Invected: as engrailed, points facing inwards.

▲ Dancetty: large saw-like points.

▲ Indented: small saw-like points.

▲ Wavy: like a wave.

▲ Embattled/crenelly: like battlements.

▲ Nebuly: cloudlike.

▲ Raguly: loglike.

▲ Dovetailed

▲ Rayonné: like flames.

▲ Urdy: serrated.

dividing of the shield in such a manner that it is part of a metal and part of a colour, and then by arranging the charges in such a manner that they be reciprocally of the same colour and metal. This sounds a complicated business, but counterchanging can in fact be one of the simplest and most effective ways of varying one very simple shield of arms from another.

The arms of the Anglo-Norman family of d'Abitot provide an example of how counterchanging can produce a striking design. The d'Abitot arms are Per pale Or and Gules three roundels counterchanged. They should be compared with the non-counterchanged alternatives, which are the arms of the Courtenay family (Or three torteaux) and its opposite, the arms of Dynham (Gules three bezants).

These three personal shields show how a certain configuration of charges can be changed through tincture. The families to which each shield belongs most probably bore no relation to each other, although changes of tincture were also sometimes employed for different members of the same family.

In the case of the Courtenay arms we can see how exact blazonry can be, the roundels each given its particular name, ie red roundels torteaux, and in the Dynham arms, gold roundels or bezants. Finally the d'Abitot arms combine these two designs but come up with something entirely different, by counterchanging both the field and the intersecting third roundel, resulting in a very distinctive shield.

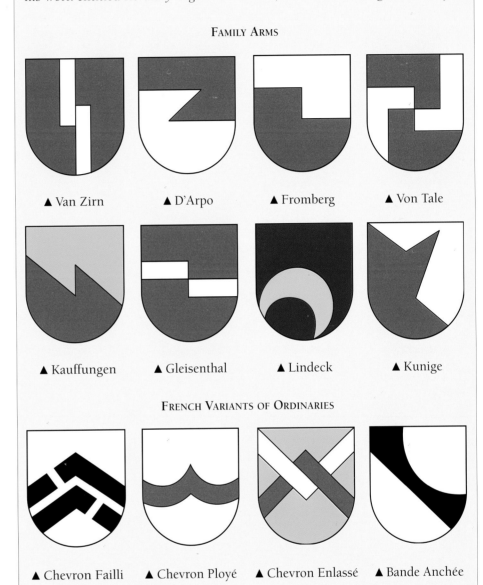

EUROPEAN VARIANTS OF LINES OF PARTITION

Certain charges, divisions of the shield, partition lines and so on, are peculiar to a particular area or nation. In 1886, in his work entitled *Heraldry English and Foreign*, Robert Jenkins gave the following examples of variants and the names of some ordinaries that would seldom, if ever, be met with in English heraldry.

FAMILY ARMS

▲ Van Zirn ▲ D'Arpo ▲ Fromberg ▲ Von Tale

▲ Kauffungen ▲ Gleisenthal ▲ Lindeck ▲ Kunige

FRENCH VARIANTS OF ORDINARIES

▲ Chevron Failli ▲ Chevron Ployé ▲ Chevron Enlassé ▲ Bande Anchée

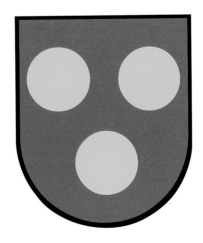

▲ *The shield of the Courtenay family: Or three torteaux.*

▲ *The Dynham shield – a reversed version of the Courtenay shield: Gules three bezants.*

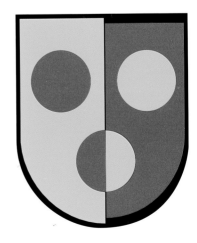

▲ *Finally the shield of the d'Abitots: Per pale Or and Gules three roundels counterchanged.*

BLAZONRY

The term blazonry refers to the special and distinct language that is used in the description of heraldry. Many a casual visitor to the world of heraldry can be baffled and put off by the nature of blazonry, but in fact it is a very user-friendly language, so exact in its phraseology that, once learnt, it enables one heraldist to impart to another an accurate and full description of any coat of arms through a concise verbal picture. Blazonry is a precise language, which it needs to be, for the nature of heraldry itself depends on the uniqueness of each coat of arms.

DESCRIBING A SHIELD

Any charge can be married to any other in any number of ways to make up a shield of arms. Often, the more ancient the arms, the simpler the design. It is in fact possible to have a shield of arms bearing no charges at all. The d'Albret arms were originally simply Gules (a plain red shield) though in 1389 they were "augmented" with the arms of France, becoming Quarterly one and four Azure three fleurs de lis Or two and three Gules (the shield was divided into four, quarters one and four were blue with three gold fleur de lis in each, quarters two and three remained the original red colour).

We have seen some of the fundamental charges employed in heraldry. Let us now see how they are "blazoned". The blazon needs to include all the details of tincture and number that an artist would need in order to reproduce the shield accurately. It always follows a set pattern:

1 The field, including any divisions
2 The ordinary
3 The principal charges on the field, followed by any lesser charges
4 Any charges on the ordinary
5 Any sub-ordinaries
6 Any charges on the sub-ordinaries

A further refinement of the language of blazonry is the means of describing the exact position on the shield any charge might take. The names of these parts and points of the shield are explained in the box.

THE PARTS AND POINTS OF THE SHIELD

For the purposes of accurate description, the heraldic shield is divided into different areas.

The dexter (right-hand) and sinister (left-hand) sides of the shield are always described from the point of view of the bearer of the shield, a throwback to the days when shields were actually carried. So from the reader's viewpoint, right is left and left is right. Most heraldic charges, particularly animate ones, are drawn so they are facing dexter, as it is considered the more "worthy" side. So from the point of the viewer, rather than a bearer, any lions, for example, on the shield, would usually face the left-hand side of the shield.

A B C: chief (top part of the shield), sub-divided into:
    A: dexter chief point
    B: middle chief point
    C: sinister chief point
D: honour point
E: fess or heart point
F: nombril or navel point
G H I: base, sub-divided into:
    G: dexter base point
    H: middle base point
    I: sinister base point

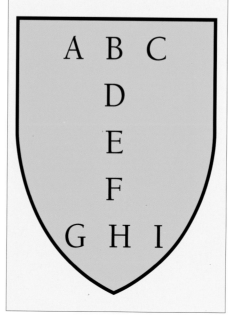

Here are three examples of how blazonry describes a shield. The first example is the arms of the family of Winneberg: Gules a bend Argent indented between six crosses couped Or.

1 The field is described first: Gules – a plain red background.

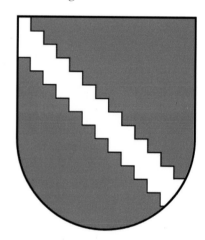

2 The next most important feature is the ordinary, in this case a bend Argent, noting any partition line, here indented.

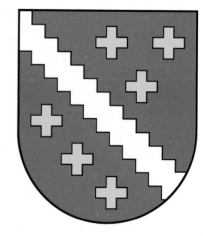

3 Any lesser charges follow: between six crosses couped Or.

The arms of the town of Gerville, Seine-Maritime, France, is described as: Argent on a bend Azure between two Phrygian caps Gules three mullets of six points Or.

The more complex arms of the Johnson family, Suffolk, are described as: Sable on a fess between two double manacles Argent three pheons Gules on a chief Or a demi lion between two lozenges Azure.

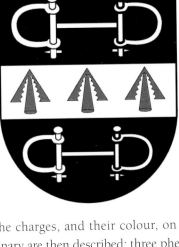

4 The charges, and their colour, on the ordinary are then described: three pheons [arrowheads] Gules.

1 The field is silver, the ordinary: on a bend Azure. ("On" anticipates point 3 below. As the lines of partition are straight they are not mentioned.)

1 The field: Sable.

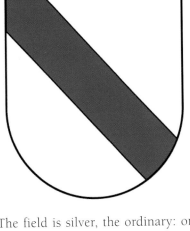

2 The lesser charges on the field: between two Phrygian caps Gules.

2 The ordinary: on a fess.

5 If a chief is borne in addition to another ordinary, as here, it is mentioned next: on a chief Or.

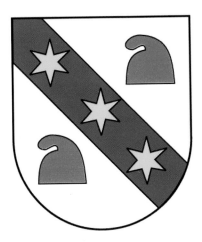

3 If any charges are borne on the ordinary, these are mentioned next: three mullets [stars] of six points Or.

3 The lesser charges on the field: between two double manacles Argent. (As both fess and manacles are silver, the colour is mentioned only once.)

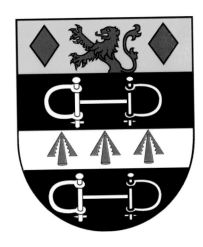

6 Any charges that appear on the chief now follow: a demi lion (the head and top half of a lion) between two lozenges Azure.

HERALDIC BEASTS

Although the earliest heraldry consisted mainly of simple geometric patterns – for easy identification at a distance – beasts, birds and monsters had begun to figure as emblems on shields and flags long before the birth of heraldry itself. We know that in ancient Greece the Athenians took an owl as their city's symbol. In ancient Egypt many of the gods were depicted partly or wholly in the forms of animals that lived alongside human beings, such as the jackal, cobra and hawk. The Bible records the instruction, "Every man of the children of Israel shall pitch by his own standard, with the ensign of their father's house" (Numbers 2:2), and of the 12 tribes of Israel no less than half took an animal as their symbol.

THE LION
Lions were in evidence at the very birth of heraldry – perhaps they were even the very first charge. When knighted in 1127 by his father-in-law, King Henry I of England, Geoffrey, Count of Anjou was given a shield bearing fanciful golden lions. The lion, believed to be the king of beasts, was

▼ *The lion, king of beasts: a page from a Dutch ordinary of 1570 shows family arms charged with the lion rampant.*

naturally a favourite symbol among the fighting men of medieval Europe, and was one of the more exotic beasts of the medieval heraldic menageries.

All postures or inclinations of an armorial charge are termed "attitudes", and this is especially relevant to creatures. Not surprisingly the lion is afforded the greatest number of attitudes – some writers have given it as many as 60 different positions. Besides its attitude, a lion or any other creature may also be distinguished by attributes. For example, a lion "passant" (attitude) may also be "langued" (tongued) in a tincture other than the normal red, and "armed" with teeth and claws.

Heraldry is an exact science. It needs to be if the individuality of a shield of arms is to be preserved, therefore attributes and attitudes are important. It could be that one family's blue shield bears a gold lion "rampant", another's a gold lion "rampant guardant" (looking at the viewer), while a third has a gold lion "rampant reguardant" (looking backwards): there is enough difference in the position of the head to give three distinct arms. Adding a forked tail ("queue fourchée") to the lions provides three more distinct arms.

OTHER BEASTS
Obviously many an early bearer of a lion chose the creature to reflect his own ferocity and bravery. The same may be said of those who chose bears, wolves and other carnivorous animals. Strength could be suggested by other creatures. The noble Moravian family of Pernstein bore on a white shield a black auroch's head "couped affronty" (with no neck visible, facing the viewer). According to a family legend the founding father of the Pernsteins was a charcoal burner of extraordinary strength called Vénava. He managed to catch a wild auroch and led it to the court of the king at Brno, where he cut off the poor beast's head with a single blow of his axe. The king was so impressed that he gave Vénava great estates and the right to commemorate his feat on his shield of arms.

▲ *This 1823 Bavarian grant of arms, to Baron Peter Kreusser, includes a variety of beasts from the heraldic menagerie.*

LIONS OR LEOPARDS
In 1235 the German emperor Frederick II presented Henry III of England with three leopards as a living shield of arms. Was this a reflection of the English arms at that time? If so, are the creatures in the English arms meant to be leopards? Confusion arises from the interpretation of heraldic terms describing the attitude of the lion. In English heraldry, the creature most often shown rearing up on one hind foot and boxing with its front paws is a lion "rampant", whereas if it is walking sedately across the shield it is a lion passant. In the arms of England the three lions are "passant guardant", walking and looking at the viewer. In French heraldry, the lion is always assumed to be rampant, while the creature that appears passant guardant is always a leopard. Furthermore, in French heraldry a rearing lion, looking at the viewer (in English "rampant guardant"), is called a *lion léopardé*, and a lion passant is a *léopard lionné*!

MOST COMMON ATTITUDES OF THE LION

▲ Statant

▲ Combatant

▲ Rampant

▲ Rampant guardant

▲ Couchant

▲ Passant

▲ Salient

▲ Rampant double-queued

▲ Rampant reguardant

▲ Rampant queue fourchée

▲ Sejant

▲ Cowed

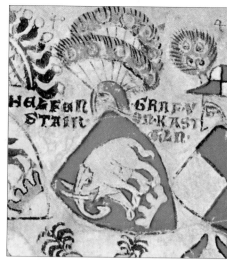

▲ *A taste of the local flora and fauna from the Baltic States: left: Polvamaa, Estonia; middle: Balozi, Latvia; right: Auce, Latvia.*

Like many heraldic stories, it is impossible to know whether the auroch appeared on the Pernstein shield before or after the legend arose, but it is carved on the family's former castle at Pardubice.

While many men of warlike disposition would not have minded being represented by a bull, there must be few that would have chosen to bear its castrated equivalent, the ox. However, if Nicholas Upton, the 15th-century English heraldic writer, is to be believed, he was instrumental in the granting of a shield charged with three oxheads to a gentleman who had had the misfortune to have been maimed in the testicles by the thrust of a spear.

Another creature that Upton might have thought equally suitable for this client

▼ *A marvellous depiction carved in stone of the porcupine badge of King Louis XII of France, 1498–1515, Château de Blois.*

would have been the beaver, whose scent glands, located near its rear, were sought after for various medicinal cures. Upton, along with other medieval writers, believed that these glands were in fact the beaver's testicles and that, when it realized that men were after them, it sensibly chose to sacrifice them by castrating itself with its teeth. Beavers, once common in much of Northern Europe, are now found only in the forests of Scandinavia and the Baltic States, and they appear in the arms of the Estonian district of Polvamaa.

Heraldry gives symbolic protection to all creatures, great and small, and whereas warriors might choose martial beasts such as lions, bears and wolves, country communities

▲ *The elephant in the arms of the Counts of Helfenstein, an unusual animal charge, chosen as a delightful pun on the family's name.*

often prefer to commemorate gentler creatures. In Latvia, the rivers and forests yield up their wildlife to local heraldry. The arms of Auce – a black crayfish on a red field – enjoyably break the colour-on-colour rule. In the arms of Balozi a frog sits below a chief charged with water-lily leaves, while squirrels in the arms of Baldone and hedgehogs in those of Vilaka recall the creatures found in many gardens.

◀ *The arms of the Pernstein family of Moravia bear the popular bull's head as both a charge and a crest.*

▲ *Vénava kills his auroch in a relief carving at the family seat, the Castle of Pardubice.*

▲ *The camel on the arms of the city of Petropavlovsk, in the old Russian Empire, at the cross-roads where East met West.*

EXOTIC BEASTS

Of the more unusual animals, elephants were relatively well known to medieval heraldists (Henry III of England was given one for his menagerie by Louis IX of France in 1254). The elephant was used as a symbol of strength and dependability, and as such it was chosen for the arms of the city of Coventry in England. A particularly enjoyable example appears in the Zurich armorial roll (1335–45) for the von Helfenstein family of Swabia, chosen for its punning value with the family name.

Other exotic beasts in the heraldic menagerie include that of the eastern territories and cities of the old Russian Empire (such as Petropavlovsk) who favoured the camel in their civic heraldry, and when Sir Titus Salt, Baronet, of Saltaire, Yorkshire was granted arms, he chose as a crest the alpaca, from whose fine wool he had made his fortune.

ANIMAL PARTS

It is not only whole creatures that are used in heraldry; various parts of their anatomy make their way on to shields. Wolves' teeth famously appear on the Kinsky arms of Bohemia, while others include the bones of fish, and various types of amputations. The bits of animals that are all quite commonly used in heraldry include heads that are either "erased" (torn off at the neck) or "couped" (clean cut), various horns and antlers, and even the paws ("gambs") of bears and lions, which can also be either erased or couped.

DOMESTIC ANIMALS

Cats, dogs and horses are all corralled into heraldry, as are the unfortunate victims of the hunt: boar, deer, hares and rabbits. The stag hunt was for centuries the exclusive sport of the nobility, so it is no wonder that, after lions, deer probably appear most commonly upon shields and are therefore afforded the next largest group of personal attitudes. The English Cottington family enjoy two hinds in their arms "counter-tripping", which have the rather comical appearance of a Push-me-Pull-you.

Greyhounds are popular in Italian heraldry, while in British heraldry the talbot, a large and powerful ancient hunting hound, is often found. However, man's best friend comes no truer than the dog on the crest of a Mr Phillips of Cavendish Square, London, who early in the 19th century was swimming in the sea off Portsmouth when he got into a strong current and was in danger of being drowned. A perceptive Newfoundland hound saw his predicament, leapt into the water and dragged him to safety. When Mr Phillips found that his canine saviour was a stray, he took the brave dog home and gave him every kind attention that he deserved. Furthermore, the Phillips family recorded this happy outcome in a new heraldic crest and motto, the full blazon being: Upon a mount Vert in front of a Newfoundland dog sejant, reguardant proper an escutcheon thereon, in base waves of the sea, and floating therein a naked man, the sinister arm erected all proper. The motto is *Auspice Deo extuli mari*, "God being my leader, I brought him out of the sea".

▼ *A tigress looks in the mirror at itself (third quarter) in the arms of the English family of Sibell. While she was beguiled by her own image her cubs were left unprotected.*

▼ *The wolf's teeth on the shield of the Czech Count Kinsky, seen here on a beautifully crafted embellishment on a wrought-iron gate. The teeth themselves are very stylized.*

▼ *Mr Phillips' faithful friend, the dog who saved his life and became his crest.*

HUMAN FIGURES

Human beings – and parts of them – appear often in heraldry, mainly reflecting enemies of the medieval period. The human figure is usually shown fully clothed or, if nearer to nature, is girded around the loins with an extremely uncomfortable "vestment of leaves" described by one English heraldic writer as "vegetable knickers". However, a naked man in all his glory appears in the arms of the Scots baronets Dalyell of the Binns and a breast of sorts, distilling milk, appears in the arms of the English family of Dodge.

Hungarian heraldry affords many instances of the human being in action, whether it be of the bloody kind – slitting the throat of an unfortunate deer or shooting a Turkish soldier – or gentler pursuits such as playing the organ, or reaping corn.

KINGS AND QUEENS

Naturally, the appearance of kings and queens in heraldry is counted to be the highest of all honours. In most cases the monarch commemorated tends to be anonymous, but the Castilian family of de Avila has in its arms an imprisoned king in chains, representing King François I of France, taken prisoner by Don Diego de Avila in 1528 during the Battle of Pavia. The Savoyard family of Amoreto also keeps a Moorish king chained to the chevron in its arms.

The Weldons, Baronets of Rahenderry in Ireland, have the bust of the Virgin Queen, Elizabeth I of England, as their crest. Family records say only that it was given as a mark of distinction by the Queen herself for some great service done to her by a Weldon.

VICTIMS AND VILLAINS

The Spanish family of Miranda commemorates a famous legend on its shield of arms. It bears the busts of five virgins, rescued from rape and murder by Alvar Fernandez de Miranda, while on pilgrimage to Santiago de Compostella. The arms of the city of Lichfield in England record a less favourable fate than that of Alvar's virgins: on old seals of the city council the shield bears "on a landscape proper several martyrs in divers manners massacred."

The English family of Davenport of Capesthorne Hall in Cheshire has what is thought to be a unique crest of a felon's head within the noose from which he is about to be hanged. It refers to the power of life and death, "without delay and without appeal", which the Davenports exercised over vast areas of forest land in north-east England.

HEARTS AND OTHER ORGANS

Human hearts often make their appearance on shields of arms, one forming the central charge in the arms of the Scots family of Douglas. Sir James Douglas was a close companion of King Robert the Bruce of Scotland (1306–29); at the end of his life the king, who had long wished to take part in a Crusade, gained Sir James's promise

▲ *The wildmen in the arms of the Wood family, traditionally girded with oak leaves.*

▼ *The all too realistic nature of Hungarian arms borne out here in a grant of 1636.*

▼ *King François I of France stands in chains on the shield of the de Avila family.*

▼ *The virgins saved from a "fate worse than death" by a member of the Miranda family.*

▲ The crest of the Davenport family of Capesthorne – showing an anonymous felon on his way to execution.

that he would carry the King's embalmed heart to Jerusalem and bury it in the Holy Sephulchre. When the King died in 1329, that is just what Sir James set off to do, but was killed in battle on his journey. Some say he threw King Robert's heart into the fight before following it to certain death. The Douglas family added a red heart to their arms, which was later crowned.

The north Italian family of Colleoni bore three pairs of testicles on their shield. In

▼ The three pairs of testicles of the Colleoni family, adorning the ceiling of their castle of Malpaga, near Bergamo, north Italy.

the virile and thoroughly human Middle Ages this was no disgrace, but the dubious gentility of the late 19th century led these vital charges to be described in some ordinaries as three upside-down hearts.

Female genitalia appear on the shield of the medieval Italian family of Conati, but perhaps the most bizarre example of heraldic "vivacity" can be seen on the shield of a Hungarian gentleman, István Várallyay, who in 1599 was granted arms of male sexual organs beneath an arm grasping a mallet. As many Hungarian family arms vividly portray the severed parts of dead Turks, this shield could be taken to represent some particularly unpleasant fate befalling yet another Turkish soldier captured in battle. In truth, however, these particular parts are those of a stallion – Várallyay was a farrier and gelder in the Hungarian army and, being proud of his swiftness and expertise in castrating horses, wished the fact to be recorded in heraldry.

The Indian state of Wankaner has in its arms a representation of the Hindu adoration of the god Shiva, through the veneration of the male phallic symbol of the *lingam*. The arms show Shiva's *trishul*, or trident, wrapped around with snakes, and the round-ended raised stone sculpture that represents the *lingam*, or generative force.

ARMS AND LEGS

Parts of the human body feature regularly in heraldry. The most common are arms or legs. The arms of the Isle of Man are Gules three legs conjoined in fess point in armour proper. They were borne by the ancient kings of Man, and appear as a quartering in the arms of Montagu, Stanley and Murray, all later Lords of Man. The legs probably derive from a Norse symbol for luck introduced by Man's Viking invaders.

A curious human appendage is the wooden leg of the Swede, Per Larsson, who when fighting during the Thirty Years War had his leg amputated. On his eventual ennoblement he took the name Stöltenhielm (*stolt* means "stilt") and a wooden stilt was a main feature in the arms he adopted.

▲ István Várallyay's shield, with the curious charges that actually celebrate the bearer's profession of farrier and gelder of horses.

▲ The arms of the Indian state of Wankaner bring the Hindu worship of Shiva to heraldry.

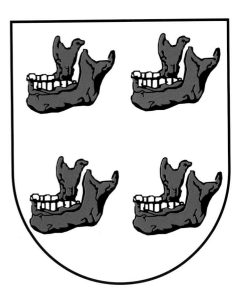

▲ The highly literal arms of the Portuguese family of Queixada, whose name means simply "jawbone".

FOWL, FISH AND PLANTS

After animals, the second most popular heraldic charge is birds – most usually the eagle but also less exalted species. Fish of various kinds also sometimes appear, and flowers, trees and even vegetables have also played their part in the heraldic story. Of flowers, the rose and the lily are most commonly met with, and each has a stylized form – the five-petalled heraldic rose and the fleur de lis.

▲ *The stork in its vigilance on the arms of the Hungarian family of Ballint of Técső. If it slept the stone would fall and waken it.*

▼ *The heraldic aviary in the coat of arms of the Barons Arundel shows the imperial eagle behind the shield, the owl as a supporter, and six hirondells (swallows) on the shield.*

HERALDIC BIRDS

If the lion is the king of beasts, the eagle, for medieval heraldic writers, was the queen of birds. From Roman times it was associated with empires, and black eagles were said to be the bravest of all. Both the Byzantine and Holy Roman emperors considered it personal to them.

Many other birds, real, fanciful or fantastic, inhabit the heraldic menagerie, particularly the martlet or *merletten*. The martlet, a swift-like creature, has no feet when depicted in heraldry (and the *merletten* has neither feet nor beak), because it was believed by medieval writers never to land. Such birds were spoken of by Crusaders who claimed to have seen them in the Holy Land. The martlet was often given as a heraldic charge to younger sons of the English nobility, as a reminder to "trust to the wings of virtue and merit, and not to their legs, having no land of their own to put their feet on."

The pelican also displays a mixture of fact and fancy. In heraldry it is often depicted using its beak to wound itself in the breast ("vulning"), using the blood it sheds to feed its young. Such a symbol of self-sacrifice is therefore often found in religious arms.

CREATURES OF THE WATER

The dolphin, the most commonly occurring sea creature in heraldry, is classed as a fish by heraldic writers, as is the whale, although both are, of course, mammals. All

◄ *The punning arms of the Portuguese family of Sardinha includes not only sardines but the crest of a whale.*

kinds of fish have appeared as various heraldic charges, but size and ferocity seems to have been foremost in the minds of the medieval heralds. Not surprisingly, therefore, numerous arms can be found bearing the pike, such as the Portuguese family of Lucio, and the Czech town of Dolni Breszov.

▲ *The ferocious and all too realistic pike devouring a smaller fish in the arms of the Czech town of Dolni Breszov.*

FLOWERS

Heraldic writers have credited the rose with many properties. It is seen as an emblem of secrecy, being good, soft, and sweet-smelling, but surrounded by evil, signified by its thorns. In medieval England the rose was a popular symbol within the royal family, reaching its zenith during the reigns of the Tudor monarchs. The white rose was a favourite badge of the royal house of York. The red rose of the rival house of Lancaster has a less certain provenance, but it is certain that Henry Tudor (later Henry VII) took it to be the Lancastrian symbol when he united it with the white rose after his marriage to Elizabeth of York in 1486.

The double Tudor rose was a favourite device of Henry VII's son, Henry VIII, and on his marriage to Catherine of Aragon he combined it with the Queen's badge, the pomegranate of Granada. An abundance of roses and pomegranates erupted throughout England, until the eventual divorce of the unhappy couple led to the defacing of any such badge in public places and churches. This must have left Herr Arnold

▼ *The fleur de lis of the French kings from their crypt in the abbey of St Denis. The shield is encircled by the Order of the Holy Ghost (St Esprit).*

▲ *Left: the rose and pomegranate charge on the arms of Herr Arnold Bilson – a design he might later have regretted after the divorce of Henry VIII and Catherine of Aragon. Right: The potato flowers of the French town of Ploudaniel.*

Bilson, presumably a German merchant in England, in an awkward situation: he had been granted arms charged with a Tudor rose and pomegranate "dimidiated" (halved).

The fleur de lis, the heraldic lily, was associated with the royal house of France long before the advent of heraldry. It is possible that the fleur de lis is a heraldic representation of the flag iris, though one of the many legends surrounding the symbol is that it evolved not from flowers but from three toads, supposedly the arms of Pharamond, King of the Franks in the first half of the 5th century.

As part of the French royal insignia, the fleur de lis can be traced back to the reign of Robert II, "the Pious" (996–1031), son of Hugh Capet. The royal coat of arms, of a blue shield strewn with golden fleurs de lis (semy de lis), made its first appearance during the reign of Louis VIII (1223–6). It is supposed that the number of lilies was reduced to three during the reign of Charles V (1364–80) in honour of the Holy Trinity, although his successor, Charles VI (1380–1422) is known to have used both semy de lis and three fleurs de lis on different occasions.

In modern heraldry, the semy variant is called "France ancient", the three fleurs de lis "France modern". It is possible that the change was an attempt by the French monarchs to distance their arms from their old enemies the English kings, who, starting with Edward III (1327–77) had asserted their claim to the throne of France by quartering the French arms (France ancient) with the lion of England. If such

a ploy was indeed attempted, it did not work, for Henry V of England (1413–22) changed the French quarters in his arms to France modern.

HERALDIC PLANTS

As for other plant life in heraldry, it can lead from the exotic – as with the palm trees in the arms of Maintirano, Malagasy Republic – to the humble, including the potato flower of Ploudaniel, Finistere, France, and the thorn bush (*Spina*) of the Italian family of Malaspina.

The broom plant, or *planta genista* is the emblem of humility, and became the badge adopted by the royal house of Plantagenet. Wheatsheaves, or "garbs", according to Guillaume, were the symbol of plenty and could signify the "harvest of one's hopes". Fruits also symbolized plenty.

The clover leaf, or "trefoil" frequently appears, not least as the shamrock, the plant symbol of Ireland. If a narrow tapering stem is shown projecting from it (or from any other leaf or flower), it is said to be "slipped". Heraldic variants of the trefoil have different numbers of leaves: the quatrefoil (four leaves), cinquefoil (five leaves) and the octofoil (eight leaves), which in England is the mark given to the ninth son.

▼ *The arms of the Italian Princes di Massa, which includes the thorn tree of the arms of the Malaspina family.*

MONSTERS AND FABULOUS BEASTS

People like to be thrilled by the unknown or strange, so it is not surprising to find in medieval armorials many examples of mythological creatures such as griffins, dragons, centaurs, unicorns and mermaids. Such monsters may have been the product of pure imagination, but it is more likely that they were the result of the need to exaggerate – most medieval heraldists and their patrons having heard at second-, third-, or even fourth-hand of the strange and wonderful creatures discovered in the far-off Indies or Americas.

▶ *The arms granted to Josef Moise in 1867 during the reign of Emperor Franz Josef of Austria includes a fire-breathing panther.*

▼ *The vibrancy and imagination of medieval heraldry is shown here in the wyvern crest of Sir John Grey de Ruthin.*

We have seen how medieval heraldry treated the relatively familiar lion, putting it into positions that would probably cause the real beast to fall over backwards. The panther was depicted equally fantastically, usually spouting flames from nostrils, mouth and even ears. Medieval bestiaries were the fuel for further heraldic fancies. These works, often wonderfully illustrated, told of cockatrices, bonacons and wyverns: fabulous creatures best encountered only in books and manuscripts. So ferocious were they that often they could turn people to stone on sight, or kill with their breath. Most medieval folk believed these creatures really did exist, and for someone who considered even the next village to be foreign territory, monsters provided just one more reason not to venture far from their own doorsteps.

THE DRAGON

Said to be the greatest of all serpents, the dragon had a scaly body and wings (usually depicted as bat-like). Its head was often horned and tufted, its tail thorny and pointed. It is quite possible that it had its origins in the unearthed fossils of prehistoric beasts. The sheer size of the skeletons that would have been found from time to time throughout the known world, would have been enough to overawe the finder, and real dragons are still alive and well on the island of Komodo off Indonesia, tales of which must have passed between traders many centuries ago.

Dragons lived in caves or deep in the earth's core, where fire was their constant companion; no wonder then that dragons themselves could breathe fire. In British heraldry the dragon is shown with four legs, but this is a late development, for

▲ *A centaur with a bow aiming skywards, an apt charge to appear on a badge for a German Army anti-aircraft unit.*

▲ *The wyvern, a heraldic beast used in England who in earlier times may well have been a dragon.*

▲ *The heraldic griffin, often seen as the guardian of treasure.*

▲ *The bonacon here seems gentle, but its unique defensive technique was all too awesome and far from benign.*

before the 15th century it was usually shown as having just two. In English heraldry the two-legged dragon tends to be called a wyvern or a basilisk, though in the rest of Europe the matter is not so distinct.

THE GRIFFIN

The heraldic monster with the forepart of an eagle and the hindquarters of a lion is called a griffin, or gryphon. Although not quite as popular as the dragon in heraldry, it nevertheless captured the imagination of many noble minds, for the griffin was the guardian of gold and hidden treasure, and was therefore a creature to be met on many a medieval quest.

▲ *The unicorn on the arms of the Polish noble tribe of Boncza – one of the few mythical beasts in Polish heraldry.*

In British heraldry a so-called male griffin is shown without wings, its body covered in tufts of formidable spikes, which are usually of a different colour to the rest of its body. Confusingly, the ordinary griffin is also normally depicted as having male sexual organs: just what a female griffin should look like is not made clear by heraldic writers. In English heraldry the griffin when in the rampant position is described as being "segreant".

THE UNICORN

Many a medieval prince kept a so-called unicorn's horn in his collection of curios, though in reality this was likely to be the tusk of a narwhal. The subject of many noble fantasies and legends, the unicorn is considered by many to be the most beautiful creature in the heraldic menagerie. In effect it is part horse, part heraldic antelope, with a large twisting horn or tusk issuing from its forehead. It is also depicted as having a lion's tail and a little tuft of hairs under its chin. So pure a creature is the unicorn that it is often entirely white, apart from its horn, tufts, mane and hooves, which are gold. When regally collared and chained, unicorns are the supporters beloved of the Scots monarchs.

In medieval romances, tales were told of how the usually untameable unicorn would befriend a gentle damsel of noble birth whom it sensed to be a virgin. When the noble creature had found such a lady it would lay its head in her lap and go to sleep. It was only at such a moment that hunters could steal in and capture or kill this wonderful prey.

The purity of both the unicorn and virgin was made much of by medieval writers, who compared the two symbols to Christ and the Virgin Mary. Because of this sacred connection some heraldic authors of the medieval period considered that the unicorn should not be sullied by placing its image on shield or crest. However, by the 16th century it had become a popular charge in heraldry all over Europe, appearing on shields as far apart as Poland, where it is borne by the Herb (clan or tribe) of Boncza, and Italy, borne by the Bardi family of Florence.

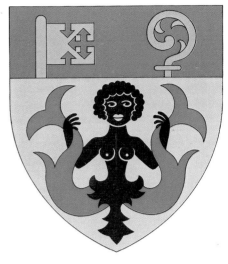

▲ *An exotic flavour is given to the ancient theme of the mermaid in the arms of Mouila in the Gabon, where a sirene was said to haunt the local river luring men to her lair.*

OTHER BEASTS

Like the salamander, depicted as a lizard surrounded by flames, the phoenix often appears in the arms of towns and cities that have been rebuilt after destruction in war. Classical writers asserted that only one phoenix existed at a time, and lived for 500 years. Knowing its end to be near, it made a nest that the sun's rays ignited, frying the poor bird. Out of the embers came its successor.

A creature peculiar to English heraldry is the bonacon. Somewhat like a bull with blunted horns that were turned inwards, the bonacon was said to defend itself by emitting burning excreta which could cover an enormous area.

MARINE MONSTERS

The mermaid was busy luring sailors to various fates, happy or decidedly nasty, from earliest times. Said to be half woman, half fish, she probably arose from sailors' sightings of the dugong or sea-cow.

The sirene seems to be a curious cousin of the mermaid with two tails. A version is found in the arms designed in the late 20th century for the commune of Mouila in the Gabon. Said to appear from time to time to claim a local man for her husband, the sirene displays two splendid scarlet tails. The white sister of Mouila's sirene appears in the arms of several European families, including the Amari of Sicily.

INANIMATE CHARGES

Heraldry has always made full and free use of every kind of object, and coats of arms reflect life's events from the cradle to the grave. The arms of the French town of St Germain-en-Laye include a very grand baby's cradle that also bears the date – 5 September 1638 – on which the future Louis XIV was born. At the other extreme, the last resting place of one of the earliest humans, found during mining activities in northern Rhodesia (now Zimbabwe), is suggested by a skull in the arms of Broken Hill, granted in 1954. A complete skeleton in a somewhat reflective pose in the civic arms of Londonderry, Northern Ireland, recalls the unhappy fate of a local nobleman, Walter de Burgo, who was starved to death in a dungeon on the orders of one of his own family members.

CLOTHING AND ACCESSORIES

All kinds of dress can be met with, from the mundane (the breeches in the arms of the family of Van Abbenbroek from Zeeland) to the curious (a French wife's hood, the heraldic badge of the English 16th-century nobleman Lord Ferrers). As early as the 14th century, fashion was appearing on the nobleman's shield. The lady's sleeve or "maunch", which had a pendulous pocket to house the owner's prayer book or missal, was a popular charge in English and French heraldry throughout the late medieval period.

A medieval lady might well also have treasured a necklace of Baltic amber, such

▲ From the cradle – Louis XIV of France's birth is remembered in the arms of the town of St Germain-en-Laye.

▲ To the grave – a rather bored skeleton of Walter de Burgo in the arms of the city of Londonderry, Northern Ireland.

▲ A pair of sandals is the charge for the Spanish family of Abarca.

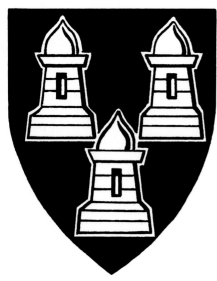

▲ The buildings of the gentry – three of the cotes that they kept their doves in, the punning arms of the English family of Sapcote.

▲ The way we earn our bread – the sewing machine in the arms of Clydebank, Scotland, home of Singer sewing machines.

▲ The inventor, proud of his works – the corrugated boiler flue that made a fortune for Samson Fox of Harrogate.

as the one found in the arms of the Lithuanian coastal resort of Palanga, where lumps of the fossilized resin are often washed up on the beaches.

BUILDINGS AND WORK

Fortresses and bridges appear on shields, as do homes, from the stone building in the arms of the town of Frontenhausen, Bavaria, to the Inuit igloo that forms the crest of the Territory of Nunuvut, Canada. Even the turrets of Indian homes, or *gonkhs*, find their way on to the arms of Halvad Dhrangadhra in Gujarat. A church features in the punning arms of the Asturian family of Iglesia.

The workplace, whether it be the coal mine of the community of Bütten (in the arms of Landkreis Peine, Westphalia) or a

▲ *The food we eat – the sugar loaves of Waghausel, Landkreis Karlsruhe, Germany, appearing here in the trademark of the sugar refinery of that town.*

▲ *The warrior chef. The cheese grater and noodle flattener crest of the Master of the Kitchens to the Holy Roman Emperor.*

sewing machine made in a factory at Burgh of Clydebank, Scotland shows that heraldry can reflect the lifestyle of the worker just as well as that of a medieval knight. Whether the corrugated boiler flue of Samson Fox of Harrogate, England or the section of bracing in the arms of the Bossom baronets (also English) constitute good heraldic charges, is open to dispute.

Both knight and motorway magnate need to eat, and the kitchen has often figured in heraldic imagination, sometimes turning the most mundane objects into comical or bizarre charges. Even the proverbial kitchen sink probably features on a shield somewhere – certainly the table does. Charges taken from the kitchen include the sugar loaf of Waghausel, Landkreis Karlsruhe, Germany; the standing dishes in the punning arms of the English family of Standish; a trivet (Trivet of Cornwall); and a kettle hanger for the town of Zwijndrecht in the Netherlands. So important was the medieval kitchen in the running of a noble or royal household that the Master of the Kitchens to the Holy Roman Emperor was afforded his own very distinctive crest – a cheese grater and a noodle flattener.

TRANSPORT

In the last two centuries the railway has cut its way across the heraldic shields of towns from Swindon in England to Kaisiadorys in Lithuania. The former has a conventional locomotive of the late 19th century (there was much correspondence between the town council and the College of Arms in London over the exact make of the locomotive), while in the arms of the latter, four stylized silver steeds, streaming steam and smoke, pass back and forth across a black shield to represent the two major railways running through the town.

Cars also found their way on to the proud shields of factory towns such as Koprovince in the Czech Republic, the home of the first Czech car, the President, which rolled off the production line in 1897. Air travel was to make its mark on shields from the early 20th century onwards, a startling example being found in the arms of the commune of Sandweiler

▲ *The four rather dashing stylized iron horses of Kaisiadorys, Lithuania.*

▼ *The President car on the arms of Koprovince in the Czech Republic.*

▲ *A jet lands on the runway of the airport at Sandweiler, Luxembourg. Traditional heraldic ordinaries with a modern flavour.*

▲ *The arms of the aviator, Mary, Duchess of Bedford, drawn up and insisted upon by her husband, in spite of the heralds' disapproval.*

in Luxembourg. Sandweiler is home to Luxembourg's international airport, so a passenger jet lands on an intersection of runways in the arms.

One aircraft that had rather a bumpy journey through the heraldic skies, made its maiden flight in the unofficial arms of Mary, wife of the 11th Duke of Bedford. The Duchess was a well-known lady aviator in the 1930s and her husband wished the College of Arms to record the fact in a grant of arms to his wife, but the heralds would not sanction the design, which the Duke had himself helped to create, including the Duchess's favourite plane, the Spider. This seems not to have bothered His Grace one jot: he claimed that his family, the Russells, had long ago used arms not granted by any herald, and what was done in the past was good enough for his dear wife in her own time.

Even the parachute has been used as a heraldic charge, most notably in the arms of Ste Mére-Eglise in Normandy, commemorating the day in 1944 when the paratroopers of the US Army's 101st Airborne Division landed in and around the town's church – one man even found himself draped across the church tower, an event memorably depicted in the film *The Longest Day.*

SPORTS AND GAMES
Heraldry can also catalogue the lighter side of life, such as the tennis-playing youths in the arms of the Tosetti family of Massiola, northern Italy. In Britain where the weather is not so propitious for outdoor sports, board games find their way on to the heraldic shield, as in the arms of the Pegrez family with its backgammon boards, and the arms of the Matthias family of Lamphey in Pembrokeshire: Gules on each of three dice in perspective Argent 11 ogresses six in front three on the sinister two on top.

▲ *A tennis match in the arms of the north Italian family of Tosetti, in which, for reasons unknown, the players are not wearing any clothes.*

▼ *Three backgammon boards appear in the arms of the English family of Pegrez.*

◄ *The arms for the French village of Ste Mère Eglise in Normandy commemorates the landing of American paratroopers at the church, during the liberation of the region from Germany in 1944.*

▲ A skiing warrior in the arms of the town of Lillehammer, Norway.

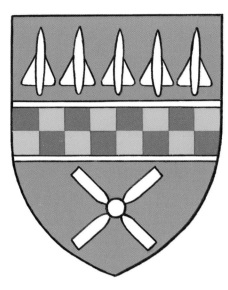

▲ Arms of Sir George Edwards – blue skies and Concordes for a life in aviation.

▲ The town of Spa in Belgium, famous for its waters, has the old spa as its arms.

▲ The local coal mine in the arms of Bülten in Landkreis Peine, Germany.

▲ Oerlese and ...

▲ ... Rietze, towns in Germany that maintain a heraldic link with local farming.

▲ The sails of the ships in the arms of the Scottish Royal Burgh of Elie and Earlsferry are charged with the arms of local lords.

▲ The ship, star and crescent in the arms of the Danish port of Nörresundby were originally on a seal and adapted to a shield.

▲ A detailed depiction of an oared 18th-century sailing ship for the Crimean port of Kostroma.

PUNNING HERALDRY

The richness of heraldic imagery and imagination is nowhere more apparent than in those arms that have been devised as a play on the bearer's name. Punning or, as it is known in Britain, "canting" heraldry, can account for almost half the designs of some nations' heraldry.

Although the great majority of arms dating from the early days of heraldry were of a simple geometric nature, the heraldic imagination at work in the arms of León and Castile (which have always featured a lion and a castle) is a good example of the simplicity of the practice.

A PLAY ON WORDS

The motto of the Scudamores is *Scuto amore divinis* ("The shield of divine love"): the shield bears a gold field with a red cross patty fitchy. The Montagus (or Montacutes) bear three fusils (elongated lozenges) conjoined in fess, the tops of which are supposed to suggest the tops of mountains or *mons acutus*. The prize for the most tortuous wordplay must probably go to the arms of the powerful Mortimer family, whose arms include blue and gold bars with a white escutcheon over all. The blue represents the skies of

▶ *The simplicity of punning or canting – the quartered arms of Castile and León, Toledo Cathedral, 16th century.*

▲ *The three bear's paws of Trebarefoote.*

▲ *The three hands of Tremayne.*

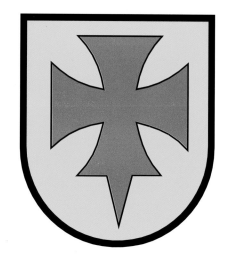

▲ *The Scudamore shield of divine love.*

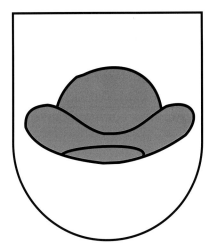

▲ *The family arms of Rotenhuet (red hat) of Silesia.*

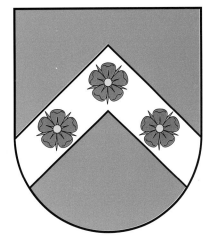

▲ *The arms of the Rosensparre (rose chevron) family of Denmark.*

▲ *The family arms of Swinhufvud (swine head) of Sweden.*

the Holy Land, the gold its sands, while the escutcheon is said to represent the Dead Sea or *mortuo maris*.

In Cornwall, the local place names offer plenty of opportunities for good puns on the number three through their common prefix "Tre". Trebarefoote has Sable a chevron between three bear's gambs (feet) erect and erased Or, and Tremayne has Gules three dexter arms conjoined at the shoulders and flexed in triangle Or, fists clenched Argent.

One of the most delightful examples has survived through the skill and imagination of the late medieval English stonemason who, asked to fashion the crest of a member of the Mordaunt family for a tomb in Northamptonshire, produced a grinning Moor showing all his teeth – literally "Moor's dents". A modern-day equivalent is the former Aeroplane and Armaments

▼ *The Moor shows off his splendid set of teeth in the Mordaunt crest.*

Experimental Establishment based at Boscombe Down in England. The English heralds came up with the local bird, a bustard, standing in a coombe (valley) on a down. That left the "Bos" which was provided by pinning the poor bustard's wing with the boss from a horse's bridle.

A EUROPEAN TRADITION

Medieval wordplay ranges from the commonplace to the curious. The Zurich armorial roll, held in the Swiss National Museum, supplies many splendid examples of punning German arms from the early 14th century. The Rand family arms are Sable a turnip Proper leaved Vert (*Rande* is German for "turnip"). The von Helfensteins of Swabia have Gules on a quadruple mount Or, an elephant statant Argent and as the Old German word for "beggar" is *betler*, the Betler family arms are Argent a beggar habited in Sable, his

shoes Or, on his shoulder a knapsack of the field, suspended by a cord Gules, a pilgrim's staff in his sinister hand, and in his dexter a begging bowl, both of the last.

Scandinavian heraldry has a long history of punning, and has made excellent use of the device. The medieval period produced the simple arms of the Swedish noble families of Sparre – Azure a chevron Or (*sparre* is a roof span, or chevron) – and Swinhufvud: Azure a boar's head couped Or (*swinhuf* meaning swine's head).

Probably the most innovative of modern punning heraldry emerged in Finland in the latter half of the 20th century. A good example is the arms of the municipality of Aanekoski, which translates from the local dialect as "sounding river" (*ääni* means "voice" and *koski*, "rapids"): Sable on a bend wavy Argent three horns stringed Gules.

▲ *The bustard stands in his coombe.*

▲ *The sounding rapids of Aanekoski, Finland.*

TIBI FIDELIS

ROYAL HERALDRY AND NOBILITY

The heraldic achievement presents a picture of the family history and alliances

that have placed a monarch on the throne or a duke and duchess in their castle.

Royal and noble families have always been keen to display this effective indicator

of their lineage and title, and occasions of state ceremonial provide welcome

opportunities for the full splendours of heraldry to be seen and enjoyed. Much of

the pomp of such occasions derives from the strict observance of distinctions of

rank; as heraldry has developed, its refinements have included numerous

details that define positions in a social hierarchy, whether of royalty,

nobility, military order or the church.

◄ *The arms of a British peer, Lord Howe, with the*
supporters, coronet of degree and helm allowed by
his rank – that of baron.

ROYAL HERALDRY

For centuries royalty has been seen as the fount of all noble titles and grants of arms, so it is not surprising to find that monarchs availed themselves of heraldry. Yet crowns, sceptres, orbs and other royal trappings were latecomers to the world of heraldic accoutrements. Until the late 15th century, there was seldom anything to differentiate the heraldic achievement of a king from that of a knight. However, on seals of the late 13th and early 14th centuries, crowns were sometimes depicted over the shields of royal individuals.

CROWNS

Heraldic crowns were imitations of actual headgear worn by monarchs. By the late 16th century royal crowns were often depicted with crimson or purple caps within them, and were embellished with raised "arches", decorated with gems and pearls, rising from the circlet and crossing over the head. In some royal families the number of arches was reduced for lesser members. While the English sovereign's crown has two intersecting arches, for

▲ ▼ *Subtle differences of rank can be shown by coronets surmounting the royal arms. Above is the coronet for a Swedish royal prince, below, that of the heir to the throne.*

example, the coronet of the Prince of Wales has only one. Other members of the royal family have coronets without any arches.

▼ *The coronation of the English King Henry IV in Westminster Abbey, 1399. The royal arms are held by officials before the dais.*

▲ *The arms of Anne, Princess Royal of Great Britain. The supporters and lozenge are both charged with a personal label (labels are used by both male and female members of the British royal family). The coronet is that of a son or daughter of the sovereign other than the heir apparent.*

▲ *The arms for the Counts of Rosenborg, the title given to Danish royal princes who married morganatically – marrying outside royal rank.*

The crown of the dauphins of France, after 1662, had arches formed of dolphins, taken from the charges in their arms.

Elsewhere there was less differentiation between family members. In Austria, for example, the emperor bore a curiously shaped crown with high arches enclosing jewelled "horns", but the crown prince and all the other archdukes bore identical crowns of more conventional appearance.

Today, some republics still retain the trappings associated with former royal powers. In Hungary, the 1,000-year-old

▼ *The personal arms of King Matthew Corvinus of Hungary (1458–90) are placed over quarters for Hungary ancient, Hungary modern, Dalmatia and Bohemia, and surmounted by St Stephen's crown.*

▲ *The Portuguese Duke of Coimbra (d1449) bears a label taken from the arms of his maternal family, the Dukes of Lancaster.*

▲ *The label of Prince William of Great Britain. The escallop is taken from the arms of the Spencers, his mother's family.*

crown of St Stephen, considered one of the finest examples of the medieval goldsmith's craft, is such a symbol. The crown's history is remarkable: having many times been hidden, stolen, lost and found, after World War II it was spirited out of Hungary to America, where it was kept safe from the Hungarian communist authorities. It was returned in 1978 and is now in the National Museum in Budapest.

The absence of a crown can be just as telling. The Swiss, proud of their freedom from any royal authority, often placed the peasant's hat of William Tell over a shield bearing the arms of the various cantons.

Although the crown is the most obvious sign of royal rank, the arms of the sovereign are often accompanied by a pavilion or robe of estate strewn with crowns or charges taken from the royal arms, and the shield is surrounded by the orders of chivalry specific to the monarchy. The pavilion is a domed tent surmounted

▲ *The white label of the royal line of Orléans on the arms of France was further differenced by crescents for the Counts of Angoulême, a junior branch.*

by the crown, with its sides drawn back to display the royal arms placed within it. Though it is common to the arms of most sovereigns, it has never found favour in British royal arms.

ROYAL DIFFERENCE MARKS

In Britain particularly, marks were added to the shields of sons and other relatives to distinguish them from the head of the family. The descendants of British kings also bore such marks, which were known as "brizures", which mainly consisted of labels, bordures and bends. For centuries the heir apparent to the sovereign has borne a three-pointed label. The earliest example seems to have been Azure, and the number of points could vary, but during the lifetime of Edward the Black Prince (1330–76), it became normalized as three points Argent. The Black Prince was created Prince of Wales in 1343, and the same label is still borne to this day by the heir apparent to the sovereign.

Other children of a British sovereign use labels bearing small charges that are mainly taken from royal badges, such as roses or crosses of St George. For some centuries the grandchildren of the sovereign have borne five-pointed labels, but the most recent label to be assigned to a royal grandson – that of Prince William, eldest son of

▲ *The foundation document for Henry VII's Chapel in Westminster Abbey, London. The royal arms are supported by the red dragon of Cadwallader, a badge of the Tudors.*

▼ *The arms of the Emperors of Austria and their major dominions – the arms of the Kingdom of Hungary bear the crown of King Stephen, with its bent cross.*

the Prince of Wales – has only three points. The central point is charged with an escallop taken from the arms of his mother's family, the Spencers, whose arms include three escallops Argent.

The French royal family was divided into numerous branches, each of which differenced the royal arms with their own particular brizures. These included the white label used by the House of Orleans and the red bend of the Bourbons. When the lesser branches of these lines in time put out their own branches, each differed the brizure of their branch with smaller charges. The Counts of Angoulême, for example, charged the white label of the House of Orléans with red crescents.

In Russia, members of the Romanov dynasty tended to difference their arms by means of supporters to show their proximity to the throne.

► *The arms of the monarchs of Europe in the late 18th century. This plate, taken from a French work on heraldry, places the Catholic kingdoms first, and the Protestant states lower down the page.*

ROYAL QUARTERINGS

As with most ancient families, the arms of the ruling dynasties of Europe often started with the simplest designs. The Hohenzollerns started with a shield quartered in white and black; their neighbours the Habsburgs had a red lion rampant on a gold field. At the height of their powers, when the Hohenzollerns were Emperors of Germany and the Habsburgs were Holy Roman Emperors, both were able to sport shields of many quarterings: each quarter represented a lordship, county, principality or kingdom over whose fortunes the emperor held sway. Yet at the heart of each grand design could still be found the red lion of the Habsburgs and the simple quarters of the Hohenzollerns.

Some monarchs, such as those of France, made relatively little use of quarterings in their arms. The fleurs de lis of France are thought by some to be symbols of the Virgin Mary, by others to be three toads. The creatures of the English kings, which have at times been thought of as

DANGEROUS DIFFERENCES

It seems incredible that the display of arms alone would be enough to topple men of power and influence. Yet during the reign of Henry VIII this was the fate of Henry Howard, Earl of Surrey and his near relation Edward Stafford, Duke of Buckingham. Henry had a paranoid suspicion of anyone with a claim to his throne, and while both men had the right to bear differenced versions of the royal arms, they were rash in their ostentatious use of royal heraldry. It was even suggested that the Earl of Surrey had removed the difference marks from his arms, asserting his claim to be more royal than the King. Whether guilty or not, the two aristocrats were executed.

either lions or leopards, were of equally ancient and mysterious origin. The English monarchs quartered the French royal arms with their own to back up their claim to the throne of France, even placing the French arms in the most prominent quarters (1 and 4), and the fleurs de lis remained in the British royal arms as late as the 19th century. British monarchs kept their arms simple by displaying only quarters representing their kingdoms: England, Scotland, Ireland and France. But when the British throne passed to the House of

Guelph (Hanover) in 1714 the royal shields became more complex, including quarters for Brunswick, Lüneberg and Hanover. Over the last three was a small escutcheon charged with the crown of Charlemagne, indicating the office of Archtreasurer of the Holy Roman Empire, held by the British monarch as Duke of Brunswick and Lüneberg.

Members of the Swedish royal family include as quarterings the arms of the province from which they take their ducal title, for example Varmland or Uppland.

THE BRITISH NOBILITY

Evolved over a millennium, the British nobility has developed a multitude of mannerisms, styles of address, dress, insignia and duties so complex and contrived that few outside its ranks understand them. While noble families no longer wield the power and wealth they once commanded, even a Labour government continues to see a need for lords and ladies of sorts: although it removed most of the hereditary holders of peerages from the House of Lords in 1998, it offered some ordinary citizens the chance to become "people's peers", and deck themselves out in scarlet and ermine.

Naturally, members of the nobility do not go around from day to day wearing their robes and coronets. In fact most of them will now have little chance of wearing their robes officially ever again, unless it is for the coronation of a sovereign. However, at least one of their number was, until quite recently, given to having his daughter dress up in his coronation robes and thrill impressionable visitors by processing down corridors when his ancestral home was open to the public.

PEERS AND PEERESSES

The word "peer" is derived from the Latin *pares*, meaning "equal" and it refers to the collective nature of the upper aristocracy. This is because despite their different ranks – from duke to baron – all holders of peerage titles were until recently entitled to a seat and vote in the House of Lords, one of the two chambers of the British Parliament. Only a few of these hereditary peers are still chosen to sit and vote in the upper House. Since the passing of the House of Lords Act, 1998, the majority of those entitled to such a seat and vote are holders of a life peerage, and their titles become extinct upon their death.

RANKS AND TITLES

The British peerage is divided into five ranks. In order of seniority, these are duke, marquess (or marquis), earl, viscount, and baron. Life peers rank as barons, and are entitled to wear the robes and coronet of that rank. Many people assume that a British lord has to live on, or own, the estate from which he derives his title: that the Duke of Somerset must own that county, or that the Earl of Plymouth lives in that city. This is certainly not the case, though in the medieval period such men may well have derived their titles from the land they governed on behalf of the king.

Of the five ranks, the highest, duke, derives its name from the Latin *dux*, or war leader. Dukedoms have always been bestowed sparingly and there have been

◄ *Until the 18th century, the funerals of the nobility were occasions for a prominent display of heraldry. The funeral trappings included the hatchment, a diamond-shaped board bearing the arms of the deceased. This impressive hatchment is that of John, 1st Duke of Atholl, d1722.*

to a nobleman of high repute. In the Holy Roman Empire, a count of the marches, or *Markgraf*, was responsible for guarding the easternmost borders.

The middle rank, that of earl, is the oldest of the five. It derives from the *earldorma*, the Anglo-Saxon official appointed to administer a shire on behalf of the monarch. The equivalent rank in the French nobility was the *comte* (or count), and in Germany, *Graf*. The administrative duties of the earl or count meant that he was a busy man and would often have needed a deputy or "vice-count" to assist him. From this subordinate office the rank of viscount arose.

The lowest rank of the peerage, that of baron, was introduced by William I from France into England. By the 13th century the barons were "summoned by writ" to take their place in the King's Council, or Parliament. The Scottish equivalent of this rank is a "lord of Parliament", or simply a "lord". In Scotland the title of "baron" is feudal by nature, and occasionally it may be purchased; it does not now give the bearer a seat in the House of Lords but does have certain heraldic insignia.

periods since 1448, when the first non-royal dukedom was conferred, during which no holder of the rank was living. In Britain, where the rank of prince is not used outside the royal family, all male children of the sovereign are styled prince, and their daughters, princesses. It has also long been the case that the younger sons of the sovereign are each given a dukedom, those of York, Kent and Gloucester being reserved for the royal family.

David Lloyd George, British Prime Minister from 1916–22, complained that a fully equipped duke was as costly to maintain as two dreadnoughts, and less easy to scrap. Those who upheld the peerage system countered by saying that a British duke "in full sail" was twice as effective as any battleship and much more difficult to sink.

The rank below duke is marquess. It derives its name from a guardian of the marches, or borders – a sensitive and strategic office entrusted by the sovereign

▲ *The Parliament of Edward I (1272–1307) in session: the parliamentary robes worn by the lords sitting opposite the bishops are very similar to those of today's peers.*

▼ *At his 1991 introduction to the House of Lords, Lord Runcie (centre) is flanked by Garter King of Arms and Black Rod (left), and two peers of the same rank (right).*

FORMS OF NOBLE ADDRESS AND COURTESY TITLES

The wife of a duke is a duchess. The wife of a marquess is a marchioness; that of an earl, a countess; that of a viscount, a viscountess; and that of a baron, a baroness. All holders of a peerage, up to and including marquesses, are addressed in speech as "My Lord" or "Your Ladyship", and their wives as "My Lady". A duke and duchess are both addressed as "Your Grace".

In the British peerage, only the head of a family bears the title (as opposed to the practice of some other nations, where many members share the rank). However, the eldest son of a duke, marquess or earl may, during his father's lifetime, use one of his father's lesser titles (often accrued before the senior title). Such a title is known as a "courtesy title" because of its acknowledgement by the royal court, though it has no legal standing. Should the "courtesy lord" have children of his own, his eldest son may use another of his grandfather's lesser titles. For example, the Duke of Leinster's eldest son is known as the Marquess of Kildare, and in turn his eldest son is styled the Earl of Offaly; the

▼ *The Earl and Countess Mountbatten of Burma in their coronation robes, at the coronation of Elizabeth II in 1953.*

eldest son of the Marquess of Zetland is styled the Earl of Ronaldshay, and his eldest son is Lord Dundas.

A younger son of a duke or marquess is given the style of Lord, followed by his name: for example, "Lord Charles Brown". A daughter is styled "Lady Jane Brown". The younger son of an earl, or any son of a viscount or a baron, is styled "the Honourable Charles Brown". A daughter is "the Honourable Jane Brown", or "the Honourable Mrs Brown" if married. In conversation or informal correspondence, "Hons" are addressed as Mr, Miss or Mrs.

The eldest son of a peer is permitted to use his father's supporters – differenced by a label and with the consent of Garter King of Arms – only if he is summoned to Parliament in the lifetime of his father. However, there are many examples to be found of eldest sons bearing their father's supporters and even coronets of rank, despite never having received such a summons. All this is very confusing, not only to foreigners trying to understand the most complex honours system in the world, but also to the British themselves. Such arcane intricacies were dismissed by Oscar Wilde in a letter to Robert Ross:

…I have written to him [Lord Alfred Douglas] to tell him that… for him to try and pose as your social superior because he is the third son of a Scotch marquis and you the third son of a commoner, is offensively stupid. There is no difference between gentlemen. Questions of title are matters of heraldry – no more.

Peerages normally pass through the male line by direct descent, or sideways through brothers and their issue. Certain titles (usually ancient baronies or earldoms) can pass through the female line, and should the holder of such a title be a woman she is said to be a peeress "in her own right".

RIGHTS AND PRIVILEGES

The privileges of a British peer have been eroded by time, especially since 1998, when most of the "hereditaries" lost their right to sit in the House of Lords. They

▲*The Earl Marshal of England, His Grace the Duke of Norfolk in 1998. He wears his parliamentary robes and holds his gold baton of office.*

used, for example, to be entitled to trial by their peers, presided over by the Lord High Steward. The last case of this kind was that of Lord Clifford, who was accused of manslaughter in 1935. Peers are still able to claim the right of direct access to the sovereign, but the present Queen has probably not been much bothered by any lords or ladies seeking her advice.

Before the 1998 House of Lords Act, there were over 850 hereditary peers who were entitled to a seat and a vote in the House of Lords. Although those times have gone, for many the House of Lords is still the most exclusive of all London's clubs. In past centuries that sense of belonging was sometimes marked in pompous ways by the peers themselves. In the 16th century for example, Elizabeth I's Lord Chancellor, Sir Christopher Hatton, erected replicas of the arms of every one of his fellow peers at his home at Holdenby, Northamptonshire, while Lord Burghley decorated his mansion with a map showing the arms of every major landowner in the country.

ROBES AND CORONETS

There are two types of peers' robes: those worn for Parliament and those worn at a coronation. Parliamentary robes, known since the late medieval period, are worn when the peer is introduced into the House of Lords and during the state opening of Parliament. They are made of fine scarlet cloth trimmed with white fur. Each peer's rank can be deduced by the number of rows, or "guards", of fur borne on the front. The robe of a duke is "powdered", or decorated, with four guards of ermine, spaced equally, with gold lace above each row. The robe of a marquess has four rows on the right and three on the left, each with gold lace. An earl's robe has three rows of ermine and gold lace. The robes of a viscount and a baron are identical, each having two guards of plain white fur and gold lace.

Peers' robes are made by Messrs Ede and Ravenscroft, the court tailors, in London. Few people today – even peers of the realm – can afford real ermine, and rabbit fur or "coney" tends to be used instead, dyed to imitate the black spots of ermine. If the peer should take pity on the rabbit or ermine, he or she may prefer to have synthetic fur. A baron's parliamentary robe at the time of writing would cost the new peer £2,000 (US$3,000), although one enterprising peeress ran hers up on her own sewing machine, using fabric purchased in the local market. For gold lace she used gold foil patterned with the

▲ *Peers' robes charge the arms of the London firm of Ede and Ravenscroft Ltd, which has made robes for the British peerage for centuries.*

▼ *The arms of Lord Mowbray, Segrave and Stourton. As a baron, his coronet of rank bears six balls on the rim, of which four are visible. It appears surmounting his arms without helm or crest.*

points of a comb. Coronation robes are much more costly and are, of course, seldom seen, unless they happen to be placed on public display in the peer's country house. The official description states that these robes or mantles:

…are created out of crimson velvet, edged with miniver [white fur], the cape furred with miniver pure, and powdered with bars or guards of ermine according to their degree:
Barons: 2 guards
Viscounts: 2 guards and a half
Earls: 3 guards
Marquesses: 3 guards and a half
Dukes: 4 guards
The said mantles or robes to be worn over full Court dress, or regimentals.

If a duke were to ask the court tailors to make him a set of coronation robes today, he would probably have to pay more than £10,000 (US$15,000).

The wives of peers, and peeresses in their own right, wear coronation robes or mantles powdered with guards in number according to their (or their husband's) degree. The robe or mantle also has a train, which varies in length from one yard for a baroness, to two yards for a duchess.

While in other nations coronets of rank are simply heraldic ornaments, the unique distinction of the British peerage is that they do get to wear actual coronets according to their degree, albeit only on one rare occasion – at the exact moment the monarch is crowned. Coronets of rank are officially described as follows:

The coronets to be silver gilt; the caps of crimson velvet turned up with ermine, with a gold tassel on the top; and no jewels or precious stones are to be set or used in the coronets, or counterfeit pearls instead of silver balls.

• The coronet of a Baron to have, on the circle or rim, 6 silver balls at equal distance.

• The coronet of a Viscount to have, on the circle, 16 silver balls.

• The coronet of an Earl to have, on the circle, 8 silver balls raised upon points, with gold strawberry leaves between the points.

• The coronet of a Marquess to have, on the circle, 4 gold strawberry leaves and 4 silver balls alternately, with latter a little raised on points above the rim.

• The coronet of a Duke to have, on the circle, 8 gold strawberry leaves.

The coronets worn by the peers' wives are smaller variants of those of their husbands.

Although no precious stones or pearls are now permitted to adorn peers' coronets, those borne by medieval earls would almost certainly have been heavily jewelled. Most aspects of coronet design were set in the 17th century; before that time, barons did not wear coronets at all but were permitted to wear only a cap of scarlet and ermine.

▼ *The arms of Francis Russell, 2nd Earl of Bedford c1580. Little except the helmet of degree has changed since then in the composition of a peer's arms.*

+ CHE SARA SARA. +

TIBI FIDELIS

THE HERALDRY OF PEERS
Peers of the realm enjoy the right of supporters and a depiction of the coronet of their degree. The latter is placed directly above the shield and not upon the helmet, which is placed above it with the crest. The helmet of a peer is silver, garnished with gold, and set in profile showing five bars. However, it is not necessary for the helmet itself actually to appear in the achievement, which is often simplified to include only the coronet – with or without its cap – and the crest. The peer may also place a robe of estate in the armorial achievement, but this is seldom done. A Scottish peer bears crimson mantling lined with ermine.

Should a married woman be a peeress in her own right, the situation becomes more complicated. The complete marital achievement uses two sets of arms, with the husband's on the dexter side and the wife's on the sinister side. Traditionally,

▲ *The full splendour of the arms of a modern British peer, Baron (Lord) Howe, with supporters, coronet of degree and helm.*

peeresses in their own right have been, by their nature, heraldic heiresses. The peeress's husband therefore martials his arms in the normal fashion, with an escutcheon

▼ *The marital achievement of a peeress in her own right, married to a commoner, her arms appear on the right, her husband's shield with her escutcheon on the left.*

of pretence of his father-in-law's arms in the centre of his shield. The escutcheon is "ensigned", or surmounted, with the correct coronet of rank for his wife. Should the husband himself be a peer, he uses the complete achievement of his degree, with supporters, coronet and so on. If he is a gentleman he simply uses the arms of that degree. In both cases, to the sinister of the husband's achievement is that of the peeress on a lozenge borne by supporters and ensigned with her coronet. If the peeress is Scottish, she can also bear in her achievement the crest of her family.

In recent years many women have been made life peers. They are thus peeresses in their own right but – provided they have brothers to carry on their family arms – not heraldic heiresses. If such a peeress is married, her husband impales his and his wife's arms on the shield, with his wife's complete achievement alongside.

When the husband of a peeress in her own right dies, she shows her situation by bearing two lozenges, the one to the dexter with the marital coat, the sinister remaining as before. The widow of a peer who is not a peeress in her own right uses the dexter achievement only – the marital arms martialled on a lozenge – but this is still "protected" by the supporters and coronet of her husband's peerage. The wife of a lord, knight or baronet enjoys her husband's title, being "Lady So and So", yet if plain Mr Jones marries a peeress in her own right, he remains plain Mr Jones.

THE BARONETAGE

There is one other rank in the British nobility that is hereditary yet does not entitle the bearer to a seat or vote in the House of Lords. This rank, which manages to confuse many, is that of baronet. In effect, the holder of a baronetcy is treated as a hereditary knight. He is therefore known as, say, Sir John Smith, and can place "Bt" after his name. Coming somewhere in precedence between knights and peers, the baronetage was considered by some to be particularly associated with "new money". It is said that Queen Victoria found it a useful way of ennobling members of the working class. At one point in the 19th century, so many wealthy brewers were members of the baronetage that it was nicknamed "the beerage".

The baronetage had its origins with James I (1603–25), who created the degree of baronet as a way of raising funds. The title was granted on payment of a fee of £1,095 – the sum required to maintain 30 infantrymen in Ulster for three years – and the first 100 letters patent were ready in 1611. A similar idea was promulgated for Scotsmen prepared to finance the settlement of Nova Scotia. The Baronets of Nova Scotia bear the arms of a British knight (with helm affronty with visor open), augmented with the arms of Nova Scotia. This can be borne on a canton or inescutcheon, or as a badge suspended below the shield by a tawny ribbon. Baronets of Ulster – and more lately of the United Kingdom – bear in similar fashion the red hand of Ulster on a white field.

TITLES FOR SALE

The selling of baronetcies raises the question of whether it is possible to buy other titles. At certain periods the sale of knighthoods and peerages was all but blatant. It seems that anyone who could afford it could advance themselves to the ranks of knights and lords if they wished. Certain courtiers, often favourites of the sovereign, saw it almost as their duty to obtain – at a price – titles for their friends or family. Sir Robert Peel was driven to write: "The voracity of these things quite surprises me. I wonder people do not begin to feel the distinction of an unadorned name."

By Victoria's reign the business had been somewhat tightened up, but there was one more scandal over the sale of titles in the 1920s, when the Liberal Party, then in power under Lloyd George as Prime Minister, saw the sale of titles as a possible means of augmenting party funds. It was claimed that costs would vary from £10,000 for a knighthood to £100,000 for a peerage, and the go-between chosen to sound out likely clients was the "peerage broker" J. Maundy Gregory. The furore created by this shady dealing in titles for political ends ultimately assisted in Lloyd George's fall from office and the passing of the Prevention of Abuses Act (1925). This made it an offence to accept "any gift, money or valuable consideration as an inducement or reward for procuring…the grant of a dignity or title of honour".

There are few chances of seeing peers in their finery, except from the House of Lords visitors gallery when a new peer is introduced. On such an occasion, the new peer is dressed in parliamentary robes and accompanied by two fellow peers of the same rank. Garter King of Arms leads them into the chamber in full ceremonial uniform, complete with tights, tabard and chain. The centuries-old ceremony involves much bowing and doffing of hats.

▼ *The shield of a baronet of the United Kingdom is charged with an escutcheon bearing the red hand of Ulster, and the helm is that of a knight (with its visor open).*

THE ORDER OF THE GARTER

The rise in chivalry brought with it messages of loyalty, heroism, glory and brotherly love. It was seized upon by the princes of Europe, who saw it as the ideal stratagem with which to bond men of rank and military expertise, creating elite brotherhoods – the chivalric orders – that would serve them in both war and peace. One of these was the English Order of the Garter. Medieval and romantic writers, inspired by the ethos of chivalry, drew on the stories of King Arthur and the Round Table, the English connections of which served Edward III's political ambitions when he instituted the Order of the Garter. The year has been disputed but is believed to be 1348, although it has also been suggested that the Order was founded some four years earlier, when the King set up a round table for knights who had taken part in a great tournament at Windsor.

INSIGNIA OF THE ORDER

The original members of the Order were the King and the Prince of Wales (Edward the Black Prince), together with 24 companions, who each took a blue garter as their device. It has been suggested that the

garter was intended to represent a sword belt, but the more romantic story concerns an incident at a ball held in Calais, when a garter fell from the leg of Joan, Countess of Salisbury. Seeing the smirks of the courtiers and the Countess's discomfort, King Edward picked up her garter and uttered the words, "Honi soi, qui mal y pense" ("shamed be he who thinks evil of it").

It may be no coincidence that the colours of the Garter – blue and gold – were also those of the French arms, when at the time of its foundation Edward III was making a claim to the French throne. Although the earliest depictions of the Garter robes show them to have been murrey (maroon) strewn with garters, by the 15th century they were blue and bore a single garter on the left shoulder. Members of the order have also always worn an actual garter on the left leg below the knee.

Gradually the insignia were increased. Henry VII (1485–1509) introduced the splendid collar, consisting of gold knots alternating with red roses encircled by garters. From this is suspended the George, a mounted figure of St George slaying a green dragon. The star of the Order was

LADIES OF THE GARTER

During the late Middle Ages, ladies were associated with the Order and although they did not enjoy full membership they were apparently entitled to wear a garter on their left arm. Effigies of Ladies of the Garter can be found in the churches of Ewelme and Stanton Harcourt, both in Oxfordshire. One of the last to be so honoured was Henry VII's mother, Margaret Beaufort. After her death in 1509 the Order became exclusively male, except for female sovereigns, until 1901, when Edward VII made Queen Alexandra a Lady of the Garter. Since then, several reigning queens have been members. In 1987 women were made eligible for the Garter in the same way as men, styled as Lady Companions of the Most Noble Order of the Garter.

▼ *The effigy of Alice, Duchess of Suffolk. The Duchess is shown wearing the Garter around her left forearm.*

▼ *A splendid design of 1589 showing the arms of the knights of the Garter from 1486–1589, enclosed on the Tudor Rose.*

▼ *The Garter has been used to encircle not only the arms of the knights but also the prelates and chancellors of the Order.*

instituted by King Charles I in 1629. It bears the red cross of St George, encircled by the garter and surrounded by silver radiating beams.

THE INSIGNIA IN HERALDRY

Since the Tudor period it has been the norm for a Garter knight to place his arms within the garter. It is also permissible to place the arms within the collar of the Order, although this is seldom done today, possibly because the collar is such a complex item to paint accurately. Other British orders of chivalry follow this pattern, and

▲ Roger Mortimer, Earl of March (d1398) in robes of the Garter. The portrait is taken from a 15th-century document.

remains, so that the earliest of these date from the late medieval period.

The shields of the Garter knights hang in St George's Hall, also in Windsor castle, and many were destroyed during a fire in 1992. The replacement shields met with disapproval among heraldists, as the work was given to a sign painter (who afterwards said that he never wanted to see another shield in his life). The shields of those appointed since 1999 have been created by a full-time heraldic artist.

The other British orders of chivalry also have chapels attached to them. The Chapel of King Henry VII in Westminster Abbey, London, is home to the Order of the Bath, and contains the stall plates of such famous members as Lord Nelson, the Duke of Wellington and Lord Kitchener of Khartoum. The Order of St Michael and St George has a chapel in St Paul's Cathedral. St Paul's also houses the Chapel of the Order of the British Empire in its crypt, although there are no stall plates there and the banners all relate to the Royal Family. The Royal Victorian Order has its home in the Queen's Chapel of the Savoy. Its stall plates include that of Sir John Miller, showing Sir John himself – not once but twice – as supporters to his own shield.

▼ The late Major General Sir Hugh Sykes, Knight Grand Cross of the Most Exalted Order of the Star of India, encircled his arms with the collar of that Order.

their members place their arms within a circlet bearing the motto. Knights Grand Cross may place their arms within the collar of their order. Knights (and baronets) show their degree by placing above their shield a steel helmet with a plain visor, fully open.

When a knight of a chivalric order displays a marital achievement of arms, two shields (or ovals) are depicted side by side. That on the dexter has the knight's arms alone within the circlet or collar of his order, that to the sinister has the full marital achievement of husband and wife (impaled or with escutcheon of pretence) within a wreath. The helmet of degree sits at the junction between the two shields. The two coats show that the knighthood was conferred on the man and not his wife, but she through courtesy enjoys her husband's title and is addressed as "Lady" (followed by her husband's surname).

In Britain, when a woman is awarded with the equivalent of a knighthood, she is called a dame (Dame Grand Cross or Dame Commander), and may place her lozenge within the circlet of the order.

DISPLAYS OF ARMS

During his lifetime, the banner and crested helmet of each Garter knight is hung above his stall in St George's Chapel in Windsor Castle. At the back of each stall is an enamelled metal plaque bearing the knight's arms, and while the banner and crest are taken down on his death, his stall plate

THE ORDER OF THE GOLDEN FLEECE

The earliest orders of chivalry in Europe were religious, formed with the intent of creating bands of military men to fight in the Holy Land. As the structure of society in western Europe changed during the 14th century, with the dominance of the Church giving way to royal power, a number of temporal orders of chivalry were founded to strengthen and glorify the position of kings. Perhaps the most glorious of these royal knighthoods belonged to the Duchy of Burgundy, whose dukes were as powerful and wealthy as any king of Christendom.

Seeing the prestige of Edward III's Order of the Garter, Philip the Good, Duke of Burgundy (1419–67) decided to create a similar institution to bond together the highest nobles of his own realm. He gave each male member of his house, and his most trusted counsellors and friends, a bejewelled golden chain, the forerunner of the collar of the Golden Fleece. The Order of the Golden Fleece (La Toison d'Or) was founded in 1430 in celebration of Philip's marriage to Isabella of Portugal. As with the Garter knights, Duke Philip exacted a vow from the Knights of the Golden Fleece to defend the Church and his ducal house from all malignant foes.

CHAPTER MEETINGS

In common with other orders of chivalry, the knights were to meet in a chapter, which was to be held every few years in one of the great cities of Burgundy. The first chapter was held in 1431 at Lille (now in northern France) and 25 knights were installed on that occasion. As with the

▲ The 15th-century Burgundian court was "the richest in Christendom". Here, Charles the Bold, Duke of Burgundy (1466–77), presides over his council. The border around the scene bears the arms of all his territories.

Garter, stalls in the chapel of the Order were decorated with the armorial achievements of the knights. However, in the case of the Golden Fleece, where chapter meetings were held in various Burgundian cities, sets of arms dating from separate meetings can be found in churches across northern France and Belgium. The chapter meetings often coincided with other lavish spectacles laid on by the Dukes of Burgundy. These events were the envy of the princes of Europe, few of whom were able to equal Burgundian opulence.

At a meeting of the chapter the Duke of Burgundy sat as Grand Master. On either side of him, the knights would take their places, each wearing the collar of the

◀ The arms of the Dukes of Burgundy on the tomb of Charles the Bold in Bruges. The quarters are 1st and 4th Burgundy modern, 2nd Burgundy ancient with Brabant, 3rd Burgundy ancient with Limburg. The escutcheon bears the arms of Flanders.

Order. The chapter meetings were administered by officers, each with a specific duty. The Chancellor of the Order, normally a high-ranking prelate, was responsible for the great seal. He organized the meetings and reported to the Grand Master on any wrongdoings of the knights. He also spoke the funeral oration after the death of a knight. The Treasurer looked after the statute books and the collars of the Order, each of which was numbered and returned on the death of a knight. The Secretary wrote down the minutes and recorded the martial deeds of the knights.

As with most orders of chivalry, the Golden Fleece had its own herald called, appropriately, Toison d'Or King of Arms. This officer wore a badge of office, a

▲ *The stall plate of Philip II of Spain, Sovereign of the Order of the Golden Fleece, placed in St Baaf's Cathedral, Ghent for the 23rd chapter meeting of the Order in 1559.*

DIVISION OF THE ORDER

The male line of the house of Burgundy came to an end in the 15th century, when all the fortunes of that extraordinary land fell to the great heiress, Mary of Burgundy, the sister of Charles the Bold. Mary married the Habsburg Archduke Maximilian, who became Holy Roman Emperor in 1493. Mary and Maximilian's grandson, Charles, eventually succeeded to the throne of Spain in 1516.

When the Habsburg bloodline became extinct in Spain, the Austrian Emperor, Charles VI (1711–40), claimed sovereignty of the Golden Fleece from the Bourbon monarchs of Spain, and in 1713 re-instituted the Order in Vienna. From that time the Golden Fleece continued separately in each of the two countries. The Austrian branch admitted only Catholics, but the Spanish branch became a civil order in the 19th century, and current members include Queen Elizabeth II of Britain.

Despite the fall of so many European monarchies in the first half of the 20th century, several of the great temporal orders of chivalry survive, among them the Order of the Garter and the Order of the Thistle. Two Scandinavian orders, the Danish Order of the Elephant (1462), and the Swedish Order of the Seraphim (1748), maintain splendid displays of heraldry relating to current and former knights of the orders.

▼ *The collar of the Golden Fleece, shown in its full form in a Flemish armorial of the late 16th century.*

version of the collar of the Order known as the "potence", decorated with the arms of all the knights at a particular chapter meeting. The herald was responsible for much of the ceremonial associated with the Order and for making sure that the knights' heraldry was correctly marshalled.

INSIGNIA OF THE ORDER

The shield of arms of each knight of the Golden Fleece is enclosed within the collar of the Order, each link of which depicts the device or badge of the Dukes of Burgundy – a steel within a flint emitting showers of sparks. Suspended from the central flint in the collar is a representation of the golden fleece, and a line from Philip's speech: "I will disperse my enemies and strike before they are ready." One of the theories mooted for the choice of the golden fleece as the Order's device is an allusion to the wool trade, source of Burgundy's great wealth; another is that it referred to the Argonauts, whose quest for the golden fleece embodied the qualities that Philip sought in his own knights.

The potence of the King of Arms and the robes of a knight of the Order are displayed in the Kunsthistorisches Museum in Vienna, and many other museums have fabulous examples of the insignia.

HERALDRY IN THE CHURCH

Heraldry was adopted by the Church not very long after its birth on the battlefield. It hardly needed to be shown what to do with arms, since its hierarchy tended to be drawn from the nobility, the class that had already adopted heraldry. Although princes of the Church were supposed not to take part in war, two of the most militant men on the battlefield of Hastings in 1066 were Odo, Bishop of Bayeux, who was the half-brother of William of Normandy, and Geoffrey, Bishop of Coutances. These fighting prelates used their weapons in as terrible a fashion as any other Norman warrior.

Ecclesiastical users of heraldry developed their own methods of displaying their arms, tending to place them on the oval seals they had used since long before heraldry appeared. Whereas the military man displayed himself on his seal in a warlike manner, a proud prelate would show him or herself – abbesses often made use of armorial seals – in the act of blessing, accompanied by a shield of his or her personal arms. The seal of an abbey, cathedral or other institution often bore its patron saint together with the arms of the institution (if used) as well as those attributed to the saint. This is still the case for many dioceses and monastic institutions. During the

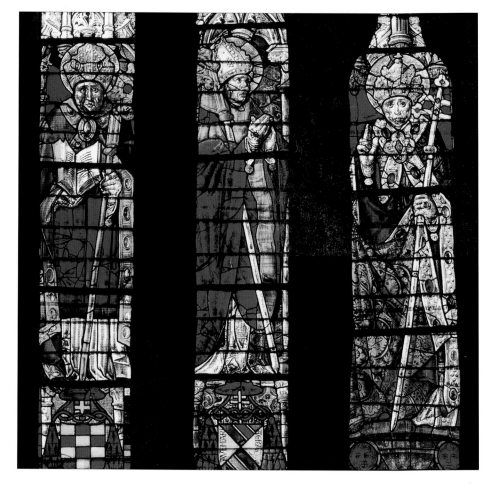

period when heraldry was being used in its true form by medieval knights in warfare, western Europe knew only one Church. The heraldry of the Catholic Church has since provided the model for other Christian denominations, including the Protestant clergy, although they tend to use simplified forms.

PAPAL ARMS

The Pope places his family arms on a shield ensigned by the papal tiara. Behind the shield are placed the keys of St Peter: a gold key points to the dexter, symbolizing papal power extending up to heaven, and a silver key points to the sinister, symbolizing power over the faithful on earth. The keys are often joined together by a red cord. During the period between the death of a pope and the election of his successor (known as the interregnum or sede vacate), the keys pass to the cardinal-camerlengo (the papal treasurer), who bears them in saltire beneath another emblem peculiar

▲ The arms of cardinals portrayed in a 15th-century window of Toledo Cathedral, Spain, are surmounted by their red hats.

to the Catholic Church, the pavilion known as the "ombrellino", which is, in fact, an umbrella. Both keys and pavilion are usually placed above the shield of the camerlengo, indicating that it is his duty to watch over the rights of the holy see until the election of the new pope.

THE CARDINAL'S HAT

Since the 13th century, the rank of cardinal has been distinguished by the wearing of a red hat, adorned with cords intended to be tied under the chin. It was long the custom for a cardinal's hat to be hung above his tomb, and you can often still see these dusty insignia hanging in cathedrals in Catholic countries. The red hat found its way into heraldry, where it ensigned the cardinal's arms. The cords hung down on either side of the shield and were often

▲ The arms of Pope John Paul II, as used for papal notepaper, display the symbols of the papacy: the crossed keys and tiara.

▲ *The oval seal design typical for a religious institution or individual here shows the punning arms of Milton Abbey, Dorset, England: a mill on a tun (barrel).*

ornamented with tassels. Their number was not fixed at first, but under Pope Pius VI (1775–99) it became the custom to set 15 tassels on either side.

▼ *Great events in the Church calendar could be recorded through heraldry. This page from the Chronicle of the Council of Constance (1414–18) shows the arms of the great clerics who sat for the election of Pope Martin V (elected November 1417).*

ARCHBISHOPS AND BISHOPS

Resident archbishops may make use of the "pallium". Originally a toga-like vestment, this shrank to a Y-shaped band worn over the shoulders. It is often used as a charge in the arms of archiepiscopal dioceses.

Archbishops can also make use of a double transfixed cross behind their shield, while bishops place a simple cross behind theirs. High prelates of the Protestant Church may choose a shield of arms ensigned with a precious (jewelled) mitre. Sometimes a crozier and cross is placed in saltire behind the shield.

In northern Europe, and especially in Britain, it is quite common for archbishops, bishops and abbots to marshal their personal arms with those of their diocese or abbey. In British dioceses, the shield is impaled (as in a marriage): the dexter half bears the arms of the see and the sinister half the arms of the bishop. As Protestant clergy are allowed to marry, the hatchment of a bishop or archbishop often shows two shields of arms, that on the dexter with the arms as just described, that on the sinister bearing the personal arms further impaled with those of the wife's family.

ECCLESIASTICAL PRINCES

For centuries, archbishops, bishops, abbots and even abbesses were able to rule over certain territories in the Holy Roman Empire. These mighty princes of the Church often used achievements of arms every bit as grand as any other ruler. Some did not even bother to show any mark of ecclesiastical dignity, preferring to use mantles, princely hats or coronets of rank. More often they combined both ecclesiastical and lay insignia, and adorned their palaces and churches with some of the grandest achievements of arms ever seen.

Their arms often include not only the symbols of their pastoral duties, such as the crozier and cross, but a sword. This seems a most unlikely object to find in the arms of a churchman, or even a churchwoman, but it signifies that they literally had power of life or death over their subjects. A sword can even be seen in the arms of Abbess Elizabeth Antonia of Saxe-Meiningen (1713–66). Though Abbess

▲ *The modern achievement, including a mitre and robe, of an archpriest of the Ukrainian Orthodox Church in Canada, the Very Revd Waldemar Kuchta.*

Elizabeth's jurisdiction was confined to the cathedral and convent of Gandersheim in Lower Saxony, and her subjects numbered fewer than twenty, she asserted her independence from the Dukes of Brunswick by placing the imperial eagle behind a cartouche of the abbey's arms. These were divided Per pale Sable and Or, the imperial colours commemorating the early abbesses of Gandersheim, who were imperial princesses.

In Britain the sword-in-arms of prelates was virtually unknown, except in the arms of the Bishops of Durham. Durham Cathedral appears in many ways to be more castle than church, and a real castle stands right behind the great church. The prince-bishops of Durham were given palatinate status by the medieval English kings, making them virtually sovereign rulers in their diocese, because they were expected to maintain their own standing army and keep vigil against the invading Scots. The prince-bishops maintained the unique distinction of placing their mitre within a ducal (or heraldic) coronet. Earlier bishops also included in their mitre an ostrich plume, thus combining a bishop's hat with a warrior's crest. Their seals showed them as knights, charging into battle, with swords held aloft.

RELIGIOUS ORDERS OF CHIVALRY

Medieval Europe was dominated by two powers, the knights and the Church. While the Church often railed against the excesses of troublesome knights, who were not averse to sacking the odd abbey, it was into the local church that the knights' bodies were eventually carried. These violent characters were the same men whose memorials often appeared in due course in the stained glass windows of the church.

THE FIRST CRUSADE

Pope Urban II (reigned 1088–99), saw a way to channel the violence of the military. Rather than beseeching men to stop fighting, he encouraged them to take their aggression out on the principal bugbear of the Christian world – the Muslims. His rough and ready evangelism appealed to the fighting men of Europe: they saw the possibility of achieving not only eternal glory, but also earthly riches.

Urban used the symbolism of the crucifix during his rallies of 1095, announcing that it should be the token of their cause. The message immediately took effect, as men tore up strips of coloured cloth and stitched crosses on their tunics. Despite many setbacks, the First Crusade (1096–99)

▼ Arms of the Hoch- und Deutschmeister (Grand and Teutonic Master) of the Teutonic Order.

▲ A seal showing two impoverished Templar knights frugally doubling up on one horse.

achieved its aim: Jerusalem was captured and its inhabitants – men, women and children – were murdered in an orgy of brutality.

While the prospect of riches was an obvious draw, there were some of high rank who espoused the noblest aims of chivalry. For several years prior to Jerusalem's capture, a group of knights had acted as protectors to pilgrims to the city. At the time of the First Crusade they lived near the Temple of Solomon in Jerusalem. In 1119 Hughes de Payns and Geoffrey de St Omer incorporated the group into a religious order, the Poor Knights of the Temple of Solomon, usually known as the Knights Templar. So poor did the early Templars claim to be that their seals often depicted two men riding a single horse. The

▼ Left to right: The arms of the Order of the Knights Templar, the Order of St Lazarus, and the Sovereign and Military Order of St John of Jerusalem (the Order of Malta).

idea of priest-knights soon caught on and led to a flowering of other military orders of chivalry. Among them were the Knights of the Order of St Lazarus of Jerusalem, who maintained leper hospitals, and the Knights of the Hospital Order of St John of Jerusalem (the Knights Hospitallers), formed to aid sick and weary pilgrims. Some of the great dormitories they built still survive. The Hospitallers and the Templars acquired great wealth and built vast castles. There was little love lost between these two powerful orders, and when not fighting the "infidel", they were apt to fight each other.

INSIGNIA OF THE ORDERS

Each religious order of chivalry settled on a cross of a particular form and colour, and some of these symbols are still familiar today, none more so than the white eight-pointed cross of the Hospitallers, now called the Sovereign and Military Order of St John of Jerusalem, and known as the Order of Malta. The British branch of the Order became the Most Venerable Order of St John, whose members are famed for their voluntary relief work as the St John's Ambulance Brigade.

The Prince Grand Master of the Order of Malta quarters his family arms with those of the Order, and his shield is placed on an eight-pointed white cross surrounded by a rosary. The whole is placed on a black princely mantle and ensigned by a princely crown of degree. Other high-ranking prelates (notably Bailiffs Grand Cross) are entitled to bear a chief of the Order – Gules a cross Argent – and have a banner of the Order carried in procession.

▲ *Arms of the 78th and current Grand Master of the Sovereign Military Order of Malta, Fra Andrew Bertie. From medieval times the grand masters have quartered the arms of the Order with those of their family.*

Protestant chapters of the Order were formed in the late 16th and 17th centuries. Their heraldry conforms in the main to the Sovereign and Military Order of St John of Jerusalem, except that various national symbols are added to the decorations, arms and banners.

Of the other religious military orders, the most famous were the Teutonic Order of Germany and the Orders of Santiago and Calatrava, both of Spain. The crosses of each order have often found their way into the heraldry of their members. The Teutonic Knights, who maintained their fighting traditions by opposing pagan tribes along the eastern Baltic, displayed a black crutched cross (cross potent) which told of their origins caring for sick and wounded knights and pilgrims who came from their homelands.

Until the 14th century, there was at least one nation – Lithuania – which the Teutonic Order could still attempt to convert through the sword, but in 1386 Grand Duke Jagiello of Lithuania converted to Christianity (having married Jadwiga, heiress to the Polish throne). However, the Order continued to invade his borders and tried his patience so much that in 1410 he exacted a terrible revenge. At the Battle of Grunwald, hundreds of the Teutonic Knights were killed. Some, it is claimed were roasted in their armour on spits by the victorious Poles.

It is sometimes supposed that in the arms of Jerusalem the gold crosses borne on a white field were originally red. This version is used by the Order of the Holy Sepulchre, which originated when knighthoods were conferred on Crusaders visiting the Church of the Holy Sepulchre in Jerusalem. It is said that the knights of the Order were dubbed with the sword of Godfrey de Bouillon, a leader of the First Crusade. Its members may place their shields on the main cross potent and include the four small crosses couped around the edge or, like the members of the Order of Malta, they can place the cross alongside their achievement of arms, as best befits the design. The highest ranking members can quarter the crosses with their personal arms.

The Knights of St John left their mark through their heraldry wherever they went, especially on Malta, where the arms of the Grand Master can be seen on many buildings. In the former Conventual Church of the Order, now the Pro-Cathedral of St John in Valetta, a collection of 400 tesselated floor plaques in multi-coloured stone indicates by their arms the burial places of many members of the Order of Malta.

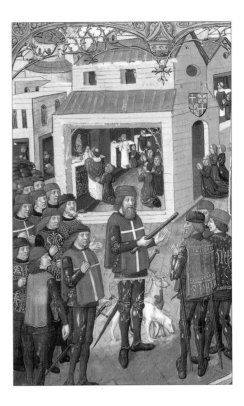

▲ *A medieval miniature shows the Knights of St John receiving orders from their Grand Master, Pierre d'Abusson (whose arms appear on the building top right), during the Siege of Rhodes by Muhammad II in 1486.*

▼ *One of the finest displays of heraldry in the world is to be found on the floor of St John's Pro-Cathedral in Valetta, Malta, where the arms of many officers of the Order of St John are executed in marble.*

CIVIC AND STATE HERALDRY

Most people feel the need to belong, whether it be to a football team, a

town or a nation. Identification with such an entity engenders a sense of

security and strength, and from that strength comes pride. The emblems

adopted by the sovereigns of Europe in the late Middle Ages soon became

identified not so much with the rulers themselves but with their entire

realms. The English were united behind the strength of the royal leopards,

the French were protected beneath their golden lilies. As the nation state

became a reality during the medieval period, the major cities and city states

of Europe also grew in wealth and power, believing themselves as rich and

mighty as any ruler or dynasty.

◀ *The civic seal, or sigil, from 1336, for the Italian*
town of Cividale.

CIVIC AND NATIONAL ARMS

Like the Church, whose religious and chivalric orders had embraced heraldry on a corporate basis, the towns and cities of Europe united their people behind devices that often reflected the protective nature of civic government. Their shields bore stylized views of municipal fortifications, with battlemented walls and turrets, or a gateway with its portcullis and other defences, asserting the defensive power and strength of the corporation.

Many early civic arms incorporate older devices found on the council's official seals. These often depicted not only the fortifications of the place, but also its patron saint, an important figure in the town or city's history. Not every town felt the need to put its protection in the hands of its patron saint alone. Where a municipality was under the influence of a local magnate or prince, who might or might not have a residence in the town, the arms of the ruler often filled the space within the gateway on the municipal shield. A combination of the arms or figures of the saint and the ruler was also common.

◄ *Many civic seals emphasized the safety of their city walls, and this was soon translated into heraldry.*

CIVIC ARMS AND EMBLEMS

As with personal arms, in the early stages of heraldry civic arms were usually adopted at will. It was only in the 15th and 16th centuries that towns started to be granted arms in a formal way, by letters patent issued on behalf of the sovereign. Provinces and counties tended to be known by the arms of their rulers, or used arms based upon theirs. Many are still in use, although major land reforms and boundary changes throughout Europe in the 19th century resulted in widespread reform of regional district heraldry.

In Britain any corporate body, from a city to a company, is entitled to apply for arms, but many towns, district councils and county councils that are not armigerous are adopting logos rather than arms, to represent themselves as dynamic and forward-looking. Perhaps this is because many of the arms granted in the 20th century were not the most imaginative of

designs, with over 70 per cent having as a principal charge a blue and white wavy line to represent some local water feature. The use of supporters is reserved for civic authorities viewed by the heralds as having some special eminence or distinction.

In Britain there is technically no such thing as "county" or "city" arms, as the arms are considered to belong to the body corporate: that is, the council or corporation in whose name they are granted. In Scottish heraldry, corporations are given a special type of helmet, called a "sallet", to differentiate them from personal arms.

NATIONAL ARMS

The need for a device representing national unity has been recognized for centuries, by both republics and monarchies. Some of the earliest republican arms must be those of the Swiss cantons. Instituted during the late medieval period, they were borne on the banners under which the famous Swiss troops marched. Swiss-trained bands were prized by other states for their prowess and discipline. Among the most famous of the cantonal arms were the white cross on red of Schwyz, the black ox head of Uri and the black bear of Appenzell.

When they were not fighting for other nations, Swiss troops kept in training by fighting those of the neighbouring cantons. One of the many disputes that arose between the cantons of Appenzell and Uri occurred when the people of Appenzell derided those of Uri by claiming – through the use of their arms – that they were as thick-headed as an ox. The inhabitants of Uri got their own back by taunting the Appenzellers, flourishing the latter's arms with the black bear missing its genitals. This was too much for the Appenzellers, who attacked Uri to avenge the insult.

WORLDWIDE HERALDRY

From the late medieval period onwards, heraldic writers gave arms to nations and rulers who had never actually encountered heraldry. To the writers this was no matter. Such was the nature of sovereignty that all

▼ *The arms of two Czech towns, Prague New Town (left) and Tábor (right), show how the motifs of civic seals were translated on to heraldic shields. Both include emblems of the kings, emperors and dynasties under which the towns prospered.*

monarchs, whether Christian or heathen, alive or dead – and their realms – were of noble status and deserving of heraldry. Thus the Shah of Persia was given a shield charged with a sun in splendour surrounded by stars, and the Sultan of Turkey was granted the Ottoman crescent, with the shield ensigned by a turban.

In time, as Europeans settled in all continents as a result of trade or conquest, heraldry was adopted by their rulers. Today, some eight centuries after the birth of heraldry in Europe, many nations and their rulers have achievements of arms. They range from the kings of Jordan to the republics of Indonesia and Bolivia. As far south as Antarctica itself, heraldry has made its mark. The English heralds designed arms for the Falkland Island Dependencies on 11 March 1952, and in 1963 the crest of the Antarctic research ship *Discovery* was added to the arms.

▲ *Arms of the major European monarchies at the beginning of the 20th century (left to right, top to bottom): Prussia, Austria, Hungary, Bavaria, Russia, Germany, Britain, Saxony, Italy, Spain, Württemberg. At the end of World War II all but two were extinct.*

▼ *The boroughs (contrades) of Siena in Italy attempt to outdo each other in magnificence at the opening procession of the festival of the Palio. This early 17th-century painting portrays the prosperity, independence and pride of the city-state.*

THE GARTER SERVICE

There are two annual events at which the full panoply of British state ceremonial can be observed by the public, and each has its own unique display of heraldry. The first is the service of the Order of the Garter in St George's Chapel, Windsor, which takes place on a Monday in mid-June, with a spectacular procession.

INVESTITURE

The investiture of new Knights of the Garter is held on the morning of the service in the Throne Room at Windsor. Two officers of the Order – Garter King of Arms and the Gentleman Usher of the Black Rod – bring in the knight or lady elect. He or she is brought, between two knight sponsors, to the sovereign, who personally invests him or her with all the insignia of the Order. For men, a garter is tied around the left leg and is held there by Garter King of Arms while the following admonition is read out, recalling a time when members of the Order formed the backbone of the monarch's military command structure:

To the honour of God Omnipotent and in Memorial of the Blessed Martyr, St George, tie about thy leg, for thy renown, this most Noble Garter. Wear it as a symbol of the Most Illustrious Order, never to be forgotten or laid aside, that thereby thou mayest be admonished to be courageous, and having undertaken a just war, with which thou shalt be engaged, thou mayest stand firm, valiantly fight courageously and successfully conquer.

THE PROCESSION

After the investiture follows lunch, after which the Garter Knights assemble in their robes in St George's Hall, the largest room in the castle, before processing to their service. They walk from the royal apartments to St George's Chapel, which lies at the foot of the hill inside the castle's outer

▲ *St George's Chapel, Windsor Castle, seen in an engraving of 1810. The stalls of the Knights of the Garter are dominated by their armorial banners, helms and crests.*

▼ *An etching by Marcus Gheeraerts the Elder, showing the procession of the Knights of the Garter in 1576.*

bailey. The first part of the procession is headed by the Constable and Governor of Windsor Castle, whose uniform includes insignia unique to his office, including a depiction of the castle's Royal Tower.

The Military Knights of Windsor follow, in their scarlet uniforms. They are the successors of the 26 impoverished ex-soldiers originally appointed as "bedesmen", people who were employed to pray for the souls of the Garter Knights. According to the letters patent instituted by Edward III in 1348, and subsequent statutes, each bedesman was to wear a red cloak with a small shield bearing the cross of St George. The cross still forms part of the insignia of the Military Knights, who also wear a silver cut Garter star and crown.

The Military Knights are followed by the officers of arms in their tabards and Tudor

bonnets, bearing a crowned Tudor rose, worn especially for the occasion. Behind the heralds come the Garter Knights in full robes, bonnets with ostrich plumes and the collars of the Order. Next are the Princes of the Blood and finally the officers of the Order leading the sovereign's procession. As with all the officers of the British orders of chivalry, each man has insignia of office, the most famous being the black rod borne by the Gentleman Usher of the Black Rod. The Garter officers wear cloaks bearing a shield with the cross of St George.

Next come the sovereign and consort, with the trains of their mantles held up by pages in the royal livery. On the sovereign's mantle is a large representation of the Garter star instead of the normal badge of the Order. The sovereign's party is followed by the Yeoman of the Guard. As the entire procession weaves its way to St George's Chapel, the festival atmosphere is maintained by military bands and the processional route is lined by troopers of the Household Cavalry. The pouches they wear on their cross belts bear the royal arms and their helmets continue the theme of the day by sporting the star of the Garter within a wreath.

The procession is met at the chapel by the clergy, and yet again the pageantry and pomp associated with royalty is manifest. The various members of the sovereign's ecclesiastical household are entitled to wear scarlet cassocks. Royal chaplains are

▲ *The standard of the Yeomen of the Guard, as approved by King George VI on 27 June 1938. It includes the badge of the House of Windsor (bottom right), newly created to appear on this standard.*

identified by a badge consisting of a silver-gilt wreath, crown and the sovereign's cypher; priests-in-ordinary wear a similar badge in silver. The steps to the chapel are lined by the officers of arms, and at the moment of the sovereign's entrance a fanfare sounds. If a new knight has been invested in the morning he will be led to his stall by Garter King of Arms. The Chancellor of the Order then calls out the knight's name, and there follows a service, after which the royal party and the rest of the participants return to the castle.

▼ *The Military Knights of Windsor leaving St George's Chapel after the Garter Service.*

MILITARY AND NAVAL KNIGHTS OF WINDSOR

All retired military officers, the Military Knights live in lodgings allocated to them in the 16th century: a row of houses built against the inner side of the castle wall opposite St George's Chapel. Apart from attending the Garter ceremony, they continue to fulfil the duties imposed on them in 1348 by attending chapel every Sunday to pray for the sovereign and the Knights of the Garter. Once known as Poor Knights, their name was changed in the 19th century, after rude and satirical verses about their alleged infirmity had been broadcast about the town of Windsor.

Between 1795 and 1892 there were also Naval Knights of Windsor. However, such was the nature of the old sea-dogs that there was much discord, not only amongst themselves, but also with the Military Knights. Far from leading a "virtuous, studious and devout life", they were wont to frequent taverns and bawdy houses in Windsor and were known to belabour each other with their crutches and wooden legs.

THE STATE OPENING OF PARLIAMENT

The ceremonial meeting of the British sovereign with parliament has its origins over 1,000 years ago, when the king consulted with his peers – other aristocrats in many ways as powerful and wealthy as he. In time the sovereign became more remote from his subjects, until events such as the signing of Magna Carta, the Civil War and the Revolution of 1688 brought the monarchy back into line.

Before the ceremony can proceed, a detachment of the Yeomen of the Guard, in their Tudor uniforms, search the cellars of the Palace of Westminster. They are looking for would-be terrorists following the example of Guy Fawkes who, on 5 November 1605, attempted to overthrow James I and his government by exploding barrels of gunpowder hidden in the cellar.

THE ROYAL PROCESSION

The sovereign is preceded by the royal regalia, which are allocated a coach of their own. In addition to the Imperial Crown, these include the Cap of Maintenance symbolizing the monarch's religious orthodoxy,

▼ *The arrival of Queen Victoria at the House of Lords to open her first Parliament. The scene includes the Lord Chancellor, with his purse, and Garter King of Arms.*

and the Sword of State which indicates his or her duty to defend justice. The sovereign follows in the Irish State Coach, escorted by the Household Cavalry.

At the moment the sovereign enters the Houses of Parliament the royal standard is raised on the Victoria Tower. The sovereign is greeted by the Earl Marshal of England, the Duke of Norfolk (or his deputy), who carries a gold baton tipped with ebony. Also present is the hereditary Keeper of the Palace of Westminster, the Lord Great Chamberlain. He wears a uniform of scarlet and gold, with blue collar and cuffs. Suspended from a hip pocket is his gold key of the Palace of Westminster, and in his right hand he bears his wand of office. Also in attendance are the Officers of Arms in their tabards. The sovereign is escorted up the royal staircase to the Robing Room. The staircase itself is a heraldic feast, its walls covered with the arms of sovereigns and their cohorts going back to the birth of heraldry.

In the Robing Room the sovereign is vested with the Imperial State Crown and dons the crimson Robe of State, whose train is carried by four pages dressed in the royal liveries, before the procession moves off. Amongst the many details to be noticed are the sticks carried by Gold Stick

▲ *At the state opening of Parliament in 1958, Queen Elizabeth II processes to the Lords Chamber, preceded by the Lord Great Chamberlain. The Yeomen of the Guard line the processional route.*

in Waiting and Silver Stick in Waiting, two senior officers in the Household Cavalry. Their office dates from Tudor times, when the sovereign was constantly protected by two chosen guards, who even slept outside the bedroom door. Charles II commemorated their devotion to duty by presenting sticks bearing either a gold or silver head inscribed with his cypher. The cypher of the current sovereign also appears in the badge of office of the Mistress of the Robes, the senior lady of the royal household.

The scene is further enhanced by the Yeomen of the Guard and the Honourable Corps of Gentlemen at Arms, who have their origin in the Band of Gentlemen Pensioners, a personal guard drawn from the king's confidants. The Gentlemen at Arms carry poleaxes with blades engraved with the royal arms. Their uniform has a scarlet coat with gold epaulettes and belt, blue trousers and brass helmet topped by white feathers. The helmet plate bears gilt royal arms quarterings within the Garter, mounted on a silver cut star. Their badge of a portcullis appears on their uniform and on their standard, devised by the

▲ *The Standard of the Honourable Corps of Gentlemen at Arms, with battle honours and the portcullis badge of Henry VIII, in whose reign the bodyguard was formed.*

English College of Arms in 1936. While it is based on the tapered shape of a cavalry standard, that of the Yeomen of the Guard is almost square. It bears the badges of the various dynasties it has served, from the crowned hawthorn bush of Henry VII to the badge of the House of Windsor, a representation of the Round Tower of Windsor Castle.

▼ *The Palace of Westminster is a haven of heraldry. Here, an artist restores the painted arms of the Chiefs of the General Staff on the Peers' Staircase.*

On the way to the House of Lords the royal procession passes by numerous armorial achievements, reflecting not only the history of the Houses of Parliament, but the leadership of the nation. At the top of the Peers' Staircase are the arms of Chiefs of the Imperial and General Staff, and at the bottom the arms of former Speakers of the House of Commons (since 1700) who have become peers.

In the Lords Chamber, the windows are set with the arms of peers and below them appear the arms of the Lord Chancellors. Much of the detail of the chamber is heraldic, from the ceiling bosses to the posts that support the curtain running around the gallery. Like much of the Palace of Westminster, the room dates from after the fire of 1834.

THE GRACIOUS SPEECH

The chamber's grandest feature, the throne, stands on a golden platform set with royal emblems. The royal party take their places and in front of them sit the peers. The Lords Spiritual (the bishops) are in their ecclesiastical robes, the Law Lords in robes and wigs, and the Lords Temporal (life peers and representative hereditary peers) in their parliamentary robes.

The Lord Chancellor approaches the sovereign holding his own insignia of office, the Lord Chancellor's Purse, embroidered with the royal arms within a border of cherub's heads. The purse formerly contained the matrix of the Great Seal of the Realm, but today it holds the text of the speech which the sovereign will read to the assembled Lords and Commons.

The sovereign is not allowed to enter the Commons, so they are commanded to attend by the Gentleman Usher of the Black Rod, who wears his chain of office and carries the Black Rod itself. The Speaker leads the Commons to the Lords, and when all are assembled in the Lords Chamber, the sovereign begins the Gracious Speech, which sets out government policy for the coming year.

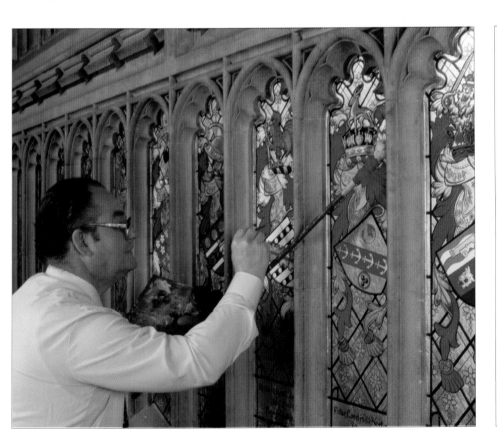

THE YEOMEN OF THE GUARD

Enhancing the pageantry of the state opening of Parliament are the Tudor uniforms of the Queen's Bodyguard of the Yeomen of the Guard. They wear the plant badges of the United Kingdom on the breast of their tunics: the combined rose, thistle and shamrock, on a background of scarlet and gold, the royal livery colours. Not to be confused with the Yeomen Warders who guard the Tower of London and wear a similar uniform but without the cross belt, the Queen's Bodyguard of the Yeoman of the Guard is the oldest royal bodyguard in existence, having served for more than 500 years. They can be observed not only at the state opening of Parliament but also at the annual Garter service in Windsor.

MILITARY HERALDRY

The military forces of the world have long been custodians of heraldic tradition. Amalgamations and changes of rulers, governments and commanding officers, have kept the heraldic designer busy devising new badges, standards or uniforms. While the medieval knight's horse bore a "trapper" or saddle-cloth resplendent with the arms of its rider, its modern equivalent – the tank – is likely to bear the heraldic liveries of a regiment.

The history of military heraldry is of course as old as heraldry itself. The military are upholders of tradition, and can give the heraldist a splendid insight into national heraldry and history. Although centuries have passed since military men wore full plate armour in battle, reminders of that remote age remain. British army officers of senior rank still wear "gorget patches" on their collars that once supported the steel gorget, or throat guard, of the medieval knight. In certain armies, some officers (normally guard commanders) still sport the gorget itself, which may bear the arms of the monarch or state.

PERSONAL LIVERIES

For centuries the military forces of Europe were recruited according to the feudal system. Lords agreed to support their leader during war through "liveries and maintenance", in return for estates with which they met the great expense of maintaining private armies. The wearing of a lord's heraldic colours and badges (liveries) was a striking aspect of the medieval scene, especially during the period of inter-dynastic strife in England now known as the Wars of the Roses (1455–85).

As late as the 19th century, certain European armies still included regiments paid for and equipped by "colonel proprietors": rich men or women, normally of high rank, who saw such private troops as liveried retainers. They naturally expected the troops to wear their heraldic colours, albeit as "facing colours" on the cuffs and collars of their uniforms. There was much jostling between the nobility to outdo not

▲ *The arm badge of the Royal Svea Lifeguards of the Swedish Army, showing the regimental arms.*

only the enemy, but also their fellow colonels, in the most recherché styles. The tradition of the colonel proprietor survives today in a muted form, in the honorary commanders of certain regiments. Even in republican France, some regiments bear the arms of former commanders from the days of the *ancien régime*.

European monarchs have long had a habit of swapping splendid uniforms with each other, making their cousins honorary colonels of regiments. By this means, almost a century after the "collapse of the eagles", these symbols of the Prussian and Austrian monarchies are still borne by British soldiers. The double-headed eagle of the Habsburgs (with their arms on its breast) is worn by the 1st The Queen's Dragoon Guards on their cap badge.

▲ *Military badges. Left, a pocket badge for the Swedish district staff of Norlands. Right, a Danish Army heraldic collar badge.*

FLAGS AND STANDARDS

The medieval tradition of a military unit going into battle under the standard of its commander is now obsolete (although Lord Lovat's piper famously led the Lovat Highlanders in the attack on D-Day in 1944, bearing His Lordship's pipe banner). However, as late as World War II, British tanks sported pennons of their regiment when going into battle.

Like all military insignia, unit flags differ from nation to nation. Some armies, notably those of republics, utilize the national flag with the addition of unit title

▼ *The shape of the standard favoured by medieval noblemen is still maintained in the flags of certain British Army units, especially artillery units.*

▲ *The simplicity of Norwegian military heraldry is exemplified in the badge of the Norwegian Army 6th Division (left) and a cap cockade (right) for the Norwegian King's Guard during the reign of Olav V.*

and battle honours. Others, as in the Swedish and Finnish armies, use the regimental badge and colours.

In the British Army, the small medieval badge-bearing flag – known as the "guidon" – has its modern equivalent in the company colours of the regiments of Foot Guards and the pennons of the regiments of the Royal Artillery. In each case the flag is long, narrowing at its end into one or two tails. Royal Artillery pennons are crossed by diagonal bands bearing the regimental motto, with the regiment's badges set in the segments between the bands, similar to the standard of a medieval English nobleman. Each company of Foot Guards has its own heraldic emblem, most of which are taken from well-known royal badges or "cognizances".

NATIONAL ARMY INSIGNIA

King Gustavus I of Sweden (1523–60) is widely credited with the formation of the first truly national army, based on a system by which each prince maintained an infantry and a cavalry regiment. By the early 19th century its units were bearing provincial arms on their helmet plates and other insignia. From the late 1970s, Swedish army units were also given formal achievements of arms, with the shield of the province surmounted by a royal crown.

Many European armies retain their national colours in the form of a metal cockade, maintaining a tradition dating back three centuries or more, of troops wearing a cloth cockade in the livery colours of their commander on their headgear. The armies of Denmark, Finland,

Norway and Sweden are all known by their cockades, splendid variants of which are worn by the troops of the guards regiments in Oslo and Copenhagen. The full military cockade worn by these troops usually comes in two parts or "buttons": the top button bears the national colours and the lower bears the national arms.

The arms of countries, provinces or districts provide the theme for many regimental badges, whether in uncoloured metal – as in the collar and shoulder insignia of the Finnish, Danish and Swedish armies – or in full colour, as on the shoulder patches also worn in the latter two forces. The Danish armed forces also wear striking heraldic collar badges, including a medieval knight on his charger and a plumed war helmet.

The insignia adoped by the Norwegian Army follow the tenets set by the leading heraldist Hallvard Trætteberg, using a shield with just two tinctures and in most cases only one charge (single or multiple), such as the crossed retorts of the NBC (nuclear, biological and chemical) Unit, or the wolf's head of Brigade North. One exception was the badge of the Royal Guard (HM Kongens Garde) during the reign of King Olav V. It bore the king's monogram (V) between two knives (swords), and was known as "the dinner service" by members of the unit.

REGULATORY SCHEMES

The two World Wars saw what amounted to a free-for-all in unofficial insignia, as soldiers sought to inject some humour, often of a bawdy and derogatory kind, into the mud and chaos of modern warfare and to enliven their drab uniforms.

Eventually, various nations came up with regulatory schemes. One of the most interesting suggestions, in 1935, was for units of the French Army to bear shields taken from the arms of the places in which they were located. However, the French government disliked the designs that we produced, in which time-honoured, pre-revolutionary symbols relating to royal and imperial power were prominent, and the scheme was shelved. Since World War II, the French Army has sought to regulate all

military insignia so that they follow certain heraldic tenets. Ideas for a unit badge normally start with the unit itself, and the suggested design is sent to the Service Historique de l'Armée de Terre in the Château of Vincennes (which maintains a collection of 15,000 unit badges), to ensure that it conforms to the ideals of clarity and sobriety cherished by the service. The insignia will often be allowed to include the arms of the local town or province. If acceptable, it is passed to the French defence ministry to be formally approved, and is given an authorized number. For a badge worn by a fighting unit the number is prefixed by the letter G (for *guerre*); for a "brevet", or specialist badge,

▼ *The pocket badge of the French 1st Parachute Hussar Regiment bears the arms of its founder, Count Ladislaus Bercheny.*

▼ *The pocket badge of the French Army's 1st Transport Regiment bears the arms of the city of Paris, where it is based.*

▲ *The heraldic beret flash and crest (now superseded) of a unit in the 172nd Infantry Brigade (Alaska) in the United States Army.*

the prefix is GS. There is even a specialist badge for a French Army war artist, which bears a shield and helm as its design.

The United States Army has its own Institute of Heraldry, which lays down specific patterns for military insignia. Each unit or battalion at regimental level is entitled to a coat of arms that is formally granted by the Institute. The grant shows the achievement of arms in full colour with its formal blazon, and also explains the symbolism behind the design.

Each colour-bearing unit in the army is entitled to its own crest as well as shield, but for new units without battle honours the crest is omitted, with the idea that, at a later date, some event in its war service will give rise to a suitable crest. The shield

should be the standard shape, as on official drawings, and the design upon it true heraldry, of a simple uncluttered nature. Embattled lines of partition are reserved for organizations that have captured a fortified objective. For National Guard units the crest is normally that of the state to which the unit belongs, and units in the Army Reserve are entitled to bear the crest of a "minuteman proper" (one of the militiamen of the fledgling Republic, so named because they undertook to be ready for action at a minute's notice).

The unit badge is normally described as a "crest", although this refers to the complete design. Worn by enlisted men on side caps and shoulder straps, it is officially known as "distinctive insignia", or DI. Each regiment or comparable unit in the US Army has its own branch colour, upon which is embroidered the arms of the United States, with the national shield and crest replaced by those of the unit.

It is stipulated that the unit motto should not include "anything of a sordid, malign or malevolent character, implying animosity or partiality towards nations or groups of nations, or which stresses the destructive nature of warfare", although many unofficial unit badges of the Vietnam era certainly did not follow this advice – "Peace", "Hell" and "Bomb Hanoi" were popular themes, as well as "Kill".

Much official American military heraldry is of excellent quality and combines the best of ancient and modern heraldic

styles. For instance, the arms of the 152nd Field Artillery Battalion are blazoned: Gules, on a canton of the same, fimbriated Or a projectile (artillery shell) bendwise, scintillant of the last. In addition to the heraldic tinctures, corps colours may also be used, as in the arms of the 201st Engineer Battalion: Per bend wavy Buff and Azure [the colours of the Quartermaster Corps] a fleur de lis Argent.

The fleur de lis is found in the arms of those units deployed in France in either or both of the two World Wars. The Institute of Heraldry designates other charges for particular campaigns, such as tomahawks for the Indian Wars or a cactus for Mexican campaigns. As an armorial charge indicative of a certain campaign, the fleur de lis can also be found in the arms of regiments of the Italian Army, which have distinctive pocket badges. The trident from the arms of the Ukraine and the lion of Abyssinia are among other charges used.

FULL ACHIEVEMENTS OF ARMS

Spanish Army units have their own achievements of arms, although only the shield tends to be used for uniforms while the full achievement is kept for more formal occasions. The insignia are regulated by the Spanish Army's Institute of History and Military Culture.

Each major unit of the Spanish Army has its own arms, a full achievement accompanied by the following exterior ornaments: the branch insignia placed in

▼ *The full armorial achievement for the 20th Anti-aircraft Regiment of the Spanish Army.*

▼ *In the arms of Bravo Group, KFOR, of the Portuguese Army, a "plate engrailed" makes an excellent parachute canopy.*

▼ *The Portuguese Army Archives Department is represented by a magpie and a shield division suggesting bookshelves.*

saltire behind the shield (such as the crossed batons of a *capitan general*, for the army headquarters). Above the shield is placed a royal crown. Any decorations worn by the unit are placed below the shield, but if the unit has the distinction of the *laureada*, the highest decoration it can win, this appears as a laurel wreath ornamented with sword blades encircling the shield. The achievement is complete when accompanied by scrolls bearing the regimental title, its nickname (if it has one), the *cri-de-guerre* (if borne) and the regimental battle honours.

The resulting arms are some of the most splendid heraldic compositions in modern military use. They show a fascinating diversity of themes, with each *tercio*, or unit, of the Spanish Foreign Legion bearing the arms of a famous warrior, such as Don Juan of Austria or the Gran Capitan Don Gonzalo Fernandez de Cordoba. The Special Operations Groups each have an animal in their arms associated with ferocity, or some means of attack: for example, SOG Valencia has a black bat, taken from the arms of Valencia but also indicating the unit's speciality – night attacks.

Other units take part or all of the arms of their home base or area of recruitment. The 50th Motorized Infantry Regiment "Canarias" includes, as well as charges taken from the arms of its base Gran Canaria, a dragon pierced by lances representing "the expulsion from the island of the English pirate, Admiral Francis Drake".

Finally, a happy combination of ancient and modern symbolism makes up the arms of Regional Engineer Unit 21. Its shield bears a bulldozer in front of a cross composed of a road intersection, while the border features the traditional punning charge of the ancient kingdom of Granada, the pomegranate.

Portuguese military units are also granted full achievements of arms, and many of their designs are simple but striking, such as a parachute canopy, which is heraldically interpreted as a "plate engrailed". The device used for the shield of the Portuguese Army's General Archives Department – books arranged on shelves shown as Paly per fess counterchanged –

is accompanied by that legendary collector, the magpie, as a crest.

In the German Army, the Bundeswehr, some freedom is allowed in insignia design. Formality is observed in the design of the arm badges of major units – divisions, brigades, corps and schools – which often bear the arms of the province in which the unit serves, but the pocket badges of smaller units are left to the commander. If he has little interest in heraldry, the designs, though always on a shield, can be complex and distinctly non-heraldic.

The matter has, however, been corrected in many cases by the "education" of unit commanders by one man with an extensive knowlege of heraldic design – Lt Col Herbert Lippert. His designs range from Teutonic Knights (from Marburg, the unit's home town) firing into the air with a bow for Air Defence Battalion 340, to a double-headed griffin (the vigilant custodian of treasure) for Direction and Replacement Battalion 855. He has made extraordinary use of counterchanging, with four semi wolves courant, for Field Replacement Battalion 24 (stationed in the town of Wolfhagen).

COMMEMORATIVE BADGES
In areas of eastern Europe that formally came under the influence of Imperial Russia, there has been a continued tradition of military insignia, much of it heraldic. The designs have a common origin in the splendid breast badges worn from the latter half of the 19th century until 1917 by units of the Imperial Russian

▲ *On a badge worn by Russian airborne troops, a parachute appears on the breast of the double-headed eagle, a legacy of the tsarist era.*

Army. It was the tradition in that army for a commemorative badge to be awarded to individuals, not so much for regimental identification but on meeting certain requirements, such as length of service. These regimental commemorative badges, made from enamelled metal, often bore imperial symbols, cyphers of the Russian sovereign and the imperial eagle, accompanied by the arms of the province or city from which the regiment recruited.

As for today's Russian Army, once again the double eagle appears on much of its insignia, both official and non-official. However, the peaked caps of the military now bear two badges – the lower one has the red star with the hammer and sickle, and the upper badge bears the double-headed eagle charged on the breast with St George and the dragon.

Between 1918 and 1939 Poland was once again a free and independent nation. The Polish Army reorganized and made use of commemorative breast badges in a similar fashion to the Imperial Russian Army. These often contained the monograms of former monarchs or *hetmen* (traditional commanders), and the arms of the town, city or province from which the regiment took its title.

◄ *A fascinating example of counterchanging in the badge of the German Army's Field Replacement Battalion 24.*

NAVAL HERALDRY

As with the armies of the world, the other fighting services have adapted their national heraldry to suit the ways in which it could be displayed on their equipment and uniforms. Warships traditionally bore the arms of the sovereign splendidly carved on their sterns. Figureheads were usually associated with the vessel's name, but could also be fashioned to hold a cartouche of arms.

The sterns of the great warships built between the 16th and 18th centuries were platforms for some of the grandest displays of heraldry ever seen. A spectacular example can be seen on the stern of the 17th-century Swedish flagship, the *Vasa*, raised from Stockholm harbour in 1961, which bears the complete achievement of arms of the sovereign, Gustavus Adolphus, for whom it was constructed. A model of a 17th-century Danish warship, in the Naval Museum in Copenhagen, shows that the ship itself bore not only cartouches of arms for all the Danish territories but also those of the Duchy of Brunswick-Lüneburg for Sofie Amalie, the Queen of Frederick III (1648–70).

ROYAL NAVY INSIGNIA

Many modern navies model their insignia on those of the British Royal Navy. As with army regiments, naval badges often started life unofficially, devised by ship's companies and their captains, and might be displayed on anything from a gun tampion to the ship's stationery. Though the Navy tried to impose some order, the Badge Committee set up in 1914 soon lapsed.

In 1916 Major Charles Ffoulkes RM, founder of the Imperial War Museum in London, was asked by the shipbuilders, Swan Hunter, to design badges for 20 ships they were building for the Royal Navy. Ffoulkes subsequently offered his services free to the Admiralty, and the Ships Names and Badges Committee was set up on 10 December 1918.

Between 1918 and 1937 Ffoulkes designed 550 ships' badges for the Royal Navy, and many contained heraldic charges associated with the ship's name and taken from

▲ Ships were considered apt platforms for heraldry, and some figureheads, such as this one on HMS Victory at Portsmouth, England, bore the royal arms.

▲ Pictures from earlier centuries suggest that flags flown from ships could be vast, like this royal standard flying from a French warship of the 18th century.

◄ For centuries the seals of admirals bore their arms on the sails of ships of the period. This fine example is the seal of Richard Duke of Gloucester (later King Richard III of England), Admiral of England, c1480.

▶ A model of the 17th-century Danish naval vessel, Sofie Amalie, *named after the Queen of Frederick III of Denmark. The white horse of Hanover is surrounded by shields of arms of the kingdom of Denmark and the Dukes of Brunswick-Lüneburg.*

personal or civic arms. The first was for HMS *Warwick* and bore the bear and ragged staff device of the Earls of Warwick. The badge of the cruiser HMS *Effingham* had a demi lion pierced through the mouth, taken from the "Flodden augmentation" of the Howard family, of which the Earls of Effingham were a branch. Other

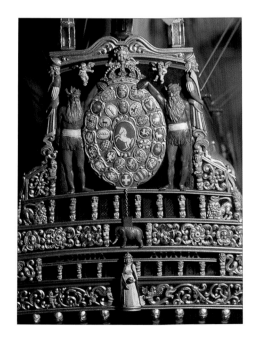

badges incorporated puns, such as a flying dove in front of a shakefork (a heraldic charge in the shape of a letter Y) for HMS *Dovey*. The symbol was placed within a frame of plaited rope, with a plaque above bearing the ship's name, surmounted by an imperial crown. The frame differed in shape for each type of vessel: battleships took a circular frame; cruisers, a pentagon; destroyers, a shield; auxiliaries, sloops, aircraft carriers and shore establishments, a diamond. During World War II the shapes were revised, and now all ships and Fleet Air Arm Squadrons take circular badges; shore establishments have diamonds and Royal Fleet Auxiliaries, pentagons.

The Royal Netherlands Navy follows the theme closely. Its badges are round, surrounded by a plaited rope tied at the base in a reef knot. The shield is surmounted by a naval crown, of the kind placed on memorials to Dutch naval heroes. Any motto is placed beneath the shield. Behind are placed crossed anchors, a device of the Dutch Admiralty since the 17th century. The anchor device is popular across the world: the Royal Danish Navy and the Royal Norwegian Navy favour a single anchor in pale behind a shield of arms, with a royal crown surmounting the shield.

One of the more bizarre RNN designs, for the gunboat *Flores*, was designed a year

▼ *The badges designed for ships of the British Royal Navy still follow the pattern set in the first half of the 20th century.*

▲ *The badge of the former Royal Netherlands Ship,* Flores, *depicts the tree of skulls from the island whose name it shares.*

after the boat's decommissioning in honour of its service during World War II. The charge is a stylized version of the extraordinary *scheldenboom*, or "tree of skulls", traditionally erected on the island of Flores and hung with the skulls of the islanders' vanquished enemies.

HERALDIC SHIPS' BADGES

Dutch naval badges are often fully heraldic in that they bear the arms of naval heroes such as Tromp or de Ruyter, or of towns, provinces or cities. United States Navy

▼ *The USS* Winston S. Churchill's *badge, named after Britain's wartime leader, bears charges from the Churchill family arms.*

▲ *Some Royal Netherlands Navy ships, such as the frigate* Bloys van Treslong, *have badges charged with naval heroes' arms.*

badges also often bear the arms of naval heroes, presidents, or other famous people. They may show the full arms or a made-up device taken from the arms of an eminent person. The badge for USS *Winston S. Churchill* (the first US Navy ship to be named after a British politician) contains a fleur de lis, cross of St George and lion passant guardant – all charges referring to Churchill's personal arms, and those of England. The ships of the Federal German Navy have maintained their own tradition of bearing the arms of cities, provinces and famous commanders on their prow, initially on the warships of World War II such as the *Graf Spee*, *Bismarck* and their class.

In recent years the Russian Navy has replaced the Soviet naval ensign bearing the hammer and sickle with one of the oldest war ensigns still in existence, the cross of St Andrew (blue on white), first adopted in about 1700 by Peter the Great. Peter also adopted for his own navy a reversed variant of the British jack, which he knew from his time spent with the Royal Navy.

An extraordinary manifestation of the tumultuous changes that have taken place in Russia may be seen on the conning towers of the nuclear submarines of the Russian Navy. These now bear the double-headed imperial eagle, with St George and the dragon on its breast.

AIR FORCE INSIGNIA

During World War I, fuselage art on aircraft showed a flair for design influenced by the most modern art of the age. Sometimes the individual unit markings designed by the pilots themselves extended along the entire length of the aircraft. French crews devised some of the most innovative air force "heraldry", and squadrons of today's Armée de l'Air bear many of the unofficial badges adopted then, amongst them the Sioux Indian chief's head chosen by the Lafayette squadron.

While the French still allow a free hand in the design of unit insignia, other air forces, such as those in Britain and the United States, maintain a much stricter control and have official authorities to design and monitor the use of formal badges. In the US Air Force, squadrons must have a pictorial device displayed on a disc, while the emblem of a flag-bearing unit (with a headquarters component) should be armorial, with the device on a shield. Unit insignia must be prepared in two versions: full colour, and subdued (olive green and black) for use in combat. Despite such strictures, towards the end of the Vietnam War there was a proliferation of non-authorized insignia, such as the badge chosen by a USAF base hospital in Korea specializing in the treatment of venereal diseases, which depicted a VD germ in a white coat bearing a syringe.

Just as close co-operation with the Royal Navy set the pattern for the insignia of various other navies, the same was the case with the allied air forces during World War II. The insignia of the Royal Flying Corps – the forerunner of the Royal Air Force – began unofficially, but an Inspector of Royal Air Force

▼ *Aircraft of the United States Air Force tend to bear the badges of wing, squadron and command.*

▲ *Two examples of pocket insignia of French Air Force airbase units: that of BA106 (top) bears the arms of Bordeaux, that of BA118 (bottom), Mont-de-Marsan.*

▲ *The badge of 22 Squadron, Royal Air Force, with its pi symbol for "22 over 7".*

Badges was appointed in 1936, and the connection with traditional heraldry was acknowledged by the selection of an officer of arms to fill the Inspector's post, as is the case today.

Every RAF badge consists of a circular frame in the form of a laurel wreath, in which the title of the unit appears, ensigned by the royal crown and bearing a motto on a scroll beneath the badge. The central plaque often contains a heraldic allusion to the unit's history and location. One of the simplest and most original charges is the *pi* symbol in the badge of 22 Squadron. In 1916 the squadron was based for a time with No 7 Wing and when the wind lay in a certain direction its aircraft had to take off over the roof of No 7 Wing's headquarters – hence 22 over 7, or the *pi* symbol.

Commonwealth air forces maintained the RAF pattern, though the laurel wreath was usually replaced by plants of national origin, such as the maple leaf for Canada, fern for New Zealand or lotus for India. Other nations have also followed this scheme. The wreath of unit badges in the Royal Netherlands Air Force is constructed out of orange leaves and fruit – the badge of the House of Orange. The Royal Danish Air Force has a coat of arms for each unit, and replaces the wreath with a wing.

Some RAF units, notably schools and colleges, have a full achievement of arms. The crest of the Central Flying School is a pelican vulning itself (feeding its young with its own blood). The arms of the former Royal Aircraft Establishment

▼ *The arms of a Royal Danish Air Force Squadron painted on an aircraft fuselage.*

symbolized its research into early flight with a pterodactyl, while the Empire Test Pilot School, at Boscombe Down in Wiltshire, had a crest of an eagle rising from an astral coronet, fondly known by the students as the "chicken in a basket". (The College of Arms grants this coronet to institutions associated with aviation, as well as senior ranks of the RAF.) Although the ETPS has been absorbed into the Defence Evaluation and Research Agency, the crest is still retained in outline on the tailfins of the school's training aircraft.

▲ *The air forces of the world tend to adopt a flamboyance not met with in navies and armies. Here a Tornado fighter bomber of the German Air Force, elaborately painted for an air show, still bears the cross of the Teutonic Knights, dating back to the time of the Crusades.*

▼ *The Empire Test Pilot School at Boscombe Down in Wiltshire, England, uses the crest from the unit's arms on its aircrafts' fuselage or tail. It shows an eagle rising from an astral coronet.*

THE POLICE AND SECRET SERVICES

So many police forces have direct or indirect connections with their nation's military forces that it is not surprising to see a marked resemblance between their insignia. However, the United Kingdom appears to be unique in that its heraldic authorities have on several occasions granted full heraldic achievements to police authorities.

POLICE INSIGNIA

The uniform worn by British police forces was standardized in 1934, although many new items of clothing have been added since then. Nearly all bear the insignia of the particular force. Many use armorial bearings or the county arms, and tend to feature the royal cypher within a circlet and star. The most prominent armorial achievement of any British police force must be that of the Metropolitan Police in Greater London, whose portcullis is distinctively featured on its police cars. The arms also include a double tressure flory counter-flory taken from the Scottish royal arms, symbolizing the Met's world-famous headquarters, Scotland Yard.

Like several other police forces that possess arms, the Metropolitan Police does not actually use them on its cap and collar

▼ *This badge follows the pattern set by the Canadian Heraldic Authority for Canada's police badges. The municipal arms and provincial flower are standard elements.*

badges. The Wiltshire Constabulary was granted full armorial bearings in 1989, but does not use them in any form on its insignia and vehicles, although it has gone to the trouble of having a splendid heraldic standard manufactured, which is borne at formal parades. Its design includes the crest of a bustard, the county bird, holding a truncheon. The arms of various other British regional forces feature cap bands, police dogs and even the pavements pounded by policemen "on the beat".

The French and German provincial police bear their provincial or department arms on arm and helmet badges, as do many other regional and municipal police forces worldwide, from New South Wales to Maryland. In France the three fleurs de lis of the Bourbon dynasty, symbols proscribed by the revolutionaries of the First Republic, now serve the police in the Paris (Ile de France) region. In recent years the Canadian Heraldic Authority has granted formal heraldic badges for Canadian municipal police services. All the designs conform to a standard pattern, which includes a shield of arms in its centre.

The police are not the only public service to make use of armorial bearings, whether their own or those of their locality. British ambulance and fire services often sport arms in their insignia, on both uniforms and vehicles. In 1995 the South Wales Fire Service was granted full armorial bearings, which are used on the service's fire engines. The design of the shield is an adaptation of the three chevrons in the arms of the de Clares, the

▲ *The design for the cap badge of the South Wales Fire Service, appropriately charged with its heraldic badge.*

ruling family in the area during the Middle Ages. In the Fire Service design, the chevrons are differenced by being "rayonny" (in flames); above and below the chevrons are "gutty de larmes" (drops of water), and the crest is a lion bearing another heraldic charge, a "water bouget" (leather water bottle) with which to extinguish the flames.

SECURITY SERVICES

The world's so-called secret services are not so secret as to want to remain heraldically invisible. Even the USA's clandestine Phoenix Programme (set up to assassinate Viet Cong collaborators) adopted that mythical bird as its device. The Phoenix

▼ *When on formal parade, the Wiltshire Constabulary fly their standard which includes the crest of the bustard with a truncheon.*

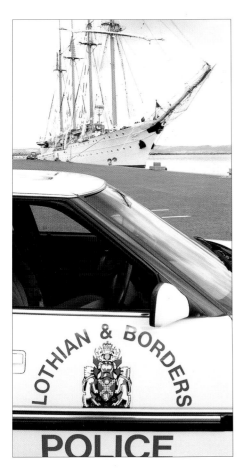

▲ *The patrol cars of Scotland's Lothian and Border Police sport the force's full arms, including the sallet helmet given by the Scottish heralds to corporate organizations.*

Programme was said to be the Central Intelligence Agency's action army during the Vietnam War, and while the phoenix insignia was unofficial, the CIA itself has had armorial bearings since 1950. The shield, Argent a compass rose of sixteen points Gules, and the crest, Or a wreath

▲ *The warning eye of the American bald eagle keeps watch over the shield of the CIA.*

Argent and Gules an American bald eagle's head erased, are officially interpreted as follows: "The American Eagle is the national bird and is a symbol of strength and alertness. The radiating spokes of the compass rose depict the coverage of intelligence data from all areas of the world to a central point." The CIA arms are displayed in many forms, both in the organization's headquarters building and on its medals: the Distinguished Intelligence Medal places the arms on the breast of the national eagle, as befits US governmental institutions.

The old and much respected foe of the CIA, the Soviet Union's Komitet Gosudarstvennoi Bezopasnosti, or KGB, also maintained its own insignia. Its mission as the sword and shield of the state was to protect the hammer and sickle of communism, and it even had its own branch colour, royal blue, the sight of which on its arms, shield and cap bands was enough to put fear in all but the bravest hearts. Its present-day successor, the Federal Security Service, has managed to keep the sword and shield in its insignia, while replacing the hammer and sickle with the old tsarist symbol of the double-headed eagle displayed.

The KGB's most loyal friend, the East German Staatssicherheitsdienst – better known as the Stasi – used the GDR's state arms on its flag and breast badge in a typically militant socialist fashion. This was cynically known amongst Soviet conscripts as "hurrah art".

In Britain the Secret Intelligence Service (MI6), has not bothered to obtain a heraldic device of its own, but has permission to use the royal arms. However, its colleagues in the Security Service (MI5) do use their own heraldic badge designed by the College of Arms. It features a winged sea-lion, reflecting the Service's association with the armed services, and portcullises, symbolic of Parliament, which allude to its function of upholding Parliamentary democracy. The portcullises are interspersed with the rose of secrecy and green cinquefoils, whose five petals refer to MI5,

▲ *The badge of the British Security Service, otherwise known as MI5.*

◄ *The breast badge of the Russian Federal Security Service, successor to the KGB. The design keeps the shield and sword used by the KGB, but replaces the hammer and sickle with the imperial double-headed eagle.*

and whose colour has been associated with intelligence at least since World War I. The Security Service's motto is *Regnum defende*, "Defence of the realm".

▲ *The dreaded East German Security Ministry, better known as the Stasi, included in its insignia the state arms with hammer and compasses.*

INSIGNIA OF OFFICE

Since the late medieval period it has been common for a man or woman of high rank who holds an official position, usually at court, to wear or carry some form of insignia as an emblem of his or her high office. The earliest form of insignia seems to have been a wand or staff, which may have had its origin in ordinary staves such as those carried by shepherds, and examples can be found in the scenes of daily life painted on the walls of Egyptian tombs. Paintings dating from the Old Kingdom (c2700–c2150 BC) depict bailiffs or tax collectors using a form of truncheon when attempting to exact payment from recalcitrant farmers. Wooden batons have also been found in the tombs of Egyptian temple officials, bearing inscriptions asking for long life, prosperity and good health.

OFFICIAL INSIGNIA IN ARMS

Some of the earliest heraldic insignia of office are depicted on the seals of medieval admirals. These use the motif of a sailing

▼ *Under the Bourbons, French court officials placed their insignia, including bottles, horns and wolves' heads, beside their shields.*

ship, with the arms of the officer placed on the ship's sails, flags and streamers. By the 17th century admirals tended to show their office by placing anchors behind their shields of arms. In France, where many insignia of office originated, even rank was indicated by them: admirals of France had a pair of anchors in saltire, the cross bars strewn with fleurs de lis, vice-admirals had one plain anchor in pale behind the shield, and admirals of the galleys placed a grappling anchor behind their shield.

There is no hard and fast rule regarding the bearing of insignia of office. Some appear only as heraldic accoutrements, while others are actual objects, borne on ceremonial occasions. The French court of the 17th and 18th centuries made use of a splendid array of heraldic insignia, ranging from the

▲ *The arms of justice of the hereditary Constables of Navarre are proudly borne at either side of the shield of the Dukes of Alba.*

crowned batons semy de lis of the Master of the Royal Household, to the extraordinary wolves' heads placed on either side of the shield of the Grand Louvetier (Grand Wolf Huntsman).

THE CONSTABLE

As the highest-ranking officer in the medieval army, one of the constable's duties was the overseeing of martial law, including the passing of the death penalty. In time, the shields of the high constables were placed between two "arms of justice" – arms in armour issuing from clouds holding their sword of office. On taking his office, the Constable of France was presented with the sword itself, in a sheath of royal blue, semy de lis. One of the greatest Constables of France was Bertrand du Guesclin, who held the office from 1370–80. When he knew that he was dying, he sent the great sword back to

Grand Boutelier Echanson
Andre de Gironde
Supprimée.

Grand Pannetier
Jean Paul Timoléon de Cossé
Duc de Brissac.

Grand Veneur
Louis Jean Marie de Bourbon
Duc de Penthievre.

Grand Fauconnier
Louis Cesar de la Baume le Blanc
Duc de la Valliere.

Grand Louvetier
le Marquis de Flamarens
le Comte de Flamarens en Survivance.

Grand Marechal de Logis
Louis Michel Chamillart
Comte de la Suze.

▲ *A painting of the thanksgiving service for George V and Queen Mary, 1935. The Lord Chamberlain leads the Court with his staff of office, and the route is lined by the Yeomen of the Guard in their Tudor tunics.*

Charles V, saying: "Take it and return it into the King's keeping, and do you tell him that I have never betrayed him or it." This the King knew, and remembering du Guesclin's loyalty gave him the rare honour for a commoner of burial in the Abbey of Saint Denis, the traditional resting place for French royalty.

In recent years the constableships of two nations, Navarre and Scotland, have been in the hands of noblewomen. In the former case, the Duchess of Alba (who is the most titled lady in the world) places her shield between the arms of justice, the clouds bearing the arms of Navarre. Her shield quarters the royal arms of the British House of Stuart in a bordure compony (a border divided into segments) signifying illegitimacy, since the Dukes of Alba are descended from a natural son of James II.

THE MARSHAL

In practice, many of the duties of the medieval constable devolved on his deputy, the marshal, who carried a black gold-tipped baton as the insignia of his office. In France, by the reign of Philip IV (1285–1314), the marshal sat in judgement on certain cases at a great marble table in the Palais de Justice in Paris, administering a blow, or *bastonarde*, to the guilty with his baton.

By the 18th century, the baton seems to have passed wholly into heraldic usage in France, for when Marechal de Duras (1715–89) attempted to try the anti-revolutionary lawyer and historian Simon-Nicolas-Henri Linguet, he threatened to use the baton to condemn him, whereupon Linguet retorted, "Monsieur le Marechal, you would not know how to use it." The marshal did not share the constable's right to the arms of justice in his heraldic achievement: instead he placed crossed batons behind his shield, a practice taken up by marshals throughout much of Europe, including the Earl Marshal of England.

The Riksmarskalsk (Marshal of the Court) of Sweden still has a staff with a maroon shaft decorated with gold crowns, which appears in the armorial achievements of recent holders of the office.

In England, where the hereditary title is held by the Dukes of Norfolk, the Earl Marshal was for centuries unable to exercise his office personally because he was a Catholic, and it was common for his duties to be administered by a deputy, who placed one baton in bend behind his shield. Such a device can often be found in the margins of patents of arms (mainly from the Georgian period). The hereditary constableship, long held by the family of Stafford, Dukes of Buckingham, was abolished by Henry VIII after the attainder of the third Duke on grounds of treason in 1521. The office is revived temporarily for the coronation of the sovereign, its ceremonial duties being undertaken on other occasions by the Earl Marshal. Conversely, in Scotland, the hereditary post of Earl Marshal, long held in the family of Keith, was lost through attainder. The hereditary constableship of Scotland is alive and well, and is held by the Hays, Earls of Erroll.

▼ *The plaque of a Knight of the Swedish Order of the Seraphim. Behind the shield are the batons of the Marshal to the Royal House and of the Chancellor of the Order.*

THE CHAMBERLAIN

At the Danish court, the Chamberlain has a staff decorated with golden leaves and bears on his court uniform the insignia common to all chamberlains, a gold key – a reminder of the time when such officers were trusted by sovereigns with the keys to their private apartments. Such keys usually have the sovereign's cypher in the bow (the ring at the top of the key). Chamberlains of the British royal household wear the key on Garter blue ribbon.

In heraldry, most chamberlains place crossed keys behind their shield, but in England a Lord Great Chamberlain places the white wands of a high court official in saltire behind the shield, while the key is placed in fess below it. (The title of Lord Great Chamberlain is hereditary but it is not a full-time post, whereas the office of Lord Chamberlain is not hereditary but the holder is involved in the day-to-day running of the royal household.)

THE STAFF OF OFFICE

A wand or staff of office was common to most court officials, and apart from marking their status, it was a useful tool for fending off the common people. Usually

▶ *Proud of his status at court as well as in the Church, Cardinal Wolsey is portrayed here holding the baton of the Lord Chancellor of England.*

▼ *Originally the key to a sovereign's personal apartments, the chamberlain's key – the highest sign of trust – has been worn on his court uniform since the Middle Ages.*

made of wood, or perhaps of ivory, it could be a short baton or as tall as the man who bore it. It was ceremonially presented to the official by his master or mistress when he took up his office, and – equally ceremonially – was broken in pieces when he relinquished the office, or on the death of those whom the officer had served.

Today, the staves of office of the British royal household are little changed from those their predecessors used centuries ago, except for one innovation: a silver ferrule halfway up the shaft, bearing the title of office, has a screw thread that allows the staff to be "broken" ceremonially when the officer relinquishes his post. The two halves are then handed back and can be screwed back together to give the ex-officer a memento of his former position.

The breaking of staves was a popular allegorical theme in former centuries. Elizabeth I of England, during one of her royal progresses around her realm, was "accosted" by a savage man covered in moss and ivy, bearing an oaken staff in his

▼ *The staff of an officer of the royal household is fitted with a screw, allowing it to be re-assembled after its ceremonial "breaking" when the officer retires from his post.*

hand. After regaling the Queen with words in praise of his patron – her favourite, Robert Dudley – the "savage" broke his staff in half, "like a dismissed Chamberlain", and threw away the pieces, unfortunately hitting the Queen's horse on the head with one of them. The ceremonial breaking of the wand of office is made much of in an account of the funeral in 1574 of Edmund, Earl of Derby: "The Steward, Treasurer, and Comptroller, when the body was buried, kneeling on their knees, with weeping tears, brake their staves and rods over their heads, and threw the shivers of the same into the grave."

OFFICIAL BADGES

While much European court ceremonial disappeared, along with the courts themselves, after the end of World War I, little changed in the British royal household. The splendid uniforms of the officers of state were retained, and upon them the jewelled badges and the great golden keys.

Among the most fascinating of the badges is that of the Marshal of the Diplomatic Corps, with its oval pendant. On one side it bears a hand grasping an olive branch, and on the other a hand grasping a sword. The story goes that in times of peace the olive branch was turned to the viewer, but when war was declared with another nation, its ambassador would receive an ominous visit from the Marshal – or rather his predecessor the Master of Ceremonies – who by this time would have swivelled his badge around to the martial side. Today, this badge may be glimpsed through the carriage windows when the Marshal of the Diplomatic Corps accompanies a new ambassador on his way to present his credentials to the Queen.

Another badge with a picturesque history is that worn by members of the Corps of Queen's Messengers. These gentlemen attend to the diplomatic mail that passes between British embassies and the Foreign Office, and the nature of their duties has given rise to many tales of bravura and adventure. Their neck badge is an oval bearing the sovereign's cypher within the Garter. Below it runs a little silver greyhound: did this originate from one of the heraldic supporters of the House of Tudor,

or did it start life as one of the stands of a silver bowl used by Charles II in exile in the Netherlands? The tale is told that, as he gave his orders to his secret messengers, one asked, "How shall we be known?" King Charles snapped the little greyhounds off the bowl, giving one to each messenger and saying, "This will be your badge."

Neither the badge of the Marshal of the Diplomatic Corps, nor that of the Queen's Messengers, is used in an armorial achievement. In Scotland, however, castle governors, the Lord High Constable and many other high officials are still granted armorial insignia.

The need to be recognized and honoured lies deep within the psyche, a fact remembered by such modern institutions as the burger-bar giant McDonald's, which awards stars to its workforce to be worn as evidence of "rank". Each star has a different design – starting with crossed mop and brush and passing on through burger bun and chip fryer to smiley face (for good customer relations) – and with it comes an increment in pay. In all, five stars can be awarded, making the bearer the equivalent in military rank of a field marshal.

▼ The badge of a former Master of Ceremonies to the English court bears the olive branch of peace on the front and the sword of war on the reverse. Nowadays, such a badge is worn by the Marshal of the Diplomatic Corps at the Court of St James.

▼ A delicate silver greyhound, perhaps one of the most romantic of all insignia, hangs from the badge of a member of the Corps of Queen's Messengers.

▼ Doormen in the Palace of Westminster wear the badges of royal messengers. The figure of Mercury below this badge denotes a door keeper of the House of Commons.

HERALDRY IN UNIVERSITIES AND SCHOOLS

Although they came later to the heraldic scene than towns or ecclesiastical bodies, universities and other major teaching establishments throughout Europe did take up heraldic devices. Often these tended to be limited to seals, but where arms were granted to or assumed by universities and schools, it was common to adopt the heraldic device of the establishment's founder and link it to a symbol of learning.

COLLEGE FOUNDERS

While most universities have arms or a seal common to the entire establishment, the colleges of the major English universities have individual arms which often have ancient origins, again usually with some obvious reference to the founder.

Amongst the most interesting arms are those of Clare College and Pembroke College, both in Cambridge. In the case of Clare College the arms of the husband and wife have been reversed, as Elizabeth, daughter of Gilbert de Clare, 3rd Earl of Gloucester, was considered far more important in estates and degree than her first husband, William de Burgh, Earl of

▲ *Margaret Beaufort's arms grace the entrance to Christ's College, Cambridge.*

Ulster. Her family arms therefore took the heraldically more important side (dexter of the marital shield). Elizabeth outlived three husbands, a fact remembered by the tears of mourning placed on a black border around the arms.

Pembroke College was founded in 1347 by Marie, daughter of Guy de Chastillon, Comte de St Pol, and wife of Aylmer de Valence, 2nd Earl of Pembroke. The

college arms have preserved the practice of dimidiation: the coats of de Valence and de Chastillon are cut down the middle and the dexter half of Valence is wedded to the sinister half of de Chastillon.

The grandest displays of heraldry in Cambridge must surely be the arms of Margaret Beaufort (1443–1509), mother of Henry VII. This proud and pious lady founded two colleges: Christ's and St John's. Both sport the Beaufort arms, complete with their yale supporters. The ground beneath the yales' hooves is scattered with Margaret's cognizance, the daisy flower or marguerite.

Oxford University is not to be outdone in heraldic honours by its younger rival. Among the shields that speak of extraordinary times in English history are the arms of that pompous prince of the Church, Cardinal Thomas Wolsey, Archbishop of York and Lord Chancellor, who founded Christ Church College. Included in the Cardinal's arms are many allusions to the institutions and individuals to which he owed his fortunes. His birthplace, Ipswich, is represented somewhat grandly by the arms of families that

◀▶ *The cloisters of the University of Padua are richly decorated with the arms of noble students of previous centuries, which have long outlived their bearers.*

▲ *The arms of Stephen Coombs, of the Katarinaskolan in Uppsala, Sweden, include the school arms (lower right) and those of his old college, Balliol, Oxford (top right).*

▲ *The arms of student fraternities from the University of Heidelberg often bear duelling swords (epées), which can be seen crossed in three of these shields.*

at one time held the Earldom of Suffolk: de la Pole (leopards' faces Azure) and Ufford (a cross engrailed). The lion passant guardant on the cross represents Pope Leo X, from whom Wolsey received his cardinal's hat. The rose stands for Wolsey's position as a royal minister and the Cornish choughs are a reference to his namesake, Thomas à Becket.

Each college displays its arms to full effect in many different places, from the façade of the building to the silver on the table. More often than not they will be encountered along with those of benefactors, ancient and modern. In Oxford, the arms of all the colleges can be seen on the doors of the Bodleian Library.

STUDENTS' ARMS

Some European universities made much of the arms of students, since many came from noble families. The finest display of students' arms appears in the precincts of the University of Padua, in northern Italy. Although it dates mainly from the 19th century, many shields still decorate the university's ancient courtyards and testify to the prestige it enjoyed all over Europe.

A unique feature of German heraldry is the arms of student fraternities displayed in the universities. These fraternities were famous for their duelling societies, and scars on the faces of young noblemen were considered a sign of honour. Each fraternity's members tended to come from the same region, so their arms included not only duelling swords, but also charges taken from the arms of their homeland. The centre of the arms often bore an inescutcheon upon which was placed a motto, or monogram, such as VCF for "Vivat, Crescat, Floreat" (Live, Flourish, Flower).

SCHOOLS

Though school arms are common in Britain, they are unusual elsewhere in Europe. The tradition does exist in Sweden, where schools display heraldic flags of their municipality. In 1993, the Katarinaskolan (St Katherine's School) at Uppsala assumed arms that were registered

in the Skandinavisk Vapenrulla (the Scandinavian Roll of Arms). They were the suggestion of Stephen Coombs, the Chairman of the Board of the School's Educational Foundation, and take as their badge a Catherine wheel surmounted by a cross formy. The wheel with its spikes refers to the martyrdom of St Katherine, but is also identified with Little Karin who, according to a Swedish folk song, was laid in a barrel with spikes.

▲ *Religion was central to the medieval scholar's life and often a school or college looked to a particular saint for patronage. The arms of Eton College, for example, are charged with the lilies of the Virgin Mary.*

MEDICAL HERALDRY

Most corporate heraldry contains a number of common symbols or charges that are particularly related to the profession or institution concerned. These charges can get very repetitive, but they do provide a clue to identity. They are a phenomenon chiefly related to British and Commonwealth heraldry, and are not often found elsewhere. The charges that frequently appear in arms related to medicine are good examples of this kind of usage.

Some medical arms, such as those of St Bartholomew's Hospital in London, have no such charges. William Wakering, Master of the Hospital from 1423–62, used the armorial bearings Per pale Argent and Sable a chevron counterchanged. These arms were not granted to Wakering or his family but because he was Master for such a long time they became associated with the hospital and are recorded as such in a 16th-century roll of arms.

SNAKES AND OTHER BEASTS

A good example of a "themed" charge is the snake, which almost invariably has a connection with medicine and is frequently used by medical institutions as well as in the personal arms of medical practitioners. For centuries the snake was thought to possess wisdom and mysterious healing powers. Temples used by ancient healers included pits of harmless snakes, thought to have healing properties.

▼ The gates of Bristol General Hospital, bearing fine representations of the city arms.

▲ Lord Leycester's Hospital in Warwick, England, maintains a fine display of heraldry, including the bear and ragged staff of the Earls of Warwick and the shield of the Dudley family above it.

As snakes periodically shed their skin, appearing to be reborn, they were seen as vehicles of immortality.

Snakes were also associated with Aesculapius, the Greek and Roman god of medicine. A legend told that as he was examining a patient, a serpent crept in, climbed his staff and imbued him with wisdom. In heraldry, the snake is usually depicted twined about a rod, known as the staff of Aesculapius. Snakes can also be found in other attitudes, such as knotted, or devouring their own tails, and may be entwined about other charges. A particular species may be blazoned occasionally, such as the red-bellied black snake of the Royal Brisbane Hospital, or the Children's python (*Liasis childreni*) in the arms of the Australian Royal Children's Hospital Board.

Two mythical creatures more or less exclusive to medical heraldry are the caladrius and the opinicus. The caladrius, a bird found in ancient bestiaries, was credited with therapeutic powers. It was pure white, and the lower part of its leg was reputed to "purge" diseases of the eye. The opinicus had lion's legs, dragon's wings, pointed ears, a long bill and a camel's tail. It was granted as a crest to the Barber Surgeons of London in 1561.

INANIMATE CHARGES

Surgical instruments have been used as heraldic charges from early times. Perhaps the best known is the fleam, a form of lancet used for blood-letting. In heraldry it resembles an elaborate figure seven. It was used in the arms of the Company of Barbers of London in 1451. A spatula was included in the badge of the Fellowship of Surgeons of London in 1492, and both instruments were incorporated in the arms of the Worshipful Company of Barber Surgeons of London in 1569.

In its arms granted in 1672, the Royal College of Surgeons of Edinburgh has a bordure charged with seven surgical instruments which, though not specified individually, are described as "several instruments indicative of the art". Scalpels, ophthalmascopes, inhalers, dental and mammary probes and syringes have all been used as charges.

The shield of the Royal College of Pathologists (1971) is Argent a bar wavy Gules between in chief two torteaux and in base a benzene ring Sable. The use of straightforward charges illustrates the four disciplines of pathology: the red wavy line suggests histopathology, one torteau represents a red cell for haematology, and the second stands for biology. Microbiology is represented by the benzene ring.

▲ *In the arms of the British Association of Urological Surgeons, the compartment is appropriately strewn with sweet peas.*

▲ *In the arms of The Faculty of Accident and Emergency Medicine, a wounded supporter sports a multitude of injuries.*

Plants naturally have a place in medical heraldry by virtue of their curative properties. The foxglove, opium poppy and cocaine plant are all associated with anaesthetics or painkillers. The mandrake is found in the crest of the Association of Anaesthetists of Great Britain and Ireland (1945). A poisonous plant of southern Europe, it was used in the Middle Ages as a sedative and painkiller. Its knobbly, forked roots were thought to resemble the human figure, and when pulled from the ground it supposedly emitted a piercing shriek that sent people mad. The pome-

▼ *The Urological Society of Australia's charge of a view up the neck of the bladder when peered at through a cystoscope.*

granate is usually depicted in heraldry as split, showing its many seeds, and is used to represent fertility. It was used in the arms of the Royal College of Physicians by Garter Barker in 1546. In more modern times, a British institution serving urologists has been granted arms in which the compartment is strewn with sweet peas.

SUPPORTERS

The supporters of medical arms include mythical beasts, real animals and birds, and real people as well as gods and goddesses. The latter, in addition to Aesculapius, include his daughter Hygeia, goddess of health. She is shown holding a bowl with a snake entwined about her arm drinking from the bowl. Machaon and Podalrius, sons of Aesculapius, are also often used. They were said to have been Greek surgeons at the Siege of Troy, where Machaon removed an arrow from the wounded Menelaus. Machaon is usually seen holding a broken arrow in his hand. Egyptian deities are represented in British arms by the goddess Isis, who appears in the arms of the National Institute of Medical Herbalists, and by Imhotep, the god of medicine, seen in the arms of the Institute of Health Service Management.

The patron saints of surgeons, Cosimo and Damian, support the arms of the Fellowship of Surgeons, and St Barbara, the patron saint of the injured, supports the shield of the Institute of Accident

Surgery. Hippocrates, founder of medical ethics, appears in several achievements.

More recent medical figures include William Harvey (1578–1657), who discovered the circulation of the blood and supports the arms of the British Medical Association, and Dr Benjamin Golding, founder of Charing Cross Hospital in 1818. British anaesthetists, Dr John Snow (1813–58) and Dr Joseph Clover (1825–82) support the shield of the Royal College of Anaesthetists. The sinister supporter of the Arms of the Royal College of Paediatrics and Child Health is Thomas Phaire, author of the first book on paediatrics written in English in 1553.

Anonymous figures include nurses in uniform and – for the Royal Victoria Eye & Ear Hospital, Australia – a surgeon gowned and ready for the operating theatre. A boy and a girl support the shield of the Australian Royal Children's Hospital.

The horn of the unicorn was believed to possess healing as well as aphrodisiac properties when ground down, and when hollowed out and used as a cup it was thought to combat poisonous substances. The horn of the rhinoceros was thought to possess similar properties, and both are displayed as the crest and supporters of the Society of Apothecaries.

▼ *The shield of a 19th-century English doctor, Thomas Smith, combines the hand feeling a pulse of the College of Physicians, with the rod and serpent of Aesculapius.*

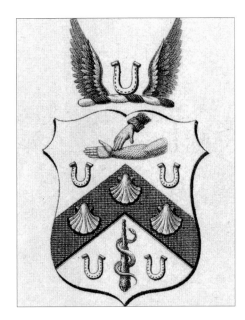

GUILDS AND LIVERY COMPANIES

In the late medieval period the growing wealth and power of the mercantile classes, and the guilds and fraternities to which they belonged, allowed them to make inroads into the preserves of the aristocracy. Naturally, the latter were none too happy about this chipping away of their prerogatives by the self-made men who had their power bases in the cities of Europe. However, various laws that attempted to safeguard the dress and other attributes of the nobility were of little use: the money of the merchants could not be ignored by lords or even kings.

Merchants and craftsmen organized themselves into guilds that safeguarded their trades, which were in some ways the forerunners of modern trades unions. A member who had served as an apprentice in his craft, and who had paid his dues and been initiated into the rites and mysteries of the guild, could expect a degree of protection against the hardships of medieval life. On his death he would know that the other guild members would give him a splendid funeral, complete with heraldry.

The wealth of the guilds, and of the individuals who made up their numbers, was vast. Merchants were often richer and lived in greater splendour than any petty European prince. It is not surprising that among the earliest English patents of arms are those of several guilds. The very same arms – such as those of the Mercers, Vintners, and all the other trades that helped to make the living in London among the richest in the medieval world – may still be seen in the annual Lord Mayor's Procession through the city. Each guild, or livery company, makes its presence known through its own particular arms and colours, or liveries.

THE GREAT TWELVE

The order of precedence of the London livery companies (of which there are now over 100) was established in 1515. The most senior companies are known as the Great Twelve, and are:

1 Mercers
2 Grocers
3 Drapers
4 Fishmongers
5 Goldsmiths
6/7 Merchant Taylors
7/6 Skinners
8 Haberdashers
9 Salters
10 Ironmongers
11 Vintners
12 Clothworkers

The Merchant Taylors and the Skinners disputed the sixth and seventh positions in the list, and as a result they change places every year at Easter (hence the expression "at sixes and sevens").

▲ Heraldry has come a long way from the medieval battlefield to the Nottinghamshire coalfield of Manton Colliery.

◀ The traditional procession in Siena, Italy, of the city's guilds, where the participants dress in medieval costume.

▲ The officers and magistrates of the city state of Florence enjoyed their own arms of office, including: 1 Masters of the Salt, 2 members of the Mercantile Tribunal, 3 officers of the monte comune (the public debt).

CRAFT SYMBOLS

All over Europe the pride men took in their professions and civic status was made manifest in symbol and colour. If he had not yet become armigerous, the merchant could content himself by showing off his individual mark, possibly placed on a shield. Many churches and houses from England to Switzerland were decorated

▼ In 1715 Thomas Doggett, a staunch Hanoverian, instituted a rowing race on the River Thames. Six royal watermen still compete for the coat and badge, shown here, which bears the white horse of Hanover.

with such marks, often in the form of initials and crosses. In England, merchants of the wool trade, or "staple", used such devices not only on their homes but also to mark their wool bales.

The arms of the guilds often included some obvious symbol of their craft, such as a pretzel for the bakers and an ox and axe for the butchers. The guild's patron saint was also often included, although after the Reformation in England several livery companies adopted new arms more attuned to the times, and any symbols overtly associated with Catholicism were judiciously shelved.

From such fraternities, other organizations emerged, such as the freemasons, in whose ceremonial heraldry plays its part.

▲ A medieval grant of arms to the Tallow Chandlers of London, 1463. The power of the city guilds was made manifest through the splendour of their arms.

Their insignia apes that of a royal household, with keys and staves of office like any court chamberlain. The "jewels" of lodge officers often include not only the arms of the town or region from which the lodge members come, but also the arms of influential local families, who may have provided past masters of the lodge.

▼ In procession in Bruges, Belgium, the guilds still make a fine showing of their arms, most of which include motifs alluding to their particular trades.

GLOBAL HERALDRY

Although heraldry uses an international language, achievements of arms have always been devised and regulated by national authorities. The royal heralds, around whom the various heraldic institutions grew up, were in the service of individual monarchs, and over the centuries many nations developed their own distinct heraldic styles. From its beginnings in northern Europe, heraldry spread all over the world during the eras of global exploration and conquest. While some countries no longer maintain their own heraldic authorities, the tradition is thriving in many parts of the world, and new ideas and artistic innovations continue to invigorate the heraldic realm.

◀ *The arms of the Jewish congregation of Shaar Hashomayim in Canada, with the crest borne on a helmet in the style of the Maccabeans.*

SCOTLAND

No country has a more diverse and fascinating application of heraldry than Scotland. It is one of the few nations with a true heraldic institution that can boast a continuous history going back centuries. Although smaller than the English College of Arms, the Court of Lord Lyon is every bit as adventurous and innovative when it comes to heraldic interpretation and application.

THE COURT OF LORD LYON

In Scotland the chief herald is Lord Lyon King of Arms. In the old kingdom of Scotland, Lord Lyon was a Privy Councillor and minister of the crown. The nature of kinship, which permeated Scottish society at all levels, gave rise to a regiment of men known as "sennachie", or bards, who called out the pedigrees and histories of the chiefs of clans and "septs" (other families loyal to a clan) at formal gatherings. Lord Lyon was Chief Sennachie of the royal line, and it was his duty to recite the king's pedigree during a coronation.

The new Lord Lyon, appointed in 2001, is considered to be more attuned to the legal side of his duties than to the heraldic side. This reflects the fact that he is concerned with many matters attached to Scottish clanship, and may often be

▼ *Scottish Officers of Arms make a proclamation in Edinburgh.*

involved in the judging of genealogies. The sacrosanct nature of heraldry in Scotland means that Lord Lyon's roar can be very loud. In recent years Sir Malcolm Innes, when Lyon, pursued anyone who presumed to bear arms not officially registered, from ice cream vendors and football teams to the owner of Harrods. In January 2000, Mohamed Al Fayed was ordered to remove the arms of the Chief of Clan Ross, which he had erected on his Scottish castle, Balnagowan, the ancestral home of the Ross family.

That case pales into insignificance compared with a 1958 grant of arms to the English town of Berwick-on-Tweed, which until 1482 was part of Scotland. The town council petitioned the English heralds for a coat of arms, but seemed to dislike the design. The townspeople then petitioned Lord Lyon, since in Scotland ancient arms are a form of heritable property, and it was held that Berwick had established an ancient right to arms in Scotland.

The heraldic author Lt Col Robert Gayre stated that Scotland could look upon Berwick as occupied territory, wrested from its own country and held as a base for further pretentious aggression against Scotland. The arms Lord Lyon matriculated included not only the bear and wych-elm, but also chained bears for supporters and the coronet and compartment applicable to a Scottish royal burgh. Eventually, the

▲ *The arms of Berwick-upon-Tweed as matriculated with the Scottish heraldic authorities in 1958.*

controversy died down and Berwick received a patent from the College of Arms in 1977: this time they ensured that the bear and wych-elm had prime position.

With the exception of Lord Lyon and Lyon Clerk, the Scottish heralds are paid only nominal fees and pursue full-time careers elsewhere, often in spheres appropriate to their heraldic duties, such as in law firms and museums or as artists. There are three heralds in ordinary: Marchmont, Rothesay and Dingwall, and four pursuivants in ordinary: Dingwall, Kintyre, Carrick and Unicorn. There are also two pursuivants extraordinary: Falkland and March. In addition, some Scottish peers of ancient title are entitled to their own private officer of arms: the herald of the Earls of Erroll, Hereditary High Constables of Scotland, is called Slains Pursuivant and bears a tabard of his master's arms, Argent three escutcheons Gules.

The Scottish officers of arms can be seen wearing their tabards and badges of office on such occasions as the installation of the Governor of Edinburgh Castle, when the standard of the Governor is unfurled above the Castle gates. The standard bears both the arms of his office and his personal arms. Also on view are the six Scottish State Trumpeters, with the royal arms of Scotland embroidered on their trumpet banners. The State Trumpeters also attend Lord Lyon at the reading of royal proclamations at the Mercat Cross in Edinburgh.

THE ARMS OF SCOTLAND

The red lion rampant within a double tressure flory counter-flory, was first used on a seal of Alexander III of Scotland in 1251, although the red lion was probably previously used by William I, "The Lion" (1165–1214), and a border of fleurs de lis was used in the arms of his son, Alexander II (1214–49). When James VI of Scotland acceded to the English throne in 1603 after the Act of Union (as James I), the ramping lion of the Scots was placed in the second quarter of the royal arms. When the British sovereign visits Scotland the quarters are reversed, Scotland taking the first quarter.

The British royal family is, in effect, the chief clan of Scotland and uses certain heraldic insignia as with any other clan. Royal Stewart tartan and its variants are worn, and the royal crest for Scotland may at times be observed. The sovereign's eldest son has his own heraldic banner for use in Scotland, where he is Duke of Rothesay, Earl of Carrick, Baron Renfrew, Lord of the Isles, Great Steward of Scotland. He uses a plain label in conjunction with his Scottish arms.

BLAZON OF THE ROYAL ARMS

As Queen of the Scots, Elizabeth II bears Quarterly 1 and 4 Or a lion rampant Gules armed Or and langued Azure, within a double tressure flory counter-flory of the second [Scotland]; 2 Gules three lions passant guardant Or [England]; 3 Azure a harp Or stringed Argent [Ireland]. Encircling the shield is the collar of the Most Ancient and Most Noble Order of the Thistle. The crest is an imperial crown proper surmounted by a lion sejant affronty Gules imperially crowned holding in his dexter paw a bared sword and in his sinister a sceptre, both proper. On a compartment vert with thistles proper are the supporters: dexter a unicorn Argent armed tufted and langued Or imperially crowned proper and gorged with an open crown chain reflexed over the back Or and supporting a banner of St Andrew; sinister a lion rampant guardant Or imperially crowned proper supporting a banner of St George. On a scroll above is the motto *In defens*; and in the compartment the motto of the Order of the Thistle, *Nemo me impune lacessit.*

THE ORDER OF THE THISTLE

Scotland's own order of chivalry is the Most Ancient and Most Noble Order of the Thistle, founded in 1540, and its Knights in their dark green mantles take their places in the stalls of the Chapel of the Order, attached to St Giles Cathedral in Edinburgh. The Chapel, inaugurated in 1911, is full of heraldic symbolism, and attached to the stall backs are the stall plates of the Thistle Knights, while their banners are grouped around the pillars in the body of the Cathedral.

THE ROYAL COMPANY OF ARCHERS

In Scotland the sovereign's bodyguard is formed by the Royal Company of Archers. Originating as a private archery club in 1676, it received a royal charter from Queen Anne, for which the "reddendo", or service in return, was to present the sovereign, when requested, with a pair of barbed arrows (an archer's "pair" numbering three). The Company's field uniform is dark green with crimson piping for men, gold for officers, and its insignia includes the reddendo of arrows and the star of the Order of the Thistle. The officers also have collar badges. Their bonnets are decorated with eagles' feathers: one for men, two for officers and three for the Captain General. The Secretary outclasses them all, by wearing a Malayan condor's feather.

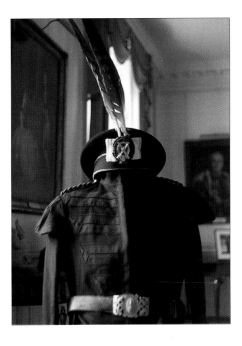

▲ *The jacket of an archer in the Royal Company of Archers, topped with the bonnet of an officer, with two feathers.*

▼ *The hat of the High Constable of Holyroodhouse, with black cock's feathers and the silver stag and cross of Holyrood.*

▶ *The baton of office of the Hereditary Master of the Household in Scotland, a position held by the Dukes of Argyll, has at its head the lion that surmounts the crest of the Scottish royal arms.*

THE SCOTTISH CLAN SYSTEM

The clan – the word stems from the Gaelic for "children" – is an enlarged family unit. It ensures that all within its ranks are equal. The common kinship of the clan, whether real or nominal, knits together every Highland community. While official records refer to the Earl of Argyll, the Lord of the Isles or Lord Lovat (as they would be known in Edinburgh), in their own lands these lords are simply called the MacCailean mor (son of great Colin), the MacDonnal (son of Donald), or the MacShimidh (son of Simon).

Although predominantly a Highland phenomenon, the clan system was also found in the Lowlands, amongst great names such as the Douglases. The terrible feuding between Highland and Lowland clans reached the highest levels of Scots society and had many victims within the royal house itself, as kings were often merely the pawns of other great families. It is a theme often reflected in heraldry. Even a playing card, the nine of diamonds, is called the "curse of Scotland" because nine lozenges appear in the arms of John Dalrymple, 1st Earl of Stair, who instigated

▼ At a gathering of Clan Donald at their ancestral seat, banners of the chief and chieftains are much in evidence.

the massacre of the Macdonalds at Glencoe in 1692. The hammer in the arms of Naesmyth and the oak tree and frame saw in the crest of Hamilton both refer to incidents during which family members had to disguise themselves as workers to avoid discovery by enemies pursuing them during Scotland's more turbulent moments.

CLAN INSIGNIA

Personal heraldry in Scotland is closely linked with the clan system, and stringent rules protect armigers and their heraldic status. The full panoply of clan insignia can be seen at annual clan gatherings, at events such as the Highland Games. Apart from wearing the clan tartan, of which there may be several versions, clan members wear on their bonnets a silver badge (or for women, a brooch) of the chief's crest within a strap and buckle, which also bears the chief's motto, slogan or war cry.

The crest on the badge is not that of the wearer but the property of the clan chief. Armigers may display their own crest within a plain circlet bearing motto or slogan, and place this behind the badge on a silver feather. The head of a large clan branch, officially recognized as such by the Lord Lyon, may bear crest, circlet and motto with two feathers. A clan chief

▲ The arms of the late Sir Fitzroy Maclean include a feudal baron's cap and insignia of the hereditary Keeper of Dunconnel.

places three feathers behind the badge, and a peer may add the appropriate coronet of rank. Even members of the royal family keep to this tradition, wearing the Scottish royal crest on Balmoral bonnets.

HERALDIC FLAGS

At a clan gathering a selection of heraldic flags will be on display, representing the clan chief, chieftains (the heads of family branches) and other senior figures. Such flags are closely regulated by Lord Lyon and come under his legal jurisdiction through an Act of Parliament of 1672. All are recorded on the matriculations of arms of those entitled to such honours.

The most important flag to look out for is the standard, which is granted only to those who have a "following", such as a clan chief. One of the most splendid heraldic accoutrements in use today, the Scottish standard has an unbroken history from the feudal standard of the late Middle Ages. It is viewed as a headquarters flag and does not necessarily mean that the chief is present: this is indicated by the square personal banner displaying his own arms. Ancient Scottish standards normally had the saltire on the hoist (the section of the flag nearest the pole), but modern standards more often bear the owner's personal arms in this area. The remainder is divided into two tracts of the livery colours for chiefs of clans or families, three tracts for very major branches – chieftains – and four for others. The standard is very long, ranging from 7 metres (8 yards) for the sovereign to 3.5 metres (4 yards) for knights and barons. It is tapered and split into two rounded ends (for peers and barons), or unsplit with a rounded end for non-baronial chiefs. It usually bears the owner's crest and heraldic badges, which include the clan's plant badge separated by transverse bands bearing the owner's motto or slogan. If the owner is a peer or feudal baron, the flagpole may be ensigned by a coronet or chapeau of degree.

The guidon is similar to a small standard, one third shorter than the standard assigned to feudal barons. It is assigned to

▼ *The Braw Lads Gathering, Galashiels – one of several "ridings" in Scotland where heraldry is much in evidence.*

lairds (the rough equivalent of English lords of the manor) who have a following.

The fourth type of flag to look out for is the "pinsel". This triangular flag denotes a person who represents the chief in his or her absence. On the chief's main livery colour is his or her crest within a strap of the second livery colour and a buckle (gold for full chiefs) bearing the motto. Outside the strap and buckle, a gold circlet is inscribed with the chief's or baron's title. On top is the coronet of rank or baronial cap. The flag also bears the plant badge and a scroll inscribed with the motto.

FEUDAL BARONIES

The clan chief or chieftain may also be a feudal baron. Lands that have been vested by charter from the Crown (or, rarely, by other high nobles) give the possessor special rights, including certain forms of public justice not normally found on ordinary estates. The holders of such feudal baronies are termed barons or baronesses. (The Scottish equivalent of an English baron is a lord of Parliament.) Before 1587, feudal barons were also entitled to sit in the Scottish Parliament, so the holders of Scottish feudal baronies enjoy certain heraldic honours akin to those of the peerage. These include a chapeau or cap of maintenance, which is placed directly above the shield between it and the helm. The colour of the chapeau shows the particular form of barony:

▲ *A matriculation of arms for Alexander Naesmyth of Posso, from the Court of Lord Lyon. This includes the feudal chapeau for an heir of a barony not in possession.*

1 Chapeau Gules, furred ermine: baron of the kingdom of Scotland still in possession of the barony.
2 Chapeau Azure, furred ermine: the heir to such a barony, not in possession.
3 Chapeau Gules, furred ermines (contre-ermine): a baron of Argyll and the Isles, or one of the older earldoms still in possession.
4 Chapeau Azure, furred ermines: the heir to such a barony, not in possession.

Scottish barons place behind their shield a feudal-baronial mantle, Gules, doubled of silk Argent, fur-edged of miniver and collar ermine, and fastened on the right shoulder by five spherical buttons Or.

The heirs of barons possessed of a barony before 1587 are entitled to clan heraldic supporters (this may also be the case for barons before 1627, but the point is not fully resolved). Feudal barons may also display a baronial helmet, "of steel with a grille of one or three grilles garnished with gold". A barony implicitly has a baron court, of which the presiding judge is baron-baillie and the executive officer is the baron-serjeant. Each has his own insignia and is entitled to heraldic mention of these when matriculating arms.

WALES

Over the centuries British monarchs have maintained in their shields heraldic references to the major nations over which they ruled: the "leopards" of England, the ramping lion of the Scots and the harp of Ireland. Yet one nation, Wales, has seldom figured within their achievements. There never was a king of all Wales, the country was split for centuries into kingdoms, principalities and lordships, and the Welsh had their own names for each degree. Under the English crown Wales has always been called a principality.

Not surprisingly, the Welsh themselves have often seen this as an example of the negative way in which the government in London regards them. It is telling that the name "Wales" comes from an Anglo-Saxon term for "stranger". The strangers in this case were the Celtic inhabitants of the British Isles who took refuge from the Anglo Saxons in the hinterland of Wales.

After 1066, the Welsh gained new neighbours, the Normans, who in time made inroads into Wales itself. The Norman and Plantagenet kings often gave the borderlands to their most trusted nobles, who marked out for themselves semi-independent territories. One of the most imperious of those Anglo-Norman dynasties was the family of de Clare, Earls of Pembroke and Gloucester. They were early enthusiasts of heraldry, and it was through the de Clares and other Norman magnates that it spread to Wales.

Although it was not as widespread and popular as among the English nobility, heraldry was certainly being used by the middle of the 13th century. In Gwynned, for instance, two sons of Llewelyn the Great used arms quartered with four counterchanged lions passant, gold and red being the favourite colours.

THE IMPORTANCE OF LINEAGE

Anyone in medieval Wales, of whatever status, was expected to be able to recite his or her own lineage for five generations. Surnames were not used, except among the English settlers. A man was Evan, son

▲ *The Welsh interest in genealogy is demonstrated by this pedigree of 1593 for Anne Harle, showing descent from Edward Vaughan, Lord Steward of all Wales.*

▶ *This 19th-century bookplate for a Welsh family includes many of the arms attributed to the princes and noble tribes.*

of Howel, son of Llewelyn, and so on. The close-knit nature of Welsh society meant that no further recognition was needed, and the local bards could always be called upon to recite a full lineage.

The all-powerful figure in Welsh lineage was the antecedent known as the noble progenitor. Most of these dated from the in general, it seemed that they would have been of armigerous status whenever they lived, and that their descendants were automatically entitled to the arms – whether real or attributed – of their noble progenitor. Such arms were invented, often using symbols taken from the potent store of bardic poetry and story-telling.

Many Welsh families still proclaim their descent from one or more of those warrior lords. One such ruler was Hywel Dda (Hywel the Good), "The Law Giver", whose 10th-century realm covered much of South Wales. Among many sensible and pragmatic laws he made was this: "It is required of those of noble descent, that their lineage be proclaimed to all in prominent places about their dwellings."

An extraordinary interpretation of this command was made around 1909 by Mrs Ada Lansdown-Williams, who used heraldry to display not only her own lineage but that of her husband, in her manor house on the Welsh coast. The house, now a hotel, contains a display of painted tiles illustrating a lineage going back to the times of the Law Giver himself. She seems to have completed her heraldic scheme in time for the 1,000th anniversary of Hywel Dda's accession. It is a glorious reminder of the staying-power of Celtic lore.

▲ *Heraldry was introduced into Wales by the late 13th century and its style was often adapted to suit Celtic taste, as here on the gravestone of Madog ap Gruffudd, Vale Crucis Abbey, Clwyd.*

▼ *One of Ada Lansdown-Williams' modern painted tiles displaying her lineage in her house near St Davids.*

Dark Ages, when the power vacuum left after the collapse of Roman power was filled by the rule of tribal leaders, strong men whose character bound the people together in desperate times. Some were real men, others semi-legendary. It has been suggested that King Arthur himself was an amalgam of several rulers. To the Welsh people of the late medieval period, men like Cilmin Troed-ddu (Cilmin of the Black Foot) of Caernarvonshire, or Hedd Molwynog of Denbighshire, were most certainly real people and a proud ancestry to be preserved and honoured.

As heraldry filtered into Wales through warfare, trade and even inter-marriage, arms were assumed by some Welsh magnates, such as Gruffyd ap Llewelyn (the Great). More often, they were attributed to chieftains who had ruled in pre-heraldic times. To the bards, and to Welsh society

THE DRAGON OF WALES
Linked with King Arthur, the red dragon was also said to have been the emblem of Cadwalader, a Welsh prince of the 7th century. The Tudor dynasty used Cadwalader's dragon in their armorial bearings, notably as a supporter, and to this day the badge of the Prince of Wales is a red dragon.

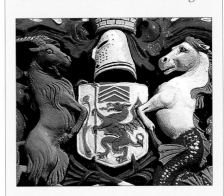

WELSH TRIBAL ARMS

In 1485 a Welshman, Henry Tudor, Earl of Richmond, succeeded by right of battle to the English throne. The Welsh nobles who followed in his wake often sought to register not only their pedigrees but their arms with the English heralds. The continuity of the oral tradition meant that a Welsh pedigree was likely to be more genuine than many of the illuminated family trees drawn up for English earls and barons. The English heralds were quick to recognize the authenticity of Welsh gentility, and maintained close relations with the bards.

The arms of the Welsh royal and noble tribes are for the most part extremely simple, with lions the favourite charges. The same arms were often borne by many families, each claiming descent from a common ancestor. It is tempting to see parallels between the Welsh noble tribe and the Polish *ród*, and it is true that several Welsh families may be grouped under one heraldic emblem. However, in Wales the arms definitely descend from just one person to his descendants alone. Whereas in Polish heraldry a shield hardly ever bears more than one distinct coat, Welsh family arms often show several quarterings, some of which (through marriage with other close-linked families) may be repeated.

For a nation rich in legend it is not surprising to find charges with stories to tell in Welsh arms. Several legends surround

the arms of Moreiddig Warwyn of Breconshire, who lived in the 12th century. The name Warwyn means "Fair Neck" and may reflect an unusual birthmark on his neck. One tale tells how his mother, while pregnant, was sleeping in her garden and awoke to find an adder sliding over her. Her fright manifested itself through her son's birthmark, hence the snake wrapped around the boy's neck which appears in his arms and those of the families claiming descent from him, notably the Vaughans of Golden Grove and Tretower.

Another famous tale concerns the arms of Cadifor ap Dinawal, Lord of Castell Hywel in South Glamorganshire. In 1165 the Lord Rhys, ruler of Deheubarth, attacked Cardigan Castle, held by one of the great Anglo-Norman families, the de Clares. Scaling ladders were put up against the castle walls and the first over the battlements was Cadifor. The Lord Rhys rewarded Cadifor with grants of land and his own daughter in marriage. The arms of Cadifor's descendants include the three ladders and a castle on a chief, with a spearhead "imbrued" (blooded).

Despite the intermittent feuding between the Welsh and English throughout much of the medieval period, families

◄ *The lesser arms of Charles, Prince of Wales. The escutcheon is charged with the arms of the last native Prince, Llewelyn the Great.*

from either side took root on the "foreign" side of the border. In time this led to English families dropping their surnames and adopting the practice of reciting their lineage. The Williams family of Abercamlais, Penpont and Aberavon in Breconshire is one such. Their arms (Argent a chevron Gules between three bulls' heads couped Sable) are the same as those of Bullen or Bollon, for the Williams claim descent from Lawrence or Thomas de Boulogne, one of the Anglo-Norman knights in the van of Bernard de Newmarch during the conquest of Breconshire. Sir Thomas Boulogne, or Bullen, was rewarded with lands in the Upper Usk Valley and his descendants live there still (one descendant of the English branch of the family was said to be Anne Boleyn, mother of Elizabeth I). In time, the name Boulogne was dropped and the son of Lawrence, following the Welsh custom, was called John ap Lawrence. Three generations later a son called William was born and his name, once again following the English custom, was adopted as a surname.

THE PRINCE OF WALES

After centuries of strife, Llewelyn the Great succeeded in unifying Wales, and was recognized as Prince of Wales by the English monarch, Henry III (1216–72). Llewelyn's grandson used his grandfather's title but was a thorn in the side of Edward I (1272–1307) and was defeated in 1282. Edward created his son, the future Edward II, the first English Prince of Wales.

The famous badge of three ostrich feathers, thought of as that of the Princes of Wales, dates from the lifetime of Edward the Black Prince, who was created Prince of Wales by his father Edward III in 1343. It is not actually the badge of the Prince of Wales but is in fact that of the heir to the English throne.

▼ *The later arms of the Tudors, with three helmets replacing Englishmen's heads: not a good design to flaunt at the English court.*

▼ *From Welsh gentry to English earl: Edmund Tudor was made Earl of Richmond by his half-brother King Henry VI.*

The following shields are a selection of the arms that appear frequently in Welsh genealogies. Some were actually used, but many were attributed later by the bards.

▲ Arms of Ynyr, King of Gwent.

▲ Arms of Rees ap Tewdwr, King of Deheubarth, used by Earls of Shrewsbury.

▲ Arms of the founder of the 15th Noble Tribe, Edynwain ap Bradwen.

▲ Arms of Cadifor ap Dinawal, reflecting his attack on Cardigan Castle.

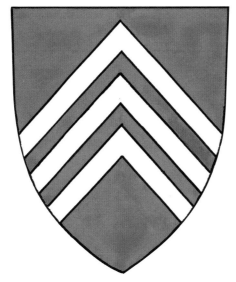

▲ Arms of Jystyn ap Gwyrgant, King of Morgannwg.

▲ Arms of Elystan Glodrudd, King between the Wye and the Severn (old Radnorshire).

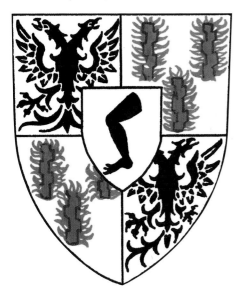

▲ Arms of Cilmin Troed-ddu ("of the Black Foot"), founder of the 4th Noble Tribe.

▲ Arms of Moreiddig Warwyn ("Fair Neck") often used by the Vaughan family.

▲ Arms of Gruffyd ap Cynan, King of Gwynedd, d1137.

IRELAND

The Irish came late to heraldry. It had little place in Gaelic culture, which had its own rich tradition of symbols. When heraldry did arrive from England, it was seen as yet another foreign import, baggage associated with the hated Anglo-Norman adventurers who managed to gain a foothold on Ireland's south-east coast during the 12th and 13th centuries. The narrow stretch of land, with its capital in Dublin, was termed "the pale": within this area the Norman lords and merchants felt secure from the native Irish who were, literally, "beyond the pale".

The arrival of heraldry in Ireland was associated with the English elite. Families such as Butler and Fitzgerald, who in time became more Irish than the Irish, spent as much time feuding against each other as they did fighting their Gaelic neighbours. The simple arms of these two families – Argent a saltire Gules for the Fitzgeralds, Or a chief indented Azure for the Butlers – reflects their early adoption.

IRISH CHARGES

In time the indigenous Gaelic nobility did become curious about heraldry, although often in a somewhat desultory fashion. Symbols that had formed part of a pre-heraldic tradition found their way on to shields of arms, where they often seem ill-placed and haphazard. Charges are cramped and squeezed into the foot of the shield, or

▲ *The arms of O'Neill, with "internal supporters", the sacred salmon and the famous red hand.*

◀ *The arms of the Fitzgeralds show the simplicity of early heraldry, which arrived in Ireland with the Norman/English aristocracy.*

▼ *A knight of the Butler family looks out upon his fiefdom from 12th-century Jerpoint Abbey, in County Kilkenny. His heraldic shield is perfectly preserved.*

▼ *A knight of the Cantwell family, wearing the dress of a well-to-do military man of northern Europe in the second half of the 13th century.*

▲ *Symbols of piety are often found in the arms of Irish Catholic families, such as those of O'Donnell.*

propped up against other main charges. A particularly Irish phenomenon is the use of animals on shields to support another charge (such as the red hand). These "internal supporters" probably started life supporting the shield in the normal way but were shifted on to the shield through a mistake on the part of the stonemason or woodcarver reproducing the arms.

Among the symbols with mystic origins favoured by the Gaelic Irish was the sacred tree, usually the oak, that grew near the entrance to a chief's home. Its divine status was shared by the salmon. Both symbols were regarded as the insignia of royalty, and the most telling gesture a victor could make was to destroy the oak tree and despoil the salmon ponds of his defeated foe.

The salmon is closely associated with the heraldry of the O'Neills, medieval kings of Ulster who also made much use of the famous red hand, a charge found in the heraldry of many Northern Irish families. The origin of the red hand has been the cause of much speculation among Gaelic historians, but many believe it to be a symbol indicative of the bloodline of a royal house. In England the red hand of Ulster, for long associated with the province of Ulster, has gained a certain notoriety through misunderstanding of its significance, especially where it appears in the arms of baronets. Tourist guides are likely to refer to it as a mark given to families who have produced an infamous murderer.

The great beasts of the chase, the stag and the boar, were also considered noble attributes worthy to be included in the heraldry of the Irish clans. Charges commonly seen in Scottish heraldry, such as ancient ships, or religious symbols coupled to warlike symbols, can often also be found across the Irish Sea, indicating the common ancestry of many old Scottish and Irish families.

CLANS AND LINEAGE

As in Scotland and Wales, the Irish Celts placed great emphasis on a royal or noble past, especially through the medium of genealogy. But while the Welsh nobles tended to trace their lineage from many different ancestors, some legendary and others real, all Celtic Irish families traced their line back to one man, Milesius, who was believed to have brought the Celts to Ireland from Spain.

Milesius was said to have had eight sons, only three of whom produced offspring. Some of the Celtic symbols that found their way into heraldry as charges were associated with the bloodlines of Milesius' sons. For instance, it was from Eirehamon, the seventh son of Milesius,

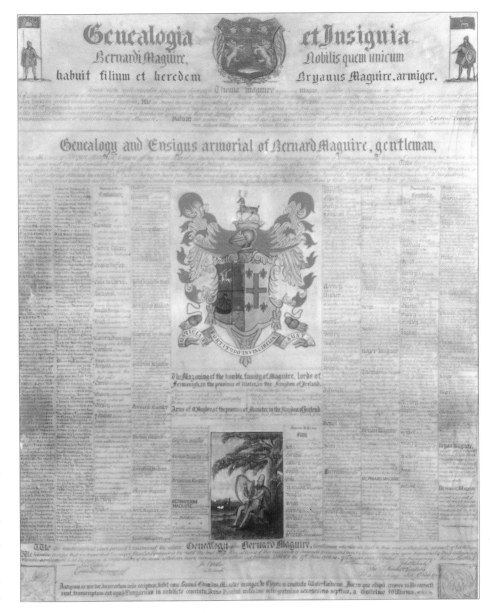

▲ A 19th-century copy of Charles Lynegar's genealogy of Bernard Maguire, originally drawn up in 1731.

that the Northern Irish tribal groupings of the Ui Neill (O'Neill) and Ui Briuin sprang. While the former took the red hand as their symbol, the latter favoured the sacred oak tree.

ENGLISH RULE

Increasing English dominance over Ireland during the Tudor period meant that heraldry was increasingly adopted by the native Irish aristocracy. Having been forced by the Crown to surrender their ancient titles and territory, the Irish nobility had their lands re-granted and new English-style titles bestowed upon them. Not everyone was prepared to take advantage

of this manifestation of foreign dominance. The London government encouraged an influx of English and Scots settlers who, as they were often drawn from the ranks of the gentry, wished to have heraldic recognition of their new local status. This led in 1552 to the establishment of a heraldic office in Dublin, housed for many years in Dublin Castle, the seat of the English government of Ireland. Ulster King of Arms, with his deputy, Athlone Pursuivant, headed the office.

Many Irishmen of Celtic stock saw the "Ulster Office" as yet another example of English arrogance. In time, native Irish historians with a particular interest in heraldry set themselves up as heralds in open opposition to it. One such, Cathal O'Luinnín (anglicized as Charles Lynegar), issued heraldic certificates and pedigrees to Irishmen who did not recognize the jurisdiction of the English-appointed Ulster King of Arms. To make his point more forcefully to the English, O'Luinnín styled himself King of Arms of Ulster. Whereas a patent of arms issued by the Ulster Office bore the English royal arms, the patents issued by O'Luinnín bore the arms of the head of the House of O'Neill, the ancient Kings of Ulster.

O'Luinnín's certificated pedigrees are interesting in that they were written not only in English, but also in French and Latin. This reflected the nature of many of his clients who, disaffected with English rule, had fled abroad to Catholic countries, notably France, Spain and Austria, where many acquired the aristocratic titles of those nations.

The drain of the native Irish aristocracy became more pronounced after the Battle of the Boyne in 1691, at which the Catholic monarch, James II, was defeated by the Protestant prince, William of Orange. The departure into exile of a new wave of Irish Catholics was known ever after as "The Flight of the Wild Geese". Many of them ended up at the court of the exiled James II at St Germain-en-Laye.

At the Stuart court in exile, heraldic matters were at first taken care of by James Terry, Athlone Pursuivant, who fled to Paris

▲ A modern grant of arms by the Office of the Chief Herald of Ireland for a Fitzgerald, based on the ancient arms of the family.

▼ Confirmation of arms of Daniel O'Donnell by James Terry, Athlone Herald at the Jacobite Court in exile, St Germain-en-Laye, 5 April 1709.

taking with him not only many documents but also the seal of the herald's office from Dublin. Many well-born Irishmen sought employment within the armed forces and government services of the Catholic monarchies of Europe, for which some proof of their nobility was required. This, together with armorial certificates, was provided by the exiled Athlone. One such patent, confirming arms from Terry to Daniel O'Donnell, is now housed in the Irish Genealogical Office in Dublin.

HERALDRY IN THE IRISH REPUBLIC

In 1921 the Republic of Ireland was born. Today it consists of the whole island except for the six counties of the northern province of Ulster, still under British rule.

In an agreement between the Irish and British governments, all heraldic records relating to Ireland remained under the control of Ulster King of Arms until 1943, when the Office of the Chief Herald of Ireland was established. Heraldic matters relating to British-controlled Ulster were then transferred to London, and the office

▲ *The arms recently granted to Leixlip Town by the Office of the Chief Herald. The charges on the shield reflect the complex history of the town: a Gaelic motto, a viking ship and the rose of a 16th-century English resident of Leixlip Castle.*

of Ulster King of Arms was merged with that of Norroy King of Arms, thus becoming Norroy and Ulster King of Arms.

The Office of the Chief Herald of Ireland is empowered to grant patents of arms and record pedigrees for all citizens of Ireland, others normally resident in Ireland, persons living abroad who have strong links with Ireland, ancestral or otherwise, and public authorities and other corporate bodies. The Genealogical Office (Office of the Chief Herald) is headed by the Chief Herald of Ireland, who also holds the office of Chief Librarian. Although he has the final say on heraldic matters at all levels, the day-to-day running of the office rests with the Deputy Chief Herald and the consulting heralds. Although the Irish heralds have no official uniform they do have insignia of office of the "paper" variety, with crossed batons depending on their degree placed behind a shield of their family arms.

Because of the nature of the relationship between Ireland and England, it may be that those with strong republican sympathies resident in the six counties of British Ulster will, if they aspire to arms, tend to apply to the Chief Herald's Office in Dublin. However, many organizations and individuals in Northern Ireland, Protestant

as well as Catholic, have also applied to Dublin for patents of arms. Whatever their interest or religion, all are made equally welcome by the Irish heralds, who have their offices in Kildare Street in Dublin. The Irish Heraldry Museum is housed in the same building, and has a fine collection of heraldic artefacts. From the walls hang the banners of the chiefs of the main Irish families as recognized.

In common with other national heraldic authorities, the Office of the Chief Herald has certain rules with regard to difference marks. Those of the English type are used, although this may change. Cadency marks are used by all children of the name. For example, if the eldest child is a daughter, she bears a label, the second child bears a mullet, and so on. Illegitimacy has no status in Irish law, so no marks of difference exist for it. Women may apply for a full grant of arms, including helm and crest.

That most Irish of symbols, the harp, is not often granted as a charge because it is associated with national institutions. Badges and standards are rarely given,

except to those with a "following". Similarly, supporters are reserved for special uses, such as in the personal arms of the State President.

DUBLIN CASTLE

As well as Irish family arms, Dublin Castle contains many reminders of the days of British rule, when the viceroys made it their home. It houses the banners of the former Knights of the Order of St Patrick, whose stall plates, together with a further set of banners, are displayed in the choir of St Patrick's Cathedral. Dublin Castle also houses a set of the coats of arms of the Irish presidents since independence, and the former Chapel Royal in the castle precincts has a fine display of armorial glass and wooden heraldic panels relating to the former viceroys and lord lieutenants.

▼ *A window in the Chapel Royal, Dublin Castle, bearing the arms of the viceroys of Ireland appointed from Westminster – the last viceroy's arms just happened to coincide with the last available panel.*

FRANCE

The French nobility were of course at the forefront of the heraldic story – heraldry itself is presumed to have had its origins in the area that today comprises northern France and Flanders. It is not surprising, therefore, to learn that, in common with other courtly culture, the French model of heraldry influenced that of other nations. The very language used to this day by heralds in the English-speaking world is predominantly medieval French. However, whereas in England the kings of arms were not only trusted by their monarch to set down and oversee most matters armorial, but were also entitled to

grant arms on behalf of the sovereign, their French counterparts never had such a right. The granting of arms in France (as in other European powers) was the exclusive right of the monarch.

In 1616 the power of the heralds was further eroded through the appointment by the king of a judge of matters heraldic, the Juge Général d'Arms de France. The judge was expected to rule over heraldic disputes and to ensure that those persons made newly armigerous by the monarch would bear arms that conformed to the principle of the noble science. The appointment soon took on a hereditary nature, and from 1641–96 it was held by a member of the d'Hozier family.

As with the heraldry of other nations, French achievements, while keeping to a certain uniformity of rule and practice,

▲ *The complete achievement of arms of the French monarchs, used at times from the reigns of Henry IV (1589–1610) to Louis XIV (1643–1715). The French fleur de lis are impaled with the arms of Navarre.*

▼ *A 19th-century illustration of the arms of the leading families of France includes variants of the French royal arms, showing a variety of bends, borders and labels.*

▲ *An illustration from the second half of the 15th century showing King Louis XI at a chapter of the Order of St Michael. The arms of France modern are depicted at the foot of the page.*

developed a distinctive national style. For example, during the medieval period crests were borne only by knights of "tournament rank" – those who actually participated in tournaments – and they are rarely found in later French heraldry. In most cases, when a helmet is shown above the shield it is topped by ostrich feathers – a convention that spilled over France's southern border into Spain.

Coronets of rank existed for each tier of the nobility, a unique addition to which was the title of "Vidame". Its holder acted as commander-in-chief to the military forces of a bishop, and was therefore responsible in time of war for the defence of a diocese. The coronet of a Vidame consisted of a jewelled circlet bearing four crosses, which is depicted in heraldry with one full and two half crosses.

Certain nobles, whatever their rank, bore the additional title of "Pair de France", for which they were entitled to place behind their shield a robe referred to as a *manteau* or robe of estate. This robe was at first depicted as being charged with the arms (including quarterings) of the bearer, but in later times it was coloured blue and edged in gold.

FRENCH ROYAL HERALDRY

No other emblem has had such a lasting and turbulent career as the French lily, or fleur de lis. The love affair between French royalty and its fleur de lis predated heraldry, and the flower's adaptability and obvious beauty has ensured its survival despite the fall of its latter propagator, the royal house of Bourbon. It has managed to weather revolutions and republics, flowering again after each, and may still be seen in one form or another in many French civic arms.

From the early 13th to the end of the 14th century the golden lilies were liberally strewn over a blue field (France ancient). During the Hundred Years War between England and France the number of lilies on the French shield was reduced to just three (France modern), when the English kings promptly reduced the lilies on their shield to the same number.

The many offshoots of the dynasties of Valois and Bourbon made use of both versions of the royal arms differenced in a number of ways, usually by bends, borders and labels. All these could be further differenced from a more senior branch by the addition of smaller charges. Today, many variants of the royal arms are still in use by the departments from which the branches of the royal family took their titles.

The French nobility viewed the lower classes with a certain suspicion and believed them always wanting "to emulate what hitherto they admired", from fine furs to armorial bearings. The bourgeoisie and even the peasantry did indeed start to adopt arms, and if originally this was frowned on by nobility and monarch alike, the latter took the somewhat pragmatic view that it might bring the throne some increased revenue. So it was that in 1696 Louis XIV enforced an edict whereby those of armigerous status would pay a tax on their arms. All newly granted arms had to be entered into an enormous register, the *Armorial Général*.

▼ *The elaborate arms of Napoleon I, Emperor of the French. A beautiful example of the heraldic artwork that was inspired by Napoleon's lavish court – in this case on the door of the imperial coach.*

THE *ARMORIAL GENERAL*

In November 1696, King Louis XIV called for the implementation of a French general armorial, an inventory of all blazons and coats of arms used in the kingdom. Anyone who failed to submit their declaration of rank and honours was to be fined 300 livres, and have their properties seized.

The real aims of this edict were financial rather than heraldic. A long period of warfare had emptied the state coffers and the heraldic census was one way of refilling them. Apart from threatening fines for failure to declare arms, the order also imposed charges for the registration of arms, with rates fixed according to status. So an archbishopric was expected to pay 100 livres, an abbey 50 livres, a parish 25 livres and an individual 20 livres.

The first results of the edict were disappointing, with most declarations coming only from nobles and parishes. Thus in 1697 a second edict was passed. This went further than the first, particularly in the power it gave to the Judge of Arms to identify any who had not declared themselves.

▼ *The Napoleonic system of heraldry laid down a large number of symbols to show rank and profession. This oval denoted a countess, and the sword in pale showed that she was the widow of a military officer.*

In heraldic terms, these laws were of mixed value. The armorials do remain a useful source of documentation on the French heraldic landscape of the 17th century. However, the official lists include large numbers of coats of arms that were never

▲ *Heraldry has long been thought a suitable medium by cartoonists – here a British caricature of Napoleon's arms incorporates the Devil and his emblems.*

actually displayed, either because their bearers did not use a coat of arms at all or because they used a different one.

From 1699, in response to issues raised by the recording of arms, particularly the complaints of those forced to pay sums higher than were justified by the revenue from their estates, many exemptions were allowed and by 1709 declarations had become little more than optional.

▼ *Examples of Napoleon's shields denoting rank (from left to right): eagle on a chief (sovereign prince); chief semy of bees (prince grand dignitary); semy of stars (duke); quarter Azure in chief dexter (count), charged for an officer in the imperial household; quarter Gules in chief sinister (baron), charged for a mayor.*

▲ *Under Napoleon, towns were divided into three degrees, identified by the style of their arms and mounts. This is the pattern for the 36 major cities ("bonnes villes").*

▲ *The designated pattern for a town of the second degree, whose mayor was appointed by the emperor.*

▲ *The designated pattern for a town of the third degree, whose mayor was appointed by the local prefect.*

THE NAPOLEONIC SYSTEM

By 1790 the French Revolution had swept away the notions of nobility and chivalric order, yet by 1802, Napoleon, who had already declared himself Life Consul if not yet emperor, had created a new chivalric order, the Legion of Honour. Once emperor, he went further. In 1806 he granted to his most loyal generals dukedoms of the lands conquered in Italy, and in 1808 he created a new nobility in France with six categories:

1 Sovereign prince (for those awarded sovereignty of a foreign principality)
2 Prince grand dignitary (for princes without sovereign power)
3 Duke
4 Count
5 Baron
6 Knight (with the Legion of Honour)

These six titles were hereditary, except for knights who were unable to prove an annual income of at least 3,000 francs.

Such was Napoleon's liking for control that a new set of heraldic rules was necessary for his brand new imperial nobility. Shields borne by the Napoleonic aristocracy showed the bearer's degree through a system of chiefs and cantons. Chiefs of rank were used for princes and dukes. Counts bore blue cantons in the dexter chief, barons bore red cantons in the sinister chief. Additional symbols borne on these cantons indicated the profession of the bearer. The arms of towns and cities of the empire were also designed according

▼ *Under Napoleon, coronets of rank for the aristocracy were replaced by embellished caps, the detail of which signified rank. Left to right, caps for: knight, baron, count, duke and prince grand dignitary.*

to set patterns indicating their size and importance. Coronets of rank were abolished and replaced by caps of dignity, called *toques*, of various degrees. This range of heraldic headgear bore no similarity to anything that had appeared before. The *toques* were not popular and were quickly forgotten after the return of the Bourbons in 1814, who promptly resurrected the pomp and ceremony of their ancestors.

Today, there is no national heraldic authority in France. The arms of towns and other municipalities are controlled and registered by the Ministry of Justice. Although no organization grants arms to individuals, this does not mean that personal arms are free to be exploited by anyone. As in other nations, there is protection of arms in French law. Anyone who finds that their arms are being used by another is entitled to seek legal redress against the usurper.

ITALY

Italian heraldry is rich with many curiosities not found in other national heraldries, making the country an armorial explorer's paradise. Many of these curiosities have their origins in the complex political and cultural history of modern Italy, a polyglot nation of former city republics and ancient family principalities and kingdoms. The separate states have been bonded together as a unified country under one ruler or government only in the last 150 years.

Since medieval times, Italian heraldry has made use of two characteristic shield shapes seldom seen in the heraldic styles of other nations: these are the teardrop shield and the horse's head shield or "chamfron". Sometimes these distinctive shapes were incorporated into the highest of art forms by the leading artists of the Renaissance in Italy, such as Brunelleschi and Donatello.

By commissioning men of such high artistic standing to execute their shields of arms, both on paper and sculpted on to the façades of their palaces and other monuments, great patrician families such as the Medicis and the Pazzis sought to outshine their rivals in heraldic statements of their wealth and power.

▲ The teardrop shield is popular in Italian heraldry, as seen in this display of the arms of leading figures in the city state of Siena.

▲ A seal of one of Florence's political factions, the Ghibelline party, shows the eagle of the empire stamping on a monstrous serpent that symbolizes their political opponents, the Guelfs.

POLITICAL RIVALRIES

A further statement might be made by placing a symbol associated with a political faction in the arms, normally on the *capo*, or chief (the band occupying the upper third of the shield). The two most famous examples were the *capo d'Angio* (chief of Anjou) and the *capo dell'impero* (chief of the empire).

From the 12th to the 15th centuries, with the German-based rule of the Holy Roman Empire extending into northern Italy, the territory was prey to the intense rivalries of two factions known as the Guelfs, who bore the *capo d'Angio*, and the Ghibellines, identified by the *capo dell' impero*. The Guelfs, supported by the papacy, advocated the independence of the powerful city states of Lombardy. The Ghibellines were the supporters of the imperial house of Hohenstaufen, most famously of Frederick I (known as

Frederick Barbarossa) 'who was Holy Roman Emperor from 1152–90, and his grandson Frederick II (1212–50). Both emperors struggled to consolidate their imperial power in Italy.

The *capo d'Angio* was formed by using a red label over three gold fleurs de lis on a blue chief – a simplified variation of the arms of the House of Anjou. (Sometimes the chief was "semy de lis", or scattered with small fleurs de lis). The *capo dell' impero* was gold charged with a black eagle, single- or double-headed.

This rivalry did not only express itself heraldically. It was also possible to tell the political persuasion of townspeople and ruling families from the architectural style of the upper storeys of their houses,

▲ *The fleur de lis and red label in the chief, known as the* capo d'Angio, *proclaim the Counts Guidi as Guelf supporters.*

churches, castles and town halls. The battlements on those erected by the Guelfs were given horizontal tops, while the Ghibellines preferred an M-shaped edge. The latter device also appeared as a charge in the arms of Ghibelline supporters.

The political nature of the chief in Italian heraldry persisted into the 20th century. Under the fascist government of Benito Mussolini (in power from 1922 to 1943), all municipal authorities were supposed to sport the *capo del littorio* in their arms. This chief included the symbol of the Fascist party, the Roman "*fasces*" – an axe surrounded by a bundle of rods – within a wreath. In fact, however, few of the authorities took up the device.

The *capo* was also used to augment the arms of supporters of the House of Savoy. The *capo di Savoia* was Gules a cross Argent. Other variants bore the dynasty's badge, the Savoy knot.

THE DUCAL CAP

In Venice the elected ruler was known as the doge (a word meaning leader that shares its derivation with the word "duke"). The doge assigned his arms with the red ducal cap or *corno dogale*. This started life as the simple conical cap of Venetian fisherfolk, but in time became a

▲ *The imperial eagle in the arms of the Venosta family, on the* capo dell'impero, *shows them to be of the Ghibelline faction.*

gorgeous object, ornamented with pearls and cloth of gold. Members of families who had at some time provided a doge were also entitled to include the ducal cap in their arms. It appeared either on the shield or, more often, as a crest, combining the two forms of headgear – the cap and the helmet – in one.

▼ *Even the shape of a castle's battlements could say something about the politics of its owner. The dovetailed crenellations in the arms of the Vismara family are typical of a Ghibelline fortress.*

ITALIAN CORONETS

One peculiarity worth seeking out within the polyglot world of Italian heraldry is the usage by noblemen who bear a lesser title than the head of a family. Two coronets of rank appear in their achievement: the one that surmounts the shield is for the bearer of the achievement, while the other is placed on the helm and is for the head of the house, as shown here in this bookplate for the family of Borio de Tigliole.

EX LIBRIS FAMILIÆ

VIGILAT QUI STRONTES SUPERAT

BORIO di TIGLIOLE

▲ *The* capo del littorio, *seen here in the arms of the province of Genoa, indicated allegiance to the Fascist party. It disappeared in 1945.*

ECCLESIASTICAL HONOURS

Much Italian heraldic practice devolved from the heraldry of the Roman Catholic Church. Italian families were proud to place in their arms one or more armorial devices signifying some high ecclesiastical honour bestowed on one or more of their ancestors or relatives. The noblest of these was the coupling of the crossed keys of the papacy and the pavilion or *ombrellino*

▼ *The arms of Prince Boncompagni Ludovisi and his wife Angela Maria, Duchess Altemps: within the princely robe the* ombrellino, *or pavilion, and keys show that members of the family have been Pope.*

(umbrella). This was placed either above the shield or on a chief, and indicated that a member or members of the family had been Pope. An example can be seen in the bookplate of Prince Boncompagni Ludovisi. The arms are a combination of the Boncompagni dragon (for the family of which Pope Gregory XIII was a member) and the bends of Ludovisi (the family of Pope Gregory XV).

Other great families, who had provided "gonfaloniers", or standard-bearers, to the papacy, were entitled to charge their shield with a pale – or vertical band – of the Church, which resembled in simplified form the banner or gonfalone itself. Originally the pale was red, charged with the crossed keys, one gold, the other silver, surmounted by the papal tiara or (later) the pavilion.

▲ *The horse's head shield typical of Italian heraldry is here engraved on a plate of 15th-century Murano glass. Above the shield is the distinctive red fisherman's cap of the doge of Venice.*

DEFACED ARMS

In northern Italy (and over the border into southern Switzerland) some evidence of the turbulent times that followed in the wake of the French Revolution is still apparent. In the area that was created the Cisalpine Republic for example, the zeal for reform was strong, and the urge to break the back of the old order was taken to such extremes that orders were sent out from the people's committees to the citizens to tear down and deface the heraldry of the former aristocracy. In many places through the new republic the order was ignored, but in others the order was taken seriously. Even though the republic did not survive, still visible in the region today are the stippled stonework and rough plaster-work scars that mark the walls that once bore carved and coloured shields.

REGULATION OF HERALDRY

In Italy today (in common with many other modern European nations) there is no official procedure for registering or granting arms to private individuals, although heraldic designers will provide arms for clients for a fee. The Italian government does still maintain a heraldic office of arms, the Ufficio Araldico, which approves arms for civic, district and regional authorities, and maintains certain rules specific to Italy. For instance, in the medieval period the gonfalone was held in special regard by Italian communities, and

▼ *The façade of a building in Brescia in northern Italy: the empty plaques originally bore the arms of the town's mayors and captains, which were defaced during the period of the Cisalpine Republic.*

◀ *The recently designed gonfalone of the province of Milan.*

still is to this day; the Ufficio Araldico monitors regulations regarding the colours and trappings of any new gonfalones, which may be gold in colour for a province and silver for a community.

Sadly, the grants of arms issued by the office today take the form of printed documents without any pictorial depiction of the actual arms. This has been the norm since the late 19th century, although before World War II the grants made under the rule of the house of Savoy did have finely coloured borders decorated with the badges and orders of the Kingdom of Italy and its ruling dynasty.

The pattern for armorial bearings is carefully regulated by the Ufficio Araldico. Submissions must be of a uniform style that should not suggest any local influence. Marco Foppoli, a heraldic artist from the northern city of Brescia, had his work rejected by the office as being too northern in style, in that it suggested Swiss and German influences.

SPAIN AND PORTUGAL

Many of the characteristics of early Spanish and Portuguese heraldry were shaped by the centuries of warfare known as the *reconquista*, or reconquest. The Iberian peninsula had been invaded from the south in 711 by the Moors, Muslim forces from North Africa, whose civilization lasted nearly eight centuries. Moorish power reached its height under the caliphs of Cordoba in the 10th and 11th centuries, but the Christian rulers of northern Spain gradually reconquered the peninsula as the Moorish empire broke up in the 13th century, and Granada alone remained Moorish. Meanwhile, the Christian rulers were unifying, a process that culminated in the marriage of Isabella of Castile and Ferdinand of Aragon in 1469. When Granada fell to the Christians in 1492, Ferdinand and Isabella became rulers of all Spain.

The presence and activity of the great military-monastic orders, such as those of Santiago, Calatrava and Alcántara, in reconquering and eventually unifying the

▲ *A fine stone achievement for the Pinto da Mesquito family in Yila Real, Portugal.*

whole of the Iberian peninsula, and the chivalric ideals that these knightly orders represented, must have facilitated the development and use of heraldic symbols in the late 12th century. The continual border conflict between the Moorish and Christian kingdoms in medieval Iberia helped to reinforce a sense of ethnic identity in the Christian forces. This was described as *limpieza de sangre*, or "purity of blood", and heraldry was just one outlet for this form of national expression.

There were attempts to make arms distinctive of class as well as ethnicity. In Portugal, King Afonso V (1438–81) restricted burgher arms to the use of colours only, while King Manuel I (1495–1521) forbade the use of arms to all but the titled classes. The Castilian sovereigns followed suit and the right to arms was restricted to members of the nobility.

QUARTERING

The need for social identification found a creative outlet in the marshalling of arms. The heraldic principle of quartering had its origins in Iberia: the Portuguese system aimed at representing every one of an armiger's ancestors, both heraldic heiresses and others. Moreover, since quarterings could be shown in any order, a system of differencings, or *briça*, was instituted by Manuel I to identify an armiger's grandparents. The quarters of paternal and

maternal grandfathers were identified with small charges and cantons (also sometimes charged) respectively; the quarters of paternal and maternal grandmothers were shown respectively with half cantons (*meia briça*) and cushions.

THE REGULATION OF ARMS

Spanish pursuivants, heralds and kings of arms were appointed directly by the sovereign. The junior officers had to be at least 20 years old and to be nominated by two heralds. They underwent a ceremony in which the king baptized them with water and wine, and after at least seven years they could be promoted, provided they had the blessings of two kings of arms and four heralds. New heralds and kings of arms had to take an oath of office and the latter were appointed only with the consent of every officer of arms.

Heralds, or *cronistas de armas*, were usually named after provinces and non-capital cities, such as Bethune and Cataluña, while kings of arms were named after the

▼ *King João II of Portugal (1481–95) holds his shield of arms. The bordure of castles was added by King Afonso III (1248–79).*

▼ *The quartered arms of Castile and León cover the robe of King Alfonso X of Spain in this 13th-century illustration.*

Spanish kingdoms, including Toledo (who bore Azure an imperial crown Or) and Granada (created in 1496 to honour the reunification of Spain). While these appointments were not hereditary, at least 15 Spanish families have produced more than one herald each in the past 500 years (compared to about the same number for England, Scotland and Ireland together).

The Portuguese King João I followed the Spanish lead in the early 15th century by appointing kings of arms, including the Englishman Arriet. The Portuguese armorial law of 1495 requiring armorial registration stimulated the production of two famous armorials, the *Livro do Rei d'Armas* and the *Livro do Armeiro-mor*.

Spanish heralds served in both palatine and private capacities, the former including diplomatic and ceremonial roles. The 17th century even saw the heralds engaged in *vistas de armas*, or visitations to the provinces and overseas colonies of Spain to locate, inspect and correct heraldic irregularities. Their regulatory powers were

such that none but the most powerful royal officials could interfere in their tours. In 1649 they castigated the Archbishop of Mexico, for irregular use of arms in the Cathedral of Los Angeles, New Spain.

The beginning of the 20th century saw many changes. The establishment of the Portuguese Republic in 1910 abolished the body of heralds in Portugal. Meanwhile, a royal decree of 1915 reformed the practice of appointing heralds in Spain. After this, heralds had to possess a degree in law or philosophy and be examined by a board of historians, notaries and archivists, while their armorial certificates were valid only if they were authorized by the Ministry of Grace and Justice.

The proclamation of the Second Spanish Republic in 1931 was soon followed by a ministerial edict abolishing the Corps of Chronicler Kings of Arms, stripping the heralds of their pensions and depositing their archives in the National Library. In Portugal, the heralds' situation improved with the founding of the Council of

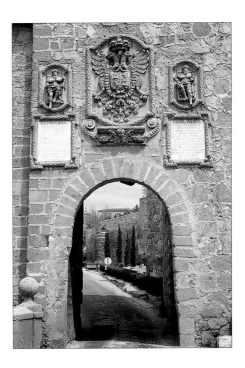

▲ *Many town walls in Spain bear the imperial arms of the Habsburg monarchs, as here on a bridge in Toledo.*

Nobility by the Duke of Bragança in 1945, but in Spain it was not until 1947 that the Spanish Ministry of Justice re-established the position of the *cronista*. By ministerial decree of 1951, the heralds were allowed to apply for recognition as private professionals (the corporate body of heralds remained dormant) and four *cronistas* were permitted to continue certifying arms for the following 30 years.

A post-republican herald, Don Vicente de Cadenas y Vicent (who also served as King of Arms to Archduke Charles of Austria-Tuscany, the Carlist pretender to the Spanish throne) was appointed in 1951. In 1992 the provincial government of Castile-León appointed Don Alfonso Ceballos-Escalera y Gila, Marqués de la Floresta, Chronicler of Arms of Castile and León. Today, these Spanish heralds, along with the heraldic commission of the Associaçao dos Arqueálogos Portugueses and the Instituto Portuguese de Heraldica, continue the history of Iberian heraldry.

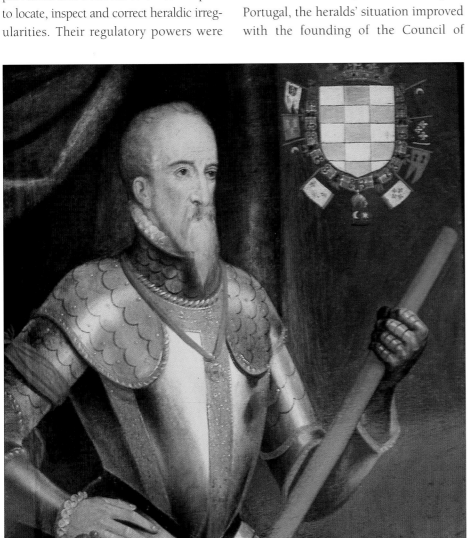

◄ *The Duke of Alva, governor of the Spanish Netherlands, with his family arms. Around the shield are banners taken in battle, usually from the Moors, often found in the achievements of Spanish nobles.*

GRANTS OF PERSONAL ARMS

As the Spanish heralds' palatine activities decreased, their private functions – namely the issuing of armorial certificates – grew in significance. Their monopoly on armorial certificates was confirmed in a royal order of 16 June 1802, which recapitulated an earlier order of 17 November 1749, and in the early part of the 20th century, kings of arms had their right recognized to certify the new armorial bearings of nobles in the name of the king.

On 17 July 1907, a royal order of the War Ministry authorized the Army Corps to solicit the kings of arms for armorial certificates with respect to their military units. The Spanish Ministry of Justice recognized the heralds' certificates and made the *cronistas* solely responsible for their accuracy in the reforms of 1915 and 1951, while at the same time organizing the different types of certificates into seven categories dealing with nobility, arms and genealogy. Citizens of South American republics and other countries that were formerly claimed by Spain have the same rights as Spaniards with respect to this legislation.

The practice of certifying and conferring armorial bearings to foreigners began with certificates issued to residents of the Spanish Netherlands in the 17th century. By the 18th century, Spanish kings of arms were certifying the arms of citizens of other countries, including France, Ireland and England. This practice was extended to the Americas in the 19th and 20th centuries. Even though the Spanish sovereigns reserve the right to grant new arms, and

▲ *The use of charges in the form of words and phrases from prayers is characteristic of Iberian heraldry, as here in the arms of the Mendoza family.*

◀ *The achievement of arms of King Juan Carlos I of Spain on the cover of a modern armorial certificate.*

▶ *The arms of Pedro Fernandez de Andrada, c1580, include a bend engoulé (being swallowed). Such a charge being devoured by wolves or dragons is a typical feature of Spanish heraldry.*

the certification of armorial bearings does not in itself constitute a new coat of arms, burgher arms (sometimes designed for a client by the *cronista*) certified by a herald are protected under Spanish law.

Today, the recipients of new Spanish titles may have armorial certificates countersigned by the king, and supporters may also be certified for those who can demonstrate a direct descent from an ennobled ancestor, or those who hold the rank of knight commander or higher in one of the dynastic or Catholic orders of chivalry.

NATIONAL HERALDIC FEATURES

Although Spanish and Portuguese arms follow rules common to all heraldry, national traits still emerge, as in the heraldry of many other European nations. Roman Catholicism is manifest through the frequent inclusion of exhortations to the saints or the Virgin Mary: often these words of prayer appear as charges on a bordure, a sub-ordinary that is much used throughout Iberian heraldry. Alternatively it may be charged with small saltires – said to be indicative of a particular battle that features in the family history.

▼ *An 18th-century viceroy of Peru, Manuel Amat de Junget, with his arms; by his time even Aztec nobility would know heraldry.*

In Spain the bordure is sometimes charged with castles and lions (for Castile and León), suggesting descent or special honours from those royal families. In Portugal the *quintas*, or escutcheon, charged with five plates taken from the royal arms, performs a similar function. Another charge peculiar to Iberian heraldry is the cauldron. In ancient times this was the sign of an *hombre rico* (rich man), who was meant to keep his cooking pot filled as a duty to the poor in times of hardship.

Grandees of Spain hold a title that is set above all others within the aristocracy, and is afforded special prerogatives at court. Heraldically, the title is suggested in an achievement of arms by a robe of estate, and a coronet of rank is placed directly upon the shield, without the helmet.

▲ *The ceiling of the Palace of Sintra bears the arms of the Portuguese aristocracy.*

▲ *In the arms of the former Portuguese overseas province of São Tome, the dexter side bears the arms of Portugal, the sinister side the provincial arms. The waves in the base signify an overseas location.*

GERMAN-SPEAKING LANDS

Through much of the period in which heraldry was in use, the German-speaking nations were loosely united under the Holy Roman Empire. Although the relationships between the emperor and the various princes, kings and other city governments were often turbulent, it was the emperor who was ultimately the fount of all honours, including arms.

The emperors delegated the granting of arms to other high-ranking personages, but they often took a keen interest in heraldic design, and kept certain honours, such as augmentation of part of the imperial arms, very much under their personal control.

Under the emperors of the house of Hohenstaufen (1138–1254), the eagle became the accepted symbol of the rulers of Germany, and through a series of embellishments was turned from a simple one-headed bird (black on a gold shield) into the glorious two-headed creature that became the symbol of the Holy Roman Emperor. From 1437 until the end of the Holy Roman Empire in 1806, the title of Emperor was held by the head of the Austrian house of Habsburg, except for the brief reign of Charles VII of Bavaria (1742–5), who placed the arms of his own family, Wittelsbach, on the eagle's breast.

▲ *The Holy Roman Emperor (centre top) and the seven electors, each shown with his arms, from the Hausekopiar, 1484, Cologne.*

THE ELECTORS

For centuries it was the practice for certain great princes to elect the Holy Roman Emperor, and for much of the period the number of electors was limited to seven. They were the Archbishops of Mainz, Trier, and Cologne (who were respectively the Arch-Chancellors of Germany, Gaul and Italy) and four lay dynasts, who each enjoyed certain offices during the coronation: the King of Bohemia (Imperial Cupbearer), the Duke of Saxony (Imperial Marshal), the Count Palatine of the Rhine (Imperial Steward), and the Margrave of Brandenburg (Imperial Chamberlain). The arms of the lay electors each tended to include the symbol of their imperial offices.

◀ *Part of the heraldic frieze in Lauf Castle, near Nuremberg, which contains an early example of an armorial hall painted in 1360.*

Therefore the Dukes of Saxony bore an escutcheon (sometimes shown as a quarter) bearing the crossed swords of the marshalcy. The Duke-electors of Bavaria bore an escutcheon with the orb of the empire, and the Margraves of Brandenburg charged their arms with an escutcheon bearing the emperor's sceptre.

These officers of the Holy Roman Empire often delegated some of their duties, and with them the right to their insignia, to lesser members of their families. This is why the Swabian branch of the Hohenzollerns (the family of the Margraves of Brandenburg) placed in the centre of their quarters a blue escutcheon charged with crossed sceptres.

IMPERIAL DIGNITIES

In the Holy Roman Empire, the granting of arms usually went hand in hand with an act of ennoblement. Families, and even prelates of the Church, who came to hold high office within the empire, were quick to include in their shields a compartment or escutcheon devoted to their regalian rights. Among these is the splendid achievement of Franz Georg von Schönborn (1729–56), Archbishop of Trier, Prince-Bishop of Worms, Prince-Provost of Ellwangen and Prince-Abbot of Prüm, who also happened to bear the glorious title of Oberst-Erblandtruchsess (Hereditary High Steward) of Austria, a fact indicated in his shield by the imperial eagle and a crowned escutcheon of the arms of Austria. Lion supporters also held high his banners of office. In common with many other high-ranking prelates of the time, his achievement includes no sign indicating ecclesiastical rank, unless, almost as an afterthought, it is by way of the cross on his princely bonnet.

Another unusual item that has found its way on to an achievement of arms is the horse's comb borne by the (now extinct) Princes of Schwarzburg-Sondershausen, who were hereditary Masters of the Imperial Stables. Also included in their achievement is a curious device like a pitchfork, which could be mistaken for an implement used to muck out the imperial horses; in fact it is associated with other rights connected with the mining of silver in the Harz Mountains.

▼ *A show of heraldic pomp for Archbishop Franz Georg von Schönborn on the entrance to the monastery of Prüm.*

The Princes of Schwarzburg also made use of a unique crest, an allegory of a very special dignity, that of the "greater *Komitiv*", which conferred the right to grant arms, to ennoble commoners, and to install barristers. Such a right was associated with the title of Hofpfalzgraf (Count Palatine of the Imperial Court). While the right to grant arms in the Holy Roman Empire rested with the emperor, some secular and ecclesiastical princes, certain universities and persons of high standing, were granted the right of *Komitiv*. The "lesser *Komitiv*" was limited to legitimizing children and granting arms to commoners. The Counts of Schwarzburg-Sondershausen were created Hofpfalzgrafen by Leopold I on 22 December 1691. On 3 September 1697, they were raised to the degree of princes, and were then granted augmented arms that included the crest denoting the greater *Komitiv*: a knight with a sword.

▲ *The complex quarterings of the princes of Schwarzburg-Sondershausen, complete with a comb to groom the imperial horses.*

▼ *The device on the shield of Andreas Gassman of Basel, c1583, has its origins in a Swiss merchant's or house mark.*

CHARGES IN GERMAN ARMS

Germanic heraldic style combines conventional geometric charges, or ordinaries, with charges of particular charm and curiosity not found in British or southern European heraldry.

The horse head gable ends of the local houses were a favourite in the arms of communities in northern Germany, together with an even older charge – a wolf's claw – based on an implement used in German forests to drag logs (of which a variant is still used).

In Switzerland and southern Germany, burgher families made use of "house marks". These took the form of various geometric figures, often appearing as a series of lines resembling numbers, and

▼ *The arms of Albrecht Dürer and his wife. Placing the helm between the two shields accolee (side by side) is typical of German marital arms.*

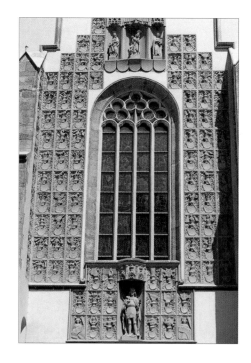

▲ *Emperor Frederick III states his control over 95 lordships in the armorial display on the façade of the Cathedral Church of Wiener Neustadt in Austria.*

they were used on property as well as market goods, often stamped alone without heraldic accoutrements. Similar marks were used by merchants on their wares. At a later date the user of such devices might place them on his shield and helmet, aping the aristocracy.

THE *WAPPENSAAL*

German-speaking nobles, perhaps more conscious of their lineage than any of their class elsewhere in Europe, often set aside a room in a mansion or castle as a *Wappensaal*, or armorial hall. Usually the shields were formally lined in a frieze around the walls in order of precedence, with the local rulers given prime position.

In Austria a popular theme was a family tree of the imperial family, often with figures depicting individual members accompanied by their shield of arms. Sometimes the scenes depicted were all too graphic, as in Tratzberg Castle in the Tyrol. Here, a frieze shows Albrecht of Habsburg, the King of the Romans, being stabbed to death by his nephew Johan "the Patricide" in 1308. The evil nature of the deed is expressed by showing Archduke Johan accompanied by a snake.

The Habsburgs themselves were keen to claim descent through heraldry, not only from the former ruling dynasty of Austria, the house of Babenburg, but also from legendary rulers of Austria. This theme is played out in its fullest form on the front

▼ *A family tree in Tratzberg Castle, Austria, showing the murder in 1308 of King Albrecht 1 by his nephew Johan.*

of the Cathedral Church of St George, in Wiener Neustadt, where the coronation of Emperor Frederick III was commemorated in 1453 through the *Wappenwand*, a heraldic frieze representing a fantastical genealogical tree of the House of Austria through 95 lordships.

The theme of maintaining the *status quo* through heraldry is awesomely expressed in the Provincial Council House of Carinthia, Klagenfurt, where each noble family, abbey and town is represented through a baroque cartouche of arms. Not content with one *Wappensaal*, the heraldic scheme, which includes nearly 700 shields in all, also finds its way into a second, smaller chamber.

GERMAN TITLES

In the Holy Roman Empire it was usual for a family's arms to be augmented with quarters as it advanced up the social scale. The original arms were usually kept as a *Herzschild* ("heart shield"). Coronets of rank were used but often a simplified variant of the arms with a crest coronet, or the family shield and crest displayed in simple medieval style, was preferred.

One unusual form of heraldic headgear worth looking out for is the cap or bonnet of the electors of the Holy Roman Empire, a scarlet cap with a large (often scalloped) ermine brim. Such a cap can be seen in the arms borne by the Hanoverian King George III of Britain, as Prince-Elector of the Holy Roman Empire.

There is some confusion outside German-speaking lands about the prefixes attached to the title of *Graf* ("count"), such as *Burggraf*, *Pfatzgraf* or *Markgraf*. These simply designate a particular territorial responsibility and were not heraldically distinguished. A *Burggraf* ruled over a *Burg* or fortress; a *Pfatz* was a palatinate and a *Mark* was a marcher, or border, land.

The prefix *von* in a name corresponds to the French *de*, both simply meaning "of". In both German and French names, the word is followed by the place name of the family home, although as an adjunct of nobility it was common practice to add the *von* and place name to a surname after ennoblement. Families of ancient nobility

▲ *A panel depicting the complete achievement of arms of the Hungarian Dukes Batthyany, Counts Strattman.*

took their surnames from their estates. No family name was required, they were simply *von*... For those families of ancient origin still in possession of their estate, *von* was replaced by *zu* ("to"), or even *von und zu*, although this style was not so commonly used. In later centuries the use of *von* in front of a name became debased, becoming almost as common as the *van* in Dutch surnames.

Since World War I, the position of the armiger, whether a private individual or a civic authority, has proved complex and curious in German-speaking lands. Before that time, a noble title was inherited by all the legitimate children of a noble father, not just the eldest son, as is the case in the British nobility. After 1919, the bearing of noble titles was banned altogether in Austria, while in Germany the title was allowed in effect to become affixed to the family's surname. Therefore, in name if not in fact, the German aristocracy may survive long after the demise of the nobility of other nations.

This change meant that for the first time the adopted children of noble fathers, who could previously use the family name but could not inherit the noble title, were now able to call themselves, for example, "Hugo Graf von..." or "Gisela Freifrau von..." and pass the name on to their own children.

THE REGULATION OF ARMS

World War I swept away not only the German and Austrian Empires, but also various other German monarchies (those of Baden, Württemberg and Bavaria), which had each maintained their own heraldic authorities. Where once the German heralds granted arms on behalf of monarchs, their place has now been taken by a number of heraldic societies (for private individuals) and state government (for local authorities), although in both cases the certification of arms is purely a registration process, without any formal authority to grant armorial bearings.

Each federal state follows its own course with regard to the registration of arms for local authorities within its boundaries. While some, such as the administration of Lower Saxony, maintain a formal register of arms deposited within their archives and are happy to advise on good heraldic practice, others demonstrate little or no interest in such matters. This has led to the adoption of quasi-heraldic symbols or even non-heraldic logos by some municipal councils in Germany.

▼ *The arms of the Counts von Zeppelin, depicted in simple medieval style with a single charge and crest.*

NAZI HERALDRY

▲ The ancient arms of Coburg on the left, replaced with the National Socialist-approved symbol on the right.

National Socialist authorities so much that in 1934 they changed the arms completely. The new shield was Per pale Sable and Or, a sword issuant from base point downwards, the pommel charged with a swastika counterchanged. In 1945 the Morenkopf of St Maurice was restored.

TEUTONIC PRIDE

Between the late 1920s and the outbreak of World War II, Germany experienced a resurgence of interest in personal heraldry. It was yet another manifestation of the Teutonic pride expounded by all members of the Nazi hierarchy, none more so than the leader of the SS, Heinrich Himmler. Though far from Aryan perfection himself, Himmler was obsessed with the cult of Germanism, and was encouraged in his

Even in relatively modern times, the power of heraldry has been acknowledged, as evidenced by the interest taken in this unlikely and archaic subject by the Nazi regime in 1930s Germany. The need to manipulate and adapt heraldry to suit the ideological ideals of Hitler and his henchmen was spelt out in a decree from the Interior Ministry dated 15 December 1937. Marked "Confidential", it gave the following direction to local Nazi party leaders with regard to the approval of arms of district authorities:

▲ The swastika, an ancient symbol taken by the Nazis as their own, dominates a rally at Nuremberg, 1933.

In accordance with the deputy/representative of the Fuhrer, I therefore request in future, that instead of overtly ecclesiastical emblems (saints, croziers, mitres, etc) other emblems be chosen for district arms which relate to other historical events, or express the particular characters of the community at present and the current state of affairs.

▼ The state of Thüringia saw the need to show approval and support of the new order by adding the swastika to the traditional arms of Hesse.

The decree stated that the cross and other symbols of the confessional aroused anger in 100 per cent of National Socialists, and local leaders were encouraged to extend their control over such institutions as community centres, once dominated by the elders of the Church.

In fact, few German councils paid much notice, and most tended to favour keeping their often ancient symbols. The government of Thüringia did, however, place a swastika between the paws of the Hessian lion in its state arms, although it was almost too small to notice. At least one town council felt bound to toe the party line. Coburg had for centuries borne a Moor's head, representing St Maurice, but such an un-Aryan character rattled the

▼ SS Brigadeführer Karl Maria Weisthor's Nazi arms, each part of which he endowed with its own mystic meaning.

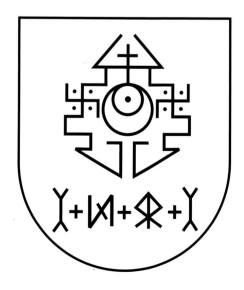

fantasies by such men as Karl Maria Wiligut (1866–1946) and Guido von List (1848–1919), a leader of the Ariosophy movement, which was an amalgam of nationalism and occultism. Both men claimed that the origins of heraldry were more remote than is usually agreed. In their view, it began in the world of the Teutonic gods – above all Wotan, the god of war, whom dead heroes met in Valhalla, and who knew the secrets of the runes.

RUNES AND MYSTICISM

The origin and meaning of runes obsessed many Nazi "theologians", and List and Wiligut, as the most famous exponents of this secret heraldry, saw to it that runes became the basis for the Nazis' own heraldry. It was no coincidence that the colours of the SS were also those of the

▶ *The apotheosis of Nazi heraldry, the arms of a new Teutonic Knight such as would have decorated the Knights' Chamber at Wewelsburg Castle.*

▼ *The bookplate of a Nazi party member – the eagle, which faced left for the state, faces right for the party.*

Teutonic Knights. At Schloss Wewelsburg, Himmler sought to combine the ideals of the Teutonic Knights and Teutonic mythology, together with the court of King Arthur, complete with round table, into a new "noble fraternity", who were to meet in a newly synthesized complex of rooms decorated with runic motifs.

Around the round table of solid oak would sit Himmler and his 12 senior SS commanders (the successors, so he believed, to the Teutonic Knights). Behind each officer would hang his own coat of arms, especially designed, as most of the 12 – including Himmler himself – lacked family arms. New arms were devised by the Ahnernerbe, the institution attached to the SS that dealt with racial purity and Teutonic history, using designs influenced by the runic translations of Karl Maria Weisthor (Wiligut had changed his name to what he believed was his ancient family name).

Among other odd outpourings, Weisthor/Wiligut claimed the power of "ancestral memory", which allowed him to trace his own unbroken family history back to the Teutonic peoples in the year 228,000 BC, his family springing from a coupling of the gods of water and air. He was also able to see the time when the earth was inhabited by mythological beings, including dwarves, giants and races such as the Lemurians – giant brown-skinned hermaphrodites with four arms. (Not surprisingly, after threatening to kill his wife, he was confined in a mental asylum.) Weisthor/Wiligut claimed to know the secret spells and meanings of the runes and used them in charges designed for his own family arms. He brought several of them together in one of the most fascinating objects associated with SS ritual (much of which he conceived): the Totenkopfring der SS, or SS death's head ring, which included both the swastika and the double sigrune of the SS.

The swastika was a mystical symbol of good fortune, used from ancient times by peoples from Tibet to northern Europe. In

▲ *The bookplate of Hans Raven, typical of the Nazi period, with the swastika much in evidence and bearing a crest straight out of the age of the Teutonic Knights.*

Europe it was associated with Donner (or Thor), god of adventurers, and became popular in 19th-century Germany as a symbol of racial and national unity. The latter would seem to have been the main reason for Hitler's love of the swastika, which he used as a heraldic device coupled with the German eagle.

The sigrunes of the SS symbolized victory and were first drawn side by side in 1931 by SS member Walter Heck, a graphic designer employed by the badge-manufacturing firm of Ferdinand Hoffstatter in Bonn. Both the swastika and the SS runes were among many devices chosen to decorate the new shields of arms in Wewelsburg Castle, although the outbreak of war seems to have placed the heraldic scheme there on hold. The only case of such arms being created would appear to be for SS Obergruppenführer Pohl, as they appear on a ring given to him by his son in 1938.

As a postscript to this account of extraordinary quasi-heraldry, it is worth looking out for signs of "human attention" on a mountainside near Schloss Wewelsburg, for it is known that in 1945, on Himmler's orders, all the remaining Totenkopfrings (which incidentally were treated as awards, and had to be returned on the death of each recipient) were blast-sealed into a mountain, and as yet they have never been found.

RUSSIA

Heraldry came relatively late to Russia, in comparison with much of western Europe. It is generally accepted that its flowering owed much to Tsar Peter I ("the Great", 1682–1725), who during his travels in Europe saw the splendour that could be achieved by its use in such media as stained glass, carved stone and furniture. The first Vice-Master of Heraldry, appointed by Peter the Great, was an Italian who saw to it that Russian heraldic practice followed that of contemporary European nations. Not that heraldic symbolism was unknown in Russia before Peter's reign: Russian cities, such as Astrakhan with its crown and sabre, and Novgorod, with its throne and flanking bears, had used pictorial devices since the early 16th century. Some civic symbols were even older, and the most famous Russian royal devices, the double-headed eagle and the horseman slaying a dragon, had appeared on the seals of the Grand Prince of Moscow, Ivan III, in 1497.

▼ *A Russian herald at the coronation in 1896 of the last tsar of Russia, Nicholas II.*

▲ *The small state seal of Tsar Ivan IV. One side bears the imperial double-headed eagle, the other a unicorn.*

EARLY HERALDRY IN RUSSIA

During his reign, Ivan IV ("the Terrible", 1547–84) required that a register of nobility was to be maintained, known – because of its cover – as the Velvet Book. At this time the Russian nobility had no titles of rank except for that of *kniaz* (prince), which was used in the main for those descended from the reigning house of Rurik. The maintenance of the Velvet Book, together with the other formal heraldic registers, was later overseen by the Heraldry Office, which was established in 1722 by Peter the Great under the control of a Master of Heraldry.

Despite Peter the Great's enthusiasm for European heraldry, Russian arms did not ape western styles and customs to the point of exactness. Indeed, Russian heraldry, like its other art forms, is a distinctive mixture of western European style and the exotic. This blend can often be observed in the official armorials of the Russian Empire, the *Obshii Gerbovnik Dvorianskikh Rodov Vserossiiskoi Imperii* (*Obschii Gerbovnik* for short) published in ten volumes between 1797 and 1840.

Peter the Great introduced the ranks of baron and count, and in 1722 decreed that all officers of the army and navy, and functionaries of the civil service above a certain rank (major in the army), were automatically entitled to enter the ranks of the aristocracy (untitled), and were thereby of armigerous status. Russian barons and counts were entitled to coronets of their degree, in European style, while princes of Russia were entitled to bear a princely crown as well as their robe of estate. The greater part of the Russian untitled nobility were entitled to bear a crest coronet from which issued three ostrich feathers.

CHARGES AND AUGMENTATIONS

The shields of the Russian nobility are often divided into several fields, each bearing one or more charges that reflect the family history. These often refer to acts of valour and may be accompanied by a citation appearing in place of a motto, such as that of the Counts Plavtov: *For fidelity, courage and indefatigable labours.* Tartar, Cossack and Polish emblems often appear in Russian heraldry, suggesting the diverse mix of nations that made up the empire.

Many Russian arms bear some direct reference to the monarch in whose reign the family was ennobled. Often the imperial eagle appears, charged on its breast with a particular emperor's cypher, and sometimes with part of one of the orders of chivalry. A distinctive heraldic honour

▼ *A variant of the arms of a Leibgardets family, with the augmentation of honour appearing in the chief.*

▲ The arms of Count Alexander Suvurov-Rymninsky (1730–1800) before his advancement to the rank of Prince; already heavily augmented, the later arms even included a map of Italy.

was created in 1741 for soldiers who had led the *coup d'etat* that placed Elizabeth Petrovna on the Russian throne. They were created *leibgardets* ("life guards") to the empress, automatically raised to the rank of nobility and given an augmentation to their arms in the form of a new coat, Sable on a chevron Or between three mullets Argent as many fire bombs or grenades Proper. The augmentation was usually borne per pale with the family arms – the augmentation on the dexter side, the family coat on the sinister. Each life guard (and his descendants) was also entitled to bear a crest of a grenadier's cap with wings and

▼ The arms, probably from a coach door, of Prince Michael Golenishchev-Kutuzov, Russian commander-in-chief in the country's campaign against Napoleon, 1812.

ostrich feathers, and the motto (in Russian), *For loyalty and zeal.*

An extraordinary example of heraldic distinction for bravery must be the shield of arms borne by one Dmitry Chuvash Narbekov who, during fighting against Kazan in the 16th century, was badly injured by a spear in the back. He was then hit in an eye by an arrow, and as if this were not unfortunate enough, as he tried to extract the arrow he had his arm blown away by a cannon ball. Amazingly,

▶ The arms of the Grand Duchy of Finland while it was under Russian rule. The Finnish lion replaces the usual warrior and dragon, and the shields on the eagle's wings are of Finnish provinces.

he survived. Among the honours he received from his grateful monarch was a grant of arms, showing in graphic detail his various acts of heroism.

IMPERIAL ARMS

By the late 19th century, the Russian heralds had formulated rules, on the orders of the emperors, regarding armorial achievements of members of the imperial family itself. Each royal personage was entitled to bear two variants of arms, greater and lesser, and their proximity to the throne was generally designated by their heraldic supporters. The immediate family – the tsar, the tsarina, the tsarevich (the heir apparent) and his eldest son – bore as

▼ The arms of Dmitry Chuvash Narbekov show in lurid detail the various wounds he received at Kazan.

▲ *A postcard of the early 20th century shows the arms of the principal cities of the Russian Empire.*

supporters the Archangels Michael and Gabriel. The younger sons of the tsar had two Varangian guards as their supporters; the grandchildren by younger sons bore two unicorns Or, and so on, down to the great-great-grandsons of the tsar, who bore two griffins Sable armed Or and langued Gules. Female descendants when unmarried were entitled to the same arms and supporters as their brothers, but on a lozenge instead of a shield. There were also marks of difference other than supporters: they mainly consisted of a lessening of the number of territorial shields that accompanied the imperial arms, and the helmets, coronets and crests that were part of the territorial achievements.

CIVIC ARMS

Between the late 18th and late 19th centuries, the authorities laid down a complex series of exterior ornaments to be borne in the arms of towns and provinces. For a lesser authority the coronet might take a simple mural form, while townships of some importance had a red mural coronet with just two crenellations. The cap of Monomakh (an ancient form of jewelled fur cap) was granted to former capitals of

the ancient Russian grand dukes. There were specific crowns for Kazan, Astrakhan, Poland, Finland and Georgia.

Most of these heraldic coronets date from an imperial decree of 1857, which also stipulated other ornaments to be placed on either side of the shield, such as crossed hammers for industrial cities, ears of wheat for cities in agricultural areas and vine leaves for those in wine-producing regions. Baron von Köehne, who invented the system, had intended that maritime municipalities should display crossed oars, but this was changed to anchors.

A special set of attributes was provided for "fortress cities", which were entitled not only to a special combination of coronet and imperial eagle, but also crossed flags. Those that had withstood a siege had the crossed flags charged with the cypher of the monarch in whose reign the siege had been conducted. Ribbons of the Russian orders of chivalry helped to complete these splendid achievements. By the same decree, civic shields were charged with a canton of the arms of the *guberniya*, or

province, in which the city lay. Prior to 1857, the arms of the latter had been charged in chief of a shield per fess, the arms in the base being of the city itself.

POST-REVOLUTIONARY ARMS

After the revolution of 1917, heraldry was still required. A commission was set up by the temporary government to look into the matter of the national arms. It suggested that although crowns, sceptres and other symbols of monarchy should be abolished, the double-headed eagle could stay, although it vied for a time with the swastika (another popular symbol signifying eternity and prosperity). The crown was replaced by a soldier's cap.

The eagle was for a short time accompanied by soldiers and peasants, although

▼ *The arms of the town of Mohyliv-Podilsky, Ukraine as borne in the late 19th century. The grapes signify its position in a wine-producing region; the moon and cross on the canton show that the town was in the guberniya (or province) of Podillya.*

▲ *The star of communism replaced the old tsarist emblems after the fall of Emperor Nicholas II in 1918.*

by spring 1918 it was felt that the imperial bird was too symbolic of pre-revolutionary Russia, and an entirely new coat of arms was needed. The hammer and sickle were selected for use on the state seal of the Russian Federation, symbolizing the alliance between the industrial workers and the peasantry. The new arms kept the old heraldic colours of red and gold, but placed the hammer and sickle in front of the rising sun of socialism.

The first regional arms, those of the Moscow regional government (*guberniya*), were approved by the praesidium of the Moscow Soviet in September 1924. They included a five-pointed star, the Statue of Freedom erected in 1918, and the hammer and sickle. On either side were blades of cereals and at the base were the attributes of labour, including anvils, shuttles and an electric motor. The Moscow arms never had a full official description and although they were supposed to set an example to be followed by other Soviet *guberny*, the idea never really took off.

The various republics of the Soviet Union took the state arms of the USSR as their model. In these a shield was not employed; a garland of wheat instead surrounded a rising sun above which was a globe charged with the hammer and sickle. The wheat blades were bound together by a red ribbon bearing the legend *Workers of*

▶ *The star of communism in the arms proposed for Volgograd when it was declared a "hero city" in honour of its citizens' bravery during World War II.*

the world unite in the various languages of the individual republics. Above the entire design shone the red star of communism. While the arms of most of the republics were devoid of any national character, some managed to achieve a localized flavour. Kirghizia had the rising sun over a local landscape, and Azerbaijan placed an oil-well against a backdrop of the rising sun. Each was dominated by the red star.

Curiously, the pre-revolutionary civic arms granted by the tsars were not abolished by the Bolsheviks; they had meant to do so but the order was never signed. In the 1960s, when many new towns and cities were created in the Soviet Union, interest in civic arms was aroused, and this was harnessed by the authorities to encourage civic pride. Soviet deputies would instigate competitions to find new designs. The arms had to include a symbol unique to the place, encapsulating a "small motherland" that exuded its own patriotic zeal. Several hundred new civic arms were designed between the 1960s and the 1980s. The designs could be quite striking, such as that of Novokusnetsk, which had a block of coal heating the furnace of a steel works.

This arousal of interest in heraldry was not welcomed throughout the Soviet Union. In the occupied Baltic States it was seen by local communist officials as a catalyst for nationalistic fervour, and was firmly curtailed.

HERALDRY AFTER COMMUNISM

Since the collapse of the communist regime and the demise of the Soviet Union at the end of 1991, many symbols that are

▲ *The new state arms of Russia were established by a presidential decree in 1993. The traditional symbols of eagle, rider and dragon have been re-established after nearly a century.*

reminiscent of tsarist times have re-emerged, particularly the double-headed eagle, regally crowned. The crown of Peter the Great appears between the eagle's heads, and it is charged on its breast with the horseman slaying a dragon. The eagle is gold (as opposed to the imperial kind, which was black) and the horseman points to the sinister, as opposed to the dexter in the later imperial arms. The figure is simply described as a rider, and before the heraldic reform of Peter I it was thought of not so much as St George but more as an allegorical representative of the sovereign overcoming his enemies.

In today's Russia, the President as head of state executes his heraldic duties through the State Heraldic Office. The office keeps a register of all state and civic arms, flags and official insignia. It does not, however, grant arms, and at the time of writing, no legal body in Russia is entitled to do so, either for personal or civic use, although various societies and heraldic colleges exist that will advise on new heraldic designs for their members. These organizations often ally themselves to one or other member of the former imperial family, which is supposed to give them some form of quasi-official status, although the State Heraldic Office does not recognize the connection.

COMMUNIST HERALDRY

Though a leveller of class, communism still saw the need for heraldry, and understood its potential power. Therefore coats of arms could be tolerated as long as their content bore no symbols that went against the cause. For the most part this meant a ban on religious or nationalistic (other than state) motifs.

▲ *In early post-tsarist Russia the old symbols of the eagle and rider remained in favour, but were soon to be swept away.*

▼ *Workers and peasants unite around the hammer and sickle of the new Soviet Union.*

In this, as in other aspects of communism, Russia led the way. The hammer and sickle, the symbols favoured by the workers' collectives in March and April of 1918, paved the way for the designs of the arms of the Russian Federation and the various Soviet Republics.

NATIONAL TRADITIONS

At the end of World War II, nations with heraldic traditions that were centuries old came under Soviet control and influence. Most symbols associated with the old order were soon banned by the increasingly hard-line regimes installed by the Soviets in Poland, Hungary, Bulgaria and Czechoslovakia, and the red star of socialism loomed large in the rhetoric of the new order. However, certain symbols were of such an emotive nature to the individual nations that even the party apparatchiks were loathe to tamper with them, although in the German Democratic Republic, the Soviet leaders' most loyal and dependent satellite, the leadership followed Soviet symbolism to the letter.

The new national arms of the GDR were an almost exact replica of the Soviet arms, except that the sickle was replaced by a pair of compasses and the ribbon that bound the ears of corn was in the German national colours of red, gold and black. These were derived from the ancient arms of the German nation: the black eagle with its red claws and beak on a gold field.

Other nations, which did not have so much reason to forget their recent past, found that their own communist bosses approved of the most curious of heraldic alliances between the past and the post-war period, even if that past was bound up with royalty. Therefore, the twin-tailed lion of the Bohemian kings continued to appear beneath the red star, as also did that most enduring of national emblems, the white eagle of the Piast dynasty that ruled medieval Poland; in the latter case the red star that replaced the royal crown was so insignificant that it looked like a crest on the noble bird's head.

▲ *The arms of the Republic of Azerbaijan in the Soviet era show the red star of socialism set high above a Soviet dawn.*

PERSONAL ARMS

The traditional users of arms – the nobility – were now taboo, and most of those who had not fled or died languished in dingy prisons or windswept gulags. Others who had dared to follow the noble science of heraldry were viewed with suspicion by the Soviet authorities. While heraldists are today usually perceived by non-heraldists as harmless cranks hankering after a romantic and improbable past, to the hard-line Marxist-Leninists of the late 1940s and 50s, anyone who professed an interest in the plaything of the nobility was probably a supporter of the old order, who wished to see the return of feudal repression. Those who enthused about heraldry were harassed by the secret police and even thrown into prison for involvement in activities "contrary to the interests of the proletariat". Personal arms were very much a thing of the past.

CIVIC ARMS

With civic heraldry the position was not nearly so clear cut. Civic pride was allowed to exist and often nurtured, since it helped citizens to focus their thoughts firmly on the immediate locality rather than further afield. The ancient arms of Prague and Pelhrimov were retained, for example, with the addition of the republic's arms on

▲ *The arms of Baja in Hungary, designed in the 1970s, conform to the style set by the community heraldry of the Soviet era.*

▲ *The arms of the cities of Marijampole (left) and Joniskis (right) in Lithuania; both shields were banned in the 1970s by the Soviet authorities because of their religious content, and replaced with new designs.*

shield or crest. Despite the treatment that was meted out to the aristocrats themselves, the arms of many ancient lords, complete with their coronets of rank, were permitted to remain on the civic shields of their old domains.

In the German Democratic Republic, civic arms were not entirely banned, but they were not permitted to be used for official purposes. Instead, the local council was to use the state arms enclosed by an inscription stating the name of the town, city, or district.

In the Soviet Union, saints and other overtly religious symbols in civic heraldry were replaced by figures representing heroism or patriotic workers. Even the heavenly eye of providence was replaced by a golden sun. If a coat of arms was so religious as to be totally offensive to the

leadership, it had to be replaced altogether. The ancient shield of the Lithuanian city of Joniskis, which bore St Michael killing a dragon, was replaced during Soviet rule by a red shield bearing a straightened scythe, the weapon of the local peasantry, between 28 pointed golden suns.

Elsewhere in Lithuania, the city of Marijampole, which bore in its ancient arms the figure of St George and the dragon, acquired not only new arms, but a new name (Kapsunkas). The new design included a canton of revolutionary red and the flame of learning.

Even these new approved designs were banned by the Lithuanian communists after a song festival in 1970, when the participants made too much show of their city arms. From then on until the fall of the Soviet regime, in Lithuania at least, city arms, and of course the old state arms, were banned.

NEW SYSTEMS OF HERALDRY

Of all the nations that had fallen under the spell of socialism, Romania was the only one that actually developed any formal system for its civic and regional arms. The arms designed by the state committee on

▼ *During the Soviet era, new arms were devised for Krasnoznamensk in the Moscow region. The USSR's supremacy in the space race made a most suitable subject for a modern Soviet town.*

▲ *The arms of the municipality of Hunedoara, Romania, are typical of the pattern of Romanian civic arms during the years of the Ceausescu regime.*

heraldry cannot be considered beautiful. Traditional heraldic symbols long associated with the ancient rulers of Wallachia (an eagle) and Moldavia (an auroch's head), found themselves sharing a shield with images of the modern industrial world, such as petro-chemical plants, blast furnaces and weavers' shuttles. Each new shield was also charged with an escutcheon bearing the symbols and colours of the Romanian state.

In 1974, Romania's neighbour, Hungary, also attempted to impose a heraldic scheme in keeping with the new way forward, replacing the ancient arms of 83 towns and cities with those with a new socialist flavour. Whereas in communist Romania, some vestige of the heraldry of the old order had often been retained, the Hungarian regime required a clean sweep on the model of the Soviet Union, with simple, stylized figures of people reaching out towards the rising sun of a socialist dawn. Parents and toddlers replaced the symbols of the nobility, with the red star triumphant over all.

It was not heraldry as we know it, but it was heraldry, sometimes innovative though usually bland. When communism collapsed, so did most of the "heraldry" that had paid it lip service for the past 50 or more years, unloved and unlamented.

POLAND

More than any other nation, Poland has maintained a heraldic "apartness", which stems mainly from the nature of its lesser nobility, or *szlachta*. This social group may be thought of broadly in the same way as the English gentry.

Those who fell into the group were members of an affiliation of noble families, known as a *ród*. Before the arrival of heraldry, each *ród* had its own standard in the form of a staff bearing a unique emblem. The devices were simple figures that cannot be described in heraldic terms: most consisted of sets of lines, curves, X- and V-shapes, which have led to the popular belief that they were adapted from Viking runes. The Vikings were just one of many peoples with whom the Poles came into contact, for the Polish area of influence was a thoroughfare for traders on their way eastwards into what is now Russia.

From the east came more warlike peoples, the Tartars and later the Turks. These roving bands had their own totemic standards – staves bearing streamers, horsetails and horns. Something similar can be seen

▼ *Herb Woroniecki, showing Christian symbols defeating the Turkish crescent. These charges would have originated as simple lines and curves that were later adapted to heraldry.*

▲ *This pedigree shows tribal arms typical of Polish heraldry. Such a document was required as proof of nobility for Poles wishing to become officers in the imperial Austrian army in the late 19th century.*

today in the Turkish crescent or "jingling Johnny", a musical instrument used by German military bands, which resembles a standard hung with silver bells and horsetails. Perhaps the eastern standards and the Viking runes were married together by the Poles to make their own distinct tribal insignia.

ADAPTATIONS TO HERALDRY

In the second half of the 10th century, Poland's first ruler, Mieszko, brought Christianity to his people, and many tribal standards had their extremities made into crosses. When heraldry eventually reached Poland, other changes were made to the symbols to produce acceptable heraldic charges, such as arrowheads and crescents. The original emblem had usually been cut out of metal, so in Polish heraldry it is very rare to find a charge that is not gold or silver. The fields of shields are almost always red or blue; green and purple are virtually unknown, and heraldic furs are not used.

Each *ród* had its own rallying cry, such as *Dolega*, *Dabrowa*, or *Pilawa*, and the tribal device came to be identified by it. In effect the war cry and the device were the same entity. When, by the late 13th century, Polish *ród* started to place their old totemic emblems on shields, the practice of identifying the arms by the relevant war

cry persisted, and for this reason there has never been a need for a system of heraldic blazon in Polish heraldry.

A single coat of arms, or *herb*, was used by all members of the *ród*, no matter their position, for in effect all members were equal. However, arms were sometimes adapted through marriage. In the case of Herb Slepowron ("blind crow"), the original arms were varied after an important marriage to a lady of the Pobog clan, by placing the black crow of Herb Slepowron on the Herb Pobog, which bore a horseshoe topped by a cross.

It is rare to find more than one charge on the shield of a Polish *ród*. Ordinaries are rare, as are quarters and supporters. Some shields were credited with legendary origins: for example, that of Ogonczyk, an arrowhead issuing from a semicircle, is said to relate to an occasion when a maiden was being abducted by Tartars, and members of the tribe pursued the Tartars at the speed of an arrow. Crests are usually ostrich plumes or peacock's feathers issuing from a crest coronet. There is no set pattern for the helmet, although the barred tourney helm is mostly used.

SOCIAL ORGANIZATION

Titles such as count or baron were forbidden to Poles. Only after the partition of Poland by its neighbours in the 18th and 19th centuries did Poles take foreign titles, although this was considered unpatriotic.

A *ród* could be any size, and could number hundreds of separate families. In theory they were all related but, as with Scottish clans, other families could sometimes be taken under their wing. If a king wished to favour a subject he might ask a *ród* to take him under its name and arms.

In later centuries when members of the *szlachta* settled in towns, villages, or on their own estates, they adopted surnames by placing Z in front of the place name, in the manner of the French *de* or the German *von*. In time the Z tended to be replaced by adding *ski* or *cki* to the end of the name, and the connection with the *ród* was kept alive by placing the tribal name before the surname, as in Sas-Tarnawski or Jastrzebiec-Marikowski.

ROYAL HERALDRY

Polish culture, art and learning were greatly admired and coveted by its larger neighbours, notably Prussia, Russia and Austria. All these powers saw the Polish state as an obstacle to their territorial ambitions, but Poland had ambitions of its own.

In 1386, Jadwiga, the daughter and heiress of the Polish–Hungarian monarch, Louis of Anjou, took as her husband Grand Duke Wladyslaw Jagiello of neigh-

▲ *At the Battle of Grunwald (Tannenberg), on 15 July 1410, a Polish–Lithuanian army decisively defeated the Teutonic knights, capturing many of the Order's standards, all of which were beautifully painted in 1448 for the Royal Archives in Kraków.*

bouring Lithuania, setting the scene for a period of great expansion. In 1413 the Union of Horodlo between Poland and Lithuania saw the adoption of many members of the Lithuanian nobility into the names and arms of the Polish tribes. The alliance was reflected heraldically in the arms of the Polish–Lithuanian sovereigns. The white eagle of the Poles had been borne on seals since the reign of Boleslaw V (1227–79), and is one of the most famous and enduring symbols in Europe. During the medieval period the eagle was often charged on its breast with a half moon device ending in stylized clover leaves or crosses, and from the late medieval period the eagle was crowned.

The arms of Lithuania were every bit as fascinating. They consisted of an armed

◄ *An illustration from the early 16th century shows the eagle of the Polish monarchs below the mounted horseman of the Grand Duchy of Lithuania; the top right shield bears the arms of the Lithuanian Gediminas dynasty.*

rider in pursuit of his enemy. Part of this device, the rider's armoured arm holding a sword, known to the Poles as the *pogonia*, was used as a kind of augmentation under the Polish–Lithuanian commonwealth, giving rise another *ród*; Pogon. The rider's shield was often charged with the double-armed cross of the Jagiello dynasty. Later, the dynastic arms of the Polish sovereigns were placed on an escutcheon on the quartered shield of Poland–Lithuania.

The last of the Jagiello line, Sigismund II Augustus, died in 1572. From then on, monarchs were elected by a general assembly of the nobility. Kings' powers were severely curtailed and they were closely watched by the nobility in this "royal republic". Elections were one of the great sights of Europe, with the *szlachta* making their way in groupings of *ród* to the Electoral Fields outside Warsaw. In 1573, no less than 50,000 nobles came to vote.

Many of the elected monarchs were chosen through the connivance of various factions allied to the interests of Poland's enemies and neighbours. In 1772 the first partition of Poland between its neighbours was instituted, and the kingdom of Poland–Lithuania disappeared. Both nations regained their independence following World War I.

▼ *The arms of Wroclaw (Breslau), bearing the lion of Bohemia, the eagle of Silesia and the city's patron saint, John the Baptist.*

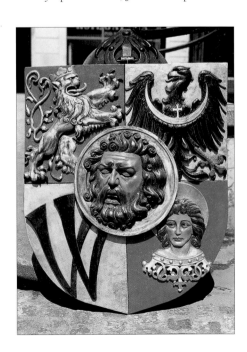

THE AMERICAS

The development of heraldry by British settlers in North America was slow, and was curtailed by the Revolution. However, the colonization of the central and western areas by the Spanish and French, in the 16th and 17th centuries, gave rise to a parallel, separate heraldic development (to say nothing of the Russian presence in the state of Alaska and the native monarchy in the state of Hawaii). The division of the continent between the major European powers fragmented the exercise of heraldic authority in what would become the United States. A comparison of the heraldic regulation exercised by the British in eastern North America, and by the Spanish in the western territories, suggests some of the differences in the colonizing methods of the two powers.

COLONIAL HERALDRY

Between Columbus's voyage in 1492 and the Declaration of American Independence in 1776, both England and Spain attempted to introduce and regulate heraldic activities in their respective

▲ *The arms of the descendants of the Aztec Emperor Montezuma II, attributed by the Spanish heralds, are a mixture of European heraldic charges and native symbols.*

spheres of authority. Among the symbols and regalia at the marriage of Philip of Habsburg and Joanna of Spain, celebrated in 1496, was a banner bearing arms for the West Indies, or the Kingdom of the Fifteen Islands. The first English grant of arms in the New World was made in 1586 to the city, governor and assistant governors of Ralegh in Virginia, while Newfoundland would receive a grant of arms about 50 years later.

These early grants made use of native scenes, wildlife and peoples, the last of which seems to have played most strongly on the heraldic imagination. Writing in 1682, Bluemantle Persuivant John Gibbon remarked on the quasi-heraldic body paint worn by Virginian natives during war-dances: "The Dancers were painted some Party per pale Gu[les] and Sab[le] from forehead to foot…at which I exceedingly wondered, and concluded that Heraldry was ingrafted naturally into the sense of the humane Race."

Meanwhile, the Spanish colonizers granted titles and arms to the native aristocracy and royalty they had conquered,

▲ *The first, rejected, design for the arms of the new United States included a rose for England, a thistle for Scotland, a harp for Ireland, a fleur de lis for France, a lion for Holland and an eagle for Germany.*

as a way of excusing them from the *encomienda* system of forced labour imposed by the Spanish rulers during the 16th century. Native American leaders could avoid this if they could successfully claim the privileges of the Spanish nobility. One remarkable instance is the case of the descendants of the Aztec emperor Montezuma II, who ruled central Mexico from 1480 to 1520. Philip II of Spain granted the title of count to Don Pedro Tesifon Moctezuma de la Cueva in 1627, and Isabel II granted the titles of marquess and duke to other descendants in 1864 and 1865. The family bore arms blazoned Vert within an orle of five roses Argent a falcon and tiger Or in pale a bordure Gules charged with thirty coronets Or, or alternately, Azure an imperial crown Or and a falcon and tiger Argent all in pale a bordure Vert charged with thirty coronets Or.

In 1984, a claimant to the Aztec throne, Don Guillermo de Grau-Moctezuma, appointed a personal herald, the Cronista Rey de Armas de la Casa Imperial Azteca.

English and Spanish heralds attempted to establish heraldic regulation in North America during the 17th and 18th centuries. In 1705, Laurence Cromp, York Herald, also became Carolina Herald, although the office expired on his death ten years later, without any grants of arms having been made. Spanish heraldic jurisdiction in the New World was more effective: in 1649, the visiting Spanish heralds censured the Archbishop of Mexico for the inaccurate display of the Spanish royal arms in the Cathedral of Los Angeles.

AFTER INDEPENDENCE

The early leaders of the independent United States and Mexico were not opposed to the principle of bearing arms. Mexico freed itself from Spanish control not as a republic but as a short-lived empire, under the rule of the armigerous cavalry officer-cum-monarch Agustín de Itúrbide. Heraldry was also esteemed by George Washington, who wrote: "It is far from my design to intimate an opinion, that Heraldry, Coat-Armor, etc. might not be rendered conducive to public and private use with us; or that they can have any tendency unfriendly to the purest spirit of Republicanism. On the contrary, a differ-

▼ *In a splendid return to medieval heraldic design, the flag of Maryland uses the arms of its founder, George, 1st Lord Baltimore.*

▲ *The great seal of the US presidents, the main design of which dates from 1782.*

ent conclusion is deducible from the practice of Congress, and the states; all of which have established some kind of Armorial Devices, to authenticate their official instruments."

Congress set Benjamin Franklin, John Adams and Thomas Jefferson to the task of designing the arms of the new republic on 4 July 1776. In the first sketch, the shield was blazoned Quarterly of six: 1 Or a double rose Gules and Argent (for England), 2 Argent a thistle proper (for Scotland), 3 Vert a harp Or (for Ireland), 4 Azure a fleur de lis Or (for France), 5 Or an imperial eagle Sable (for the German Empire) and 6 Or a lion rampant Gules (for Holland). Fortunately, perhaps, this cluttered design did not meet with approval, and the famous arms Argent six pallets Gules a chief Azure were designed in part by Charles Thompson, Secretary of Congress, in 1782.

THE REGULATION OF ARMS

Civic heraldry prospered in the independent republic, and today such symbols are protected from misuse by legislation, but personal heraldry in the USA remains unregulated. Interest is high, however, as witnessed by the success of "bucket-shop" heraldry, and both private agencies and official bodies have sought to address the current state of affairs.

In 1928 the New England Heraldry and Historic Genealogical Society of Boston's heraldic committee began to publish the inherited and adopted arms of Americans, and in 1972 the American College of Heraldry was founded. This body has been very effective in drafting and publishing arms of adoption, with a dedication to the principles of heraldic design, while the setting up of the College of Arms Foundation in the 1980s has set a good precedent.

On an official level, several European heraldic agencies have in the 20th century begun to grant and register American arms. The Office of the Chief Herald in Dublin and the Court of Lord Lyon in Edinburgh both grant arms to eminent Americans of, respectively, Irish and Scottish descent. The College of Arms in London has granted honorary armorial bearings to eminent Americans of English descent since the early 20th century, though the practice began without a general warrant from the Earl Marshal, and these documents go unrecognized by the Irish and Scottish authorities. The English College also issues devisals of arms to American corporations with the approval of their respective state governors. The Spanish Corps of Chronicler Kings of Arms issues armorial certificates recognizing the arms of citizens of American republics once claimed by the Spanish crown, including most of the USA (such certificates protect these arms under Spanish law).

These different organizations and avenues are made use of by many Americans, testifying to their heraldic interest. While there are many drawbacks to the USA's lack of a native central heraldic authority, the present unregulated situation at least allows America's plurality of heraldic traditions to develop organically.

SCANDINAVIA

The migration of heraldry from its historic centre in northern France and Flanders was rapid, and by the 13th century arms were being used by the nobility of Denmark, Sweden and Norway. Just as the nobles of Spain, Italy and England felt themselves to belong to a social group sharing a common goal that knew no borders, towns and cities throughout Scandinavia showed a common pride, taking up seals whose central motifs, such as town walls, castles and saints, could be found all over Europe.

The noble families of Finland were mainly of Swedish origin. Few were of local Finnish stock, and the indigenous families usually changed their names as they moved from estate to estate, so that sons might have different surnames from their fathers. Just one Finnish family, the Princes Menshikov, attained princely rank, a reminder of the period from 1809–1917 when the Grand Duchy of Finland was part of the Russian Empire.

The Menshikovs also reflect the polyglot nature of Scandinavian nobility in general, which assimilated into its ranks Scots, English, French and German families. Not surprisingly, the nobility of

▼ *The arms of Baron Örnsköld have the two helmets and crests accorded to a Swedish baron. The quarterings are divided by a cross throughout, in a style characteristic of Swedish heraldry.*

Scandinavia adapted the heraldic style of northern Germany, including the use of peacock feathers in crests, and arms that became increasingly augmented with quarterings as families rose to higher rank. But gradually Scandinavian heraldry took on its own flavours, and some of its charges have few equivalents elsewhere in Europe. In Denmark and Sweden, for instance, a cross throughout may divide various quarterings, and this is a practice seldom met with elsewhere, except in Scotland.

HERALDIC FUNERALS

A practice dating from the late 16th century, peculiar to Sweden, Finland and much of the Baltic coast, was the carrying of heraldic shields on poles in the funeral procession. A large achievement of the defunct's own arms, known in Sweden as the *hufvudbaner*, was carried at the head of the coffin, with smaller shields (*anvapen*) belonging to the paternal and maternal ancestors on either side.

The *anvapen* were borne separately at first, sometimes by as many as 16 bearers, but in about 1660 Queen Hedvig Eleonora decreed that such a show of pomp should be confined to the royal family. From then on just two *anvapen* were carried, but these were, if anything, more splendid: each developed into the form of a heraldic family tree, with its branches adorned with many separate shields. Both the *hufvudbaner* and the *anvapen* were carved from wood, bright with gold and silver leaf and fully coloured.

ARMORIAL COLLECTIONS

Both Sweden and Finland maintain Houses of the Nobility, in Stockholm and Helsinki respectively. Although now much reduced

▲ *A plaque for President Eisenhower of the United States, made a Danish knight of the Order of the Elephant.*

in power, they still enjoy a certain kudos and maintain splendid collections of family arms. In both cases, the arms of the nobility are grouped together through rank and chronology. Because the Finnish House of Nobility was established while Finland was under Swedish rule, it followed the Swedish system.

The Swedish Riddarhuset (the "house of nobility") contains a total of 2,320 armorial plaques, which are numbered in order of seniority. Among them is the achievement of the Counts of Wasalborg (No 5) with the curious punning charge of two crowned fish. The family was descended from Gustav Gustafsson, illegitimate son of Gustavus Adolphus, and a merchant's daughter from Gothenburg called Margareta Kabiljau (*kabelju* means

▲ *The armorial plaque of the noble family of Stöltenhielm in the Riddarhuset in Stockholm. The progenitor's wooden leg appears as one of the charges.*

"dried cod" in Swedish). The achievement includes the arms of the house of Vasa, with a bendlet sinister to show illegitimacy.

Many families have punning arms, including a troll in the arms of Trolle, and a wooden leg, or stilt, in the Stöltenhielm arms. Coats of arms of the Swedish aristocracy sometimes feature a scarlet hat, which was worn by members of the monarch's council of state. They may also include the arms of a province, if a member or members of the family had been the monarch's representative there.

ORDERS OF CHIVALRY

Many noble families of foreign extraction originated with high-ranking military officers who staffed the armies of northern Europe during the expansionist wars of the 17th and 18th centuries. They also swelled the ranks of the ancient orders of chivalry in both Denmark and Sweden.

The chapel in the Castle of Frederiksborg at Hillerød, to the north of Copenhagen, contains the armorial plaques for knights of two Danish orders: the Order of the Elephant (believed to have been founded in 1464) and the Order of the Dannebrog. The Order of the Elephant

is the senior order, and its foreign knights include Sir Winston Churchill and President Eisenhower. Its badge is a white enamelled elephant charged with a cross of five plate diamonds, guided by a mahout and bearing a golden tower. The collar of the order is charged with elephants and towers. Churchill was once seen wearing the insignia of the Elephant and when asked if it happened to be an "Order Day", he replied in the negative. He was in fact in mourning for an elephant that had just died at London Zoo.

Before 1975, Sweden maintained four orders of chivalry. The Order of the Seraphim, founded in 1748 by Fredrik I, was the highest. Each order had its own room in the royal palace in Stockholm, the wall decorations of which were taken from the collars of the orders. Today only two survive, the Order of the Seraphim and the Order of the Polar Star, but neither can be conferred on Swedish citizens other than the royal family. The Order of the Seraphim is most often conferred on foreign heads of state. Notable among non-royal knights is Nelson Mandela, whose shield bears the South African flag.

The insignia include golden seraphs, the monogram of Christ – IHS – and three nails from the Cross. Ladies of the Order and prelates have their arms within a pale

▲ *The* hufvudbaner *and* anvapen *(arms of alliance) for Diedrich Kagg (d1671) in Linköping Cathedral, Sweden.*

blue ribbon, from which the badge is suspended. Female sovereigns, like male knights, have the collar. The arms of all female members are placed on an oval. Since 1748 the Seraphim has been conferred on nearly 800 men and women, and of those over 600 have their achievements

▼ *For the memorial service of a newly deceased knight of the Order of the Seraphim, the heraldic plaque is displayed on an easel before the altar of the Riddarholmskyrka in Stockholm.*

on plaques hung, three-deep, on the walls of the Riddarholmskyrka ("Church on the Knights' Island") in Stockholm.

PERSONAL ARMS

In general the Scandinavian heraldic authorities are concerned with national, royal and military matters, rather than personal arms. Personal heraldry is usually treated like a trade mark and can be registered as such for protection, although state authorities will give advice on corporate and personal arms, especially in regard to correct blazon. Guidance can also be gained from heraldic societies and foundations. Some of the foremost heraldic experts in northern Europe collaborate under the aegis of the Societas Heraldica Scandinavica in bringing out the twice-yearly magazine *Heraldisk Tidskrift.*

Those living in Scandinavia can register their arms through the *Skandinavisk Vapenrulla,* the Scandinavian roll of arms. It has its own heraldic artists and consultants to ensure that every coat of arms is correctly treated.

CLARITY AND SIMPLICITY

While each of the Scandinavian nations enjoys its own heraldic customs and styles, during the 20th century there was a noted interaction between heraldic designers and authorities within the northern states, which provided some of the liveliest discourse and debate in the heraldic world. The most distinctive styles emanated from a handful of heraldic craftsmen and designers, notably Hallvard

Trætteberg in Norway and Gustav von Numers, Ahti Hammar and Olof Eriksson, all from Finland. Trætteberg's ideas had a profound effect not only on the civic and municipal heraldry of his own country, but also on that in neighbouring Sweden.

Norway has no state herald (the duties being undertaken by the National Archives), but Trætteberg, who worked in the Archives, may be regarded as the nearest thing to it. Between 1920 and his death in 1987, he was very much the influence behind Norwegian heraldry. His controversial stand on the matters of tincture and charges still strongly influences Norwegian military and civic heraldry.

Trætteberg advocated a number of heraldic rules, the most notable being that no more than two tinctures, one colour and one metal, should be used on a shield. He also liked the idea of one charge being used, in a singular or multiple fashion, and suggested that no shading or shadow should be applied to the charge. His theories have made modern Norwegian heraldic style the starkest and most uncompromising in use today. Those used to British arms may regard his shields as too plain, yet a Scandinavian heraldist might characterize English civic heraldry as cluttered and lacking in style.

CIVIC HERALDRY

In Finland, meanwhile, von Numers, Hammar and Eriksson were revolutionizing their nation's civic and municipal arms with a series of shields unparalleled in their symbolism and simple beauty. Taking into

▲ *Possibly the most influential of modern styles is that of Finnish municipal heraldry, with its unusual divisions of the field and combinations of charges, seen here in the arms of Liminka commune.*

account the local dialect, geographical curiosities and folklore of each place for which they devised arms, these three visionaries produced new heraldic designs that were often daring in their simplicity. Their ideas gave food for thought to the then new heraldic authorities of South Africa and Canada.

Among their innovations, ordinaries were offset in unusual fashion, sometimes combined with other charges, at other times standing alone. Among the former, the shield of the municipality of Kuivaniemi, with its single wavy flanche and seal embowed, suggests Kuivaniemi's position on the coast of the Gulf of Bothnia. Other fascinating designs include those of the municipality of Pielavesi, which features the local musical instrument – a horn made of birch bark.

Native flora and fauna are often depicted in the most unconventional forms, as in the arms of Simo in Lapland, which is one of the oldest parishes in the

 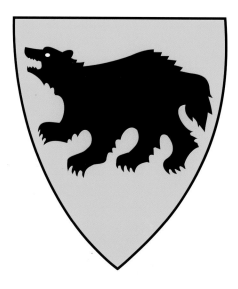

◄ *Two civic arms exemplify the simplicity of modern Norwegian heraldry: the shield of Målselv (left) includes the district's river; for Bardu (right) a wolverine represents the area's forests.*

province, and is also famed for its salmon fishing: its twin distinctions are neatly married in a cross composed of fish tails.

Lines of partition were drawn anew by Trætteberg and the Finnish designers, with the fir trees that cover so much of the country as a favourite motif. In much modern Scandinavian heraldry, the charges, trees especially, are stylized in a simple form. This can make for a refreshing clarity, as in the arms of the Swedish border town of Haparanda: these include in their design a border post between two trees, surmounted by the midnight sun, which is enjoyed by the community for several months each year.

Inevitably, the point was eventually reached when nearly all communities, of whatever size, had had arms designed for them, and the steam went out of the innovative phase of Finnish civic heraldry. Now even this heraldic nation has started to embrace the logo. But in general Scandinavia enjoys its civic heraldry and uses it to the full. It is usual for communities to place their arms not only on buildings but also on local transport and on the boundary signs on the approaches to cities, towns and villages. In Finland, fans of civic heraldry can find plenty to spot, and are often rewarded with a two-in-one "prize", for the community arms may well be twinned with those of the local province. The latter date in the main from the 16th century, when Finland formed part of the kingdom of Sweden. Many of the provincial arms appeared on banners carried in the funeral procession of King Gustav I in 1560.

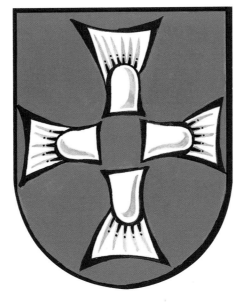

▲ *Four salmon tails in the arms of Simo in Lapland form a cross for the see of Uppsala.*

▲ *The arms of Pielavesi commune, Finland, with its birch bark horns.*

▲ *A wonderful example of a heraldic hybrid species representing forests and lakes, in the arms of the city of Zarasai in Lithuania, created in 1969.*

▲ *The arms of the Finnish municipality of Inari include an extraordinary marriage of two species raised on local farms.*

▲ *The approach to many Scandinavian towns and villages is clearly marked with heraldry, as in Haparanda in Sweden.*

▶ *The sublimely simple punning arms of the Finnish community of Sumiainen – sumu means "foggy" in Finnish.*

AFRICA

While it belongs first and foremost to the nobility of western Europe, heraldry has such an attractive character that it was bound to be taken by Europeans to the lands they invaded, subdued and settled, not the least of which were the colonial territories of Africa.

SOUTH AFRICA

Heraldry was first taken to South Africa in 1488, with the Portuguese adventurer, Bartholomew Diaz, who had stone crosses erected bearing the arms of Portugal. Although the Portuguese did not actually colonize South Africa, what was probably the first grant of arms to an indigenous armiger in this area, the Emperor Monomatapa, was made by the King of Portugal in 1569. The blazon was Gules, between two arrows Argent an African hoe barwise bladed Argent handled Or, the shield surmounted by an Eastern crown.

The Dutch ruled the land that now forms the Republic of South Africa between 1652 and 1806. They were followed by the British, who brought with them their own heraldic tradition. For much of the period of British rule, South African arms were typical of the lacklustre heraldry the British heralds of the time

▲ *The arms granted to South Africa's Emperor Monomatapa by the Portuguese king in 1569.*

were foisting on the colonies, in the fussy overladen style of the late Georgian and Victorian eras.

In 1961 the Republic of South Africa broke its ties with the British Commonwealth, incidentally cutting itself off from the authority of the British heralds. Some two years later the South African Bureau of Heraldry was established in Pretoria. The Bureau has at its head a State Herald to whom any person or corporate body may apply for grant and registration of armorial bearings. When granted, these are officially published in the Government Gazette. (Many armigers in the United Kingdom have asked for their heraldic authorities to publish such a record.)

SCANDINAVIAN INFLUENCE

The new authority looked to the Scandinavians, notably the Finnish heraldic artists, Gustav von Numers and Ahti Hammar, for inspiration. In recent years it has come up with some of the simplest and most splendid designs in modern heraldry, taking its themes from the modern Scandinavian style. In 1974 the State Herald of the time, Mr Hartman, visited Finland to meet the Finnish heraldic experts and gain insight into their local styles and design techniques. Some five years later, Hartman's successor, Frederick Brownell, followed his example.

From their time spent with their Finnish colleagues, the South African heralds decided on a fresh approach to heraldic design. Simplicity was to be the first principle, followed by new lines of partition based on the local architecture, flora and fauna. Elements of innovative Finnish design were to be incorporated into the heraldry of South Africa, where these were considered appropriate.

The marriage of the two national styles produced some strikingly simple designs. New partition lines were based on the gable ends of the Dutch-style farmhouses in the Cape and the national flower, *Protea cynaroides*, the stylized petals of which

were used to create a striking new motif reminiscent of the fir twig partition line found in Finnish and Swedish arms.

The indigenous tribes of South Africa had long marked their oval shields with a system of colour and symbol, which was not so much heraldry as armory. Such symbols were part of a "regimental" identification system, rather than a personal or family one. The South African Bureau of Heraldry has made much use of traditional native shields in the designs of arms of black townships.

HERALDRY AFTER APARTHEID

The future status of the South African Bureau of Heraldry can only be guessed at, although it is of necessity not of the first importance to the post-apartheid government. State Herald Brownell has done much to ensure that heraldry can be enjoyed by people of all creeds and colours, for in his own words, heraldry is "colourful, but colour blind".

Frederick Brownell and his fellow heralds have sought to combine English, Afrikaans and Portuguese heraldic traditions with the symbols of the indigenous African tribes. However, despite his good intentions, heraldry is bound to be viewed

▲ *Three different designs by the South African State Bureau of Heraldry based on the national flower, the protea.*

▲ *The arms of Soweto, a mixture of traditional African symbols and classical medieval European heraldry.*

▲ *The arms of the Republic of Zimbabwe include in the crest the star of socialism and behind the shield an automatic rifle.*

▼ *In the arms of Harare, capital of Zimbabwe, heraldry finds its way on to a shield of traditional African shape.*

▲ *The new coat of arms of the Republic of South Africa, a modern application of heraldry fit for the second millennium.*

by the vast majority of the population as yet another toy of the old European oppressors, fit to die a natural and unlamented death.

For the new national arms for the Republic of South Africa, the Bureau of Heraldry was bypassed and a design commissioned from a non-heraldic artist. The achievement was adopted in April 2000. The motto is in the now extinct Khoisan language spoken by the oldest known inhabitants of the land, and it means *Diverse people unite*. The shield is enclosed within elephants' tusks, symbolizing wisdom and strength, and ears of wheat to represent fertility and growth. The human figures are shown in an attitude of unity.

ZIMBABWE

In the neighbouring republic of Zimbabwe, the state arms have a traditional British flavour to them, and use the heater-shaped shield of medieval European heraldry.

However, this traditional shape has been married to typical Marxist-style militancy, with symbols of the workers and peasants side by side. An AK47 assault rifle, the weapon that armed many revolutionary struggles of the late 20th century, takes its place against the red star of socialism. In the arms of the capital city, Harare, the great Zimbabwe bird is used as a traditional charge, but has been placed on an African-style shield.

HERALDIC SURVIVALS

While some ex-colonial territories, such as the former Portuguese provinces of Angola and Mozambique, have wished to throw off heraldry, seeing it as an uninvited import of their former white rulers, others have taken it to their hearts. The former French territory of Gabon, for example, has employed a French heraldic designer to create (with local assistance) arms for its regions, districts and communities. In these, typically European heraldic practices are twinned with the most striking of local African fauna, flora, customs and art, creating fine examples of good heraldry.

CANADA

The newest of all national heraldic authorities, that of Canada, came into being in 1988 after Queen Elizabeth II, acting in her capacity as Sovereign of Canada, authorized the Governor General to exercise in Canada one of her Royal prerogatives, the right to grant arms.

The Canadian Heraldic Authority, unlike its Scottish and English counterparts, does not have a king of arms as its chief officer. That office is exercised by the Chief Herald of Canada. However, there are heralds and pursuivants, as would be found in any of the more ancient state heraldic offices.

INDIGENOUS STYLE

The Authority grants arms to Canadian nationals and corporate institutions after receiving a formal petition, presented in the same way that any English or Scots person or corporation would do to their own heraldic authority. But the arms

▼ *A splendid stained glass window showing the insignia and badges of the Canadian Heraldic Authority and its officers of arms set against a background of the arms of the Canadian provinces. Made by Christopher Wallis in 1990.*

▲ *Some years ago the College of Arms in London granted a pilot's helmet in lieu of the traditional medieval warriors' helmet – a theme taken up and expanded by the Canadian Heraldic Authority. The crests of*

granted by the CHA, though they keep to the age-old tenets of European heraldic tradition, often have a very distinct flavour. Right from its beginning, as well as employing artists and historians belonging to the European tradition in Canada (notably French, English and Scots), the CHA has sought out those of the indigenous peoples. All the West Coast Indians and Inuit tribes have fascinating histories, symbols and folklore that can be drawn from and adapted to serve the heraldic achievement of arms.

Nowhere does this happy mixture of native and imported traditions become more manifest than in the achievement of arms of the Canadian Heraldic Authority itself. Its shield bears a maple leaf charged with an escutcheon, the like of which could be found on any Scots, English or Scandinavian shield of arms, conventional

these three arms are, clockwise from top left, an Indian Shaman's headdress for Mr Norquay, a Maccabean warrior's helmet for a synagogue, and a fur parka hood for Helen Maksagak, former commissioner of the Northwest Territories.

but efficient in its effect. The supporters, however, are wonderfully aboriginal in their execution and content. They are two fantastic creatures, half polar bear, half raven, dancing energetically and resembling figures that might be found at a West Coast Indian tribal gathering or on one of its totem poles.

This combination of "first nation" and European symbolism allows the Canadian heralds a wealth of charges open to no other heraldic organization, except the South African Bureau of Heraldry, which has a similar blend of colonial and indigenous symbols at its disposal. Two more creatures straight from a totem pole support a shield charged with traditional European heraldic charges – bezants and a pallet wavy – in the arms of the Honourable Judy Gingell, Commissioner of the Yukon Territory. Elsewhere, in the arms of the city of White Rock, an iceberg can be seen along with an aboriginal representation of a killer whale.

Jewish communities are unusually well represented in Canada. While individual Jewish people have long been commemorated in the heraldry of certain European nations (notably Italy), few Jewish communities are heraldically recognized.

ACCESSIBILITY AND EQUALITY

A combination of cultures is not limited to the pictorial display of arms. In the patents issued by the Canadian Heraldic Authority, the blazon and formal declaration of the grant are written in both French and English – a legal requirement for all official Canadian documents.

The requirement to make arms known to "all and singular", whatever the reader's origin, has been taken even further by the CHA. When granting arms to the new

▼ The patents of arms for Canadian institutions and individuals are usually worded in English and French, but native languages may also be included.

▲ Cadency marks for two children of James Robson: on the left a label for an eldest son, and on the right the ermine spots in the top corners that are the mark for a second daughter in the Canadian cadency system.

Territory of Nunavut, established on 1 April 1999, the text and motto were fully translated on the patent into the native language of the local Inuit people of that region, and the wording was first approved by local linguistic experts.

Although it may be only a babe in arms in comparison with the English College of Arms and Lord Lyon's Office in Scotland, the CHA is very much the new star of the heraldic world. It has already produced its own marks of difference for women, and

it does not discriminate between men and women in respect of helms and crests: Canadian grantees of either sex are entitled to them. Women may also use the heater-shaped shield or lozenge without any mark to differentiate their arms. As sexual equality is enshrined in Canadian law, it is considered illegal for the Heraldic Authority to treat women differently.

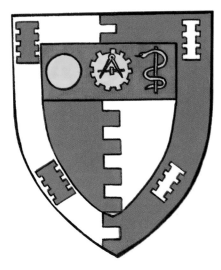

▲ The shield of arms for the British Columbia Institute of Technology is charged with computer symbols.

I·HOLD·BEFORE·YOU·AN·OPEN·DOOR

JAPAN: THE OTHER HERALDRY

Few nations and societies outside Europe have ever maintained any system of recognition comparable with heraldry in length of service and application. There is one extraordinary exception: the crests or badges used for many centuries by the Japanese courtiers and military elite. Such devices are called *mon*.

THE *MON*

To understand the precise meaning of the word *mon* it is necessary to decipher the two Japanese characters that make it up: they mean "thread" and "markings". In other words, the badges originated as embroidered costume decorations. Often, as with heraldry, they employ as symbols the simplest household objects, such as fans or kitchen implements.

Various heraldic writers have been intrigued by the similarity in usage between Japanese *mon* and European heraldry, for the former were used by Japanese warriors on their armour and battle flags, and on the clothing they wore for formal occasions. Even so, throughout the periods during which warfare raged in both

Japan and Europe, neither system can have had any influence on the other. In modern times, along with the importation into the West of so much that is Japanese, has come the triumph over heraldry of the western equivalent of the *mon* – the logo. Very often in recent years, corporations that previously sported full achievements of arms have shelved them in favour of a corporate emblem that in style would not have looked out of place on the battle banners of a 15th-century shogun.

As early as the 8th century, the emperors of Japan were using specific emblems associated with their dynasty. It followed that what the ruler did was aped by those who served him and formed his social circle: the courtiers and court officials. The early *mon* were often Chinese in flavour, with symbols such as the phoenix, cloud formations, peacocks and dragons reflecting the influence and respect felt by the Japanese court for the powerful T'ang dynasty and its court across the water.

MILITARY USE

Although in its early life the *mon* was primarily a feature kept firmly within the walls of the imperial court, its use was watched with envy by the other leading group in Japanese feudal society: the military, or warrior, class. As this group grew in strength it made inroads into the formal life of the court and adopted much courtly style as its own. Yet often the two classes viewed each other with mutual suspicion. The court saw the warrior caste as brutal and barbaric, while the warriors regarded the courtiers as effete and weak-willed.

Having started as a symbol that identified the courtier's possessions and costume, the *mon* became associated with the trappings of the military man. The three main platforms for its display were the standards or battle flags (*hata*), tall, narrow banners up to 3m (10ft) in length; cloth curtains (*tobari*) used in the military camp to partition the commander's formal enclosure; and the formal garment (*hitare*), made of silk brocade, which, although worn

▲ *The marriage of two distant and distinctive symbolic traditions: a recent grant of arms to a gentleman of Japanese origin now living in Canada has placed the family* mon *on a European warrior's shield.*

▼ *Just as in Europe heralds and heraldic writers drew up rolls of armorial bearings, in Japan the history and characters of* mon *were studied in great detail, especially by artists. This is a page from a Japanese artist's book of* mon.

▲ *The* jimbaori, *the Japanese nobleman's equivalent to the tabard or jupon. This example bears the* mon *of the Honda clan.*

beneath armour, was visible through sleeves and leg coverings. Small flags bearing *mon* were also attached to helmets.

In time, European influence did make its presence felt in Japan and the clothes worn by Portuguese and Spanish adventurers led to the development of a Japanese version of a coat of arms. The *jimbaori* was a sleeveless garment worn over armour and often decorated with the bearer's *kaemon*, a substitute, or lesser form of, *mon*. The garment was much favoured by the *daimyo*, or feudal lords, who controlled much of Japan between 1400 and 1416. The essential difference between the *jimbaori* and the medieval western warrior's "jupon", or tabard, was that the former was removed before battle commenced.

From the late 17th century onwards, the *mon*, which had up to then been thought of as the prerogative of the courtiers and warrior classes, began to be adopted by anyone, of any status, who was in some way associated with them – such as the kabuki actors and courtesans who helped the samurai or the palace official to forget his heavy day. As in Europe, where inroads

▼ *A 17th-century battle scene shows in vivid colour and detail the use of the* mon *by the Japanese clans (in this case the Minamoto and the Taira); battle flags and standards are much in evidence.*

were made into heraldry by the merchant classes, Japanese commentators of the period bemoaned the usurpation of noble dress and insignia by those of less ancient and less honourable status.

MON MOTIFS

The *mon* of the military elite were often adapted from those of the courtiers in a way that emphasized the former's martial nature. Flowers, which were associated with a more gentle way of life, therefore had their petals interspersed with sword blades; instead of butterflies or birds, the warriors might choose axe blades and a spirited representation of the helmet horns (*kuwagata*) favoured as an adornment by Japanese warriors.

The design of the *mon* is usually very simple. Multiples of motifs are rare, as are combinations of more than two different objects. The device may be left by itself or fitted into a frame formed by a ring, square, diamond, or several-sided border (as opposed to the shield shape that is essential to heraldry).

Mon are seldom of more than one colour, and the choice of this depends on the background. Black lacquer, for example, used in Japan for many articles from furniture to armour, tends to be decorated with the family *mon* in gold. Battle flags might be of white cloth charged with the

commander's *mon* in either red or black, though if the flag was black the *mon* would probably be in white.

Whatever the nature of the motif – whether it was a bird, flower, geometric pattern or ideograph (written character) – the *mon* was designed to fill the frame in which it was used. So much of Japanese life was dominated by the symbolism of superstition that, unlike European heraldry, the *mon* might consist of a character representing an auspicious meaning, such as "good luck" or "longevity".

Many a Japanese *mon* could be translated heraldically, bars and pallets being just two devices that heraldists would recognize as directly comparable with heraldic ordinaries. But there the similarity ends, for far from being simple geometric shapes, in Japan much that is simple carries a hidden meaning through symbolism that is sometimes several millennia old.

Although formal systems of difference marks for children or branches of a family do not exist as they do in European heraldry, junior branches of a Japanese family grouping often adopted modified versions of the *mon* of the senior branch or leader. In addition to their formal mark (*jomon*), families also had several substitute symbols (*kaemon*), which might, through common practice, be granted to another family related by marriage.

THE HERALDRY OF CONFLICT

From its earliest days, heraldry has been seen as an adjunct to conflict. Just as one person's freedom fighter is another's terrorist, so also the signs and symbols of either side can promote inspiration or hatred. Heraldry grew up during a period of conflict between Christian Europe and the Islamic East, and there is some evidence that it may have had its origins in Islamic emblems. Many shields bearing crosses or crescents are said to have their origins in the Crusades, but such symbols pale beside the heraldic imagery of Hungary, whose noble families saw themselves as the last bastion of Christendom against the Turks. At least a third of all Hungarian arms bear Turkish body parts.

The clash of ideologies spilled over into the arms of other noble families of the Holy Roman Empire. The Princes of Schwarzburg, for their part in defeating a Turkish army at Raab in Hungary, were given an augmentation consisting of a Turk's head having its eye pecked out by a crow. Another augmentation, granted to the Barons Hochpied, shows the hand of a Christian freed from Turkish fetters. But heraldry can be a witness to all parties, whoever the oppressor. In the arms of the Gabonaise district of Ogooué-Lolo, broken fetters represent the countless people who were forced into slavery by Europeans.

EUROPEAN CONFLICTS

More recent struggles have been commemorated on the shields of arms of many towns, from Sweden to Serbia. The struggle for freedom from Russia by the Lithuanian townspeople of Pandorys was recorded by a rising hawk blooded in one wing, while the infamy of the Nazi concentration camp at Flossenburg in Czechoslovakia is recorded in the arms of the nearby town of Holysov, featuring a red rose rising from behind barbed wire. The division of Germany between East and West was recorded with more barbed wire in the arms of Wennerode in Lower Saxony, where the watchtowers and trip mines of the East German border zone actually passed along the edge of the parish: the heraldic Saxon stallion easily leapt the manmade absurdity.

The manipulation of symbols by men of war is of course far older than heraldry itself, but recent conflicts provide vivid examples of this use of heraldic emblems.

▲ *Heralds of the Holy Roman Empire and Hungary point to the freeing of Christian slaves in the arms of the Barons Hochpied.*

▼ *An arm patch of a Croatian Special Forces unit during the conflict in Yugoslavia. The Sahovnica, the chequered shield of Croatia, appears in the background.*

▲ *The rose of freedom throws its head above the wire of the concentration camp in the arms of Holysov.*

▼ *The Saxon horse leaps to freedom over the Iron Curtain in the arms of Wennerode.*

The break-up of the former Yugoslav Federation saw heraldry that had remained dormant for many years revived with fervour. Slovenia adopted entirely new arms, despite having a national identity many centuries old. Other states such as Bosnia-Herzegovina, Serbia and Croatia, re-adopted heraldry that each associated with a glorious past, real or imaginary.

To the Croats, the Sahovnica – their shield of white and red chequers – was a symbol of pride worn since the medieval period, but during World War II it was banned by Tito for 45 years. After 1991 it re-appeared everywhere, on flags, badges,

▲ A Serbian military official denounces NATO bombing against a backdrop of the arms of the Yugoslav Federation, Serbia and Montenegro, Belgrade 1999.

key rings and car stickers, and was viewed with horror by Serbs. In turn, the Serbs replaced the red star on the Serbian flag with their ancient coat of arms – a cross between four Cyrillic letter Cs – in a direct challenge to the hated Croatian chequerboard. The Cs stand for *Samo slago Srbina spasava* ("Only unity saves the Serbs").

▼ In Northern Ireland both sides of the political divide make their presence known through heraldry. This display by a Loyalist group mixes conventional heraldic charges with local symbols such as unit numbers.

NORTHERN IRELAND

The tempestuous twinning of symbol and sensibility has nowhere been more manifest than in Northern Ireland. Both Republicans and Ulster Unionists know equally well the power of symbols. From the 1960s to the 1990s, the most vivid byproduct of the Troubles has been the development of "house art", or murals. Each side has seen this as a means of displaying the essential episodes of its history.

Heraldry has played a large part in the mural movement. The Republicans' desire to see Ireland united has often been manifested by presenting the arms of the country's four provinces – Leinster, Connacht, Munster and Ulster – on a single shield. In these cases the arms of Ulster are those of the Republic's province of that

name: a field of gold with a red cross (the arms of the de Burgh family), its centre charged with the bloody hand of the O'Neills. The British province of Ulster places the red cross on a white field, with the red hand surmounted by a crown.

Many tales are told of the origins of the red hand. It is not, as some would have it, a sign used by those who fought on the Protestant side at the Battle of the Boyne in 1690, but a charge borne in the arms of the O'Neill family. They were kings of Ireland, and the hand is said to commemorate the legend that their ancestor was part of a Viking raiding force. The Vikings had decided that whoever was first to place his hand on Irish soil would be its rightful ruler. The O'Neill ancestor, seeing that the ship of a rival would ground before his, cut off his hand and threw it on to the shore.

The hero of Protestant Loyalists is William of Orange, king of Britain 1689–1702. The Union Jack and its colours are used to decorate lampposts and kerbstones in Loyalist areas, and each Loyalist faction displays its badge combining the red hand and the crown. In murals, these may be placed beside the arms of Derry or Belfast, accompanying the portrait of a "local hero". In Republican areas, paintings of masked gunmen may be seen against a backdrop of the arms of the Republican provinces, and also of other national groups around the world.

▼ In Republican Belfast the arms of the city of Valencia are used to express solidarity with the freedom fighters of Catalonia.

THE CONTINUITY
OF HERALDRY

The heraldic tradition stretches back at least eight centuries, but for most of
that time no knight in armour has carried a coloured shield or worn a
helmet decorated with a crest to identify him in the thick of battle.
Heraldry has long outlived its original function on the battlefield, because it
has also served other purposes: the assertion of noble status, the declaration
of allegiance and the rallying of loyalty. Its vivid imagery and venerable
traditions still have persuasive power today, when even though few heraldic
authorities remain, coats of arms still lend grace and authority to many
products of the modern world, from cigarette packets to submarines.
Displays of the heraldry of earlier centuries are vivid reminders of our
cultural history and stability, and there are many who are proud to continue
heraldry's long tradition.

◀ *The achievement of arms of Robert Harrison,*
painted by Dan Escott.

HERALDRY'S PAST AND FUTURE

As the world enters the third millennium of Christian history, heraldry will soon be able to celebrate its first thousand years of being. Although the exact date of its birth is, of course, unknown, perhaps 2150 might be a good time to celebrate its first millennium. Certainly by 1150 the main tenets of heraldry – as a hereditary system of colour and symbol based on the shield – were already in place. What then will heraldry look like in 2150? How might it have progressed, and will it be used in any way that resembles its original function?

Is heraldry still the preserve of the aristocracy? Britain is now possibly the only nation that continues to renew its aristocracy, by the creation of life peers. Of those who take up their seats in the House of Lords, about two thirds still apply to the English College of Arms for a grant of arms and supporters. However, the number of peers that do not bother to take up their entitlement is growing. Their attitude may be best summed up in the words of Baroness Ryder of Warsaw, better known through her charity work as Sue Ryder, who firmly rejected armigerous status:

▲ In past centuries many arms featured body parts, and even a wooden leg was used as a charge. In the modern age, prison bars and six female legs grace the arms posthumously granted to a judge who often presided over cases involving prostitutes.

Those funny fellows the heralds asked me if I wanted a coat of arms. I saw how much they were asking for it and thought of how many food parcels I could send with the money. I cannot think what type of person would go for such an absurd anachronism.

Well, there are such people: they do still approach the College of Arms and feel a certain pride in a grant of armorial bearings. They may number in their hundreds in a single year, though this is unusual.

CHARGES OLD AND NEW

Those who do wish to become armigerous are taking part in a centuries' old tradition that has served and been adapted and fuelled by the fashion of the age. In heraldry's heyday, heralds compiled rolls of arms known as "ordinaries", which were catalogued according to the charges they bore. If an updated ordinary of arms were to be compiled by today's heralds, it would reflect the whole span of the history of heraldry, setting "then" alongside "now" on the same sheet.

It would be possible, for instance, to see medieval dress sense mixed with that of modern times, starting with the maunch, a medieval lady's sleeve that still graces the shields of the English families of Hastings and Cowper, just as it did in the days when such an item was actually worn some 700 years ago, and the Dutch family of van Abbenbroek still use their punning arms of a pair of breeches, in the style worn by the men of the family four centuries ago.

Beside the shields of those families might be placed that of an English judge from the late 20th century, who often had to pass sentence on the local prostitutes: he is commemorated in arms – granted (posthumously) by the English heralds – charged with pallets (representing prison bars) and six ladies' legs clad in fishnet stockings and garters.

Heraldry has shown itself to be a survivor, and will probably long continue to survive. Whereas once achievements of

▲ Trinity House, the corporation that administers English and Welsh lighthouses, had its arms granted in the Tudor period and now uses them on its helicopters.

arms could be seen on the coach panels of the aristocracy, today they are more likely to be painted on a lorry belonging to a supermarket chain, or a municipal garbage truck. Where once shields of arms were used to decorate the dinner services on noblemen's tables, today you are more likely to see a coat of arms on a china teacup on sale in a seaside souvenir shop, or on a pewter plate decorated with the arms of a German district.

SOCIAL STATUS

The longing for social recognition shows itself in many ways. The obtaining of a grant of arms is perhaps just the most blatant expression of such a need, and is not confined to the nobility.

In 17th-century France the middle classes, and even the peasantry, were encouraged to take up arms (though many of the latter were forced to accept such an honour, and were then taxed for the privilege). In Switzerland, heraldry of a domestic nature was commonly adopted by the townsfolk: builders, decorators, and even funeral directors were keen to curry favour with the middle classes. The gable ends of their houses might bear heraldic charges such as crosses, or even shields, and if the owner could make no claim to arms, his initials or the date of the house's construction could fill the space, which on

▲ *Imitation is the highest degree of flattery, and the use of heraldry always confers a certain respectability, even when it appears in a condom advertisement.*

the nobleman's house would bear his heraldic achievement. In death, the coffin fittings of the middle classes were shaped like shields or cartouches to lend an air of nobility to the funeral observances.

It is a theme carried on into our own age. Many companies associated with the leisure and pleasure industry, from playing card manufacturers to condom makers, look to an achievement of arms, real or

▼ *Arms designed by the English heralds for the Maharajahs of Jaipur appear on a plaque in Elveden Church, Suffolk, England. It commemorates the son of Duleep Singh, the Maharajah from whom Queen Victoria obtained the Koh-i-noor diamond.*

assumed, to give them a respectability associated with the traditional users of heraldry. Cigarette manufacturers notoriously commandeer coats of arms for their own ends – almost half of all popular cigarette brands are stamped with quasi-heraldic bearings in an attempt to distract attention from the message of the government health warnings prominently printed alongside.

The notion of conferring nobility through arms was behind the urge to bestow splendid achievements on those of royal or noble status who came from nations where heraldry was not known. One recipient of a regal achievement, whether he wanted it or not, was a young ward of the British Raj in India, the Maharajah Duleep Singh of Jaipur. Duly shipped off to Britain, in 1849 the Maharajah was persuaded to "present" Queen Victoria with the principal jewel of his treasury, the magnificent diamond known as the Koh-i-noor, now part of the British crown jewels. The grateful Queen, who treated the young Maharajah as one of her own family, saw to it that the coat of arms drawn up for him by the English heralds included an escutcheon of the Cross of St George – an allusion to his nominal conversion to Christianity. The Maharajah eventually moved to France, disillusioned with British control of his former realm.

LIVERIES AND SYMBOLS

Once upon a time men in armour watched over the land, bearing their personal devices on breastplates and shields. Today

▲ *In the medieval melée – the part of a tournament in which all the combatants took part together – heraldry was often the only way to identify the contestants.*

the armorial bearings they display are more likely to belong to a police force: the armoured man still exists, no longer a knight in shining armour but a member of a police anti-riot squad. Yesterday's war horse is today's battle tank or fighter bomber, though the modern German armed forces still bear the iron cross, the famed sign of the Teutonic Knights.

The medieval melée, or staged battle, with its milling knights and liveried troops,

▼ *The modern equivalent of a tournament melée can be seen on the crowded floor of the Chicago Board of Trade, where the traders identify themselves by wearing jackets in the liveries of their companies.*

▲ *The collapse of communism is vividly depicted in a Hungarian political party poster. The ancient shield of the kingdom of Hungary smashes through the arms of the communist state.*

▲ *The coat of arms of the Princes of Schwarzenberg, constructed by Franticek Rint in 1870 from human bones. It hangs in the remarkable ossuary at the monastery of Sedlec in the Czech Republic.*

of Bradfield Manor, Wiltshire, who chose to pen a satire on the rule of Richard III and his cronies, was just too much for the last Plantagenet monarch. Collingborne's political satire included the famous rhyme, "The Cat, the Rat, and Lovel our Dog, Rule all England under the Hog". Each name represented one of Richard's chief officials: Sir William Catesby, Sir Richard Ratcliffe, and Francis, Viscount Lovel. Sir William's crest was a cat, Lord Lovel's a dog and the King's badge was the white boar, or "hog". The author of the rhyme was seized and executed for his temerity in 1484.

ADAPTABILITY

Heraldry lends itself to a whole world of application, from the conservative to the crazy. An outstanding example of the latter can be found in the ossuary (or bonehouse) of the former Cistercian monastery at Sedlec, near Kutna Hora in the Czech Republic. Faced with a mound of up to 40,000 complete sets of human bones, the local authorities commissioned a local woodcarver, Franticek Rint, to put them in some kind of order.

Rint's original solution was to arrange them into the most bizarre decorations for the chapel, including an altarpiece and a chandelier. He started work in 1870 and,

▼ *The colours of heraldry are vibrantly rendered in a massive stained glass window displaying the arms of the Princes of Schwarzenberg in Prague Cathedral, Czech Republic.*

has been replaced by the financial market floor, where groups of traders in coloured jackets jostle and gesticulate in a scene worthy of King René's tourney book or a painting by Uccello. A similar scene is played out in modern-day horse racing, with the jockeys wearing the liveries of the racehorses' owners, much as any household retainer might have done in the medieval period.

In Italy the great horse race of Siena, known as the Palio, takes the viewer back to medieval times. Not only does each rider wear the colour of his *contrada* (ward) but the whole day is one of medieval splendour, with each *contrada* represented by banner-bearers wearing the dress of the 15th century.

HERALDRY AS A WEAPON

While those of a certain degree have long been afforded armorial bearings, the very exclusivity of armory meant that it could be harnessed by those who wished to pour scorn on its noble and royal patrons – and this has been the case from the medieval period until the present day. Cartoonists and more formal artists have had fun with

the heraldic beast, turning even the most ferocious monsters into cuddly figures of fun at the expense of the armiger.

The political satirist has frequently turned the statement "Know by arms" on its head, poking fun at the pompous, the proud and the unpopular through their heraldic bearings, but cartoonists and poets have at times needed to tread a careful line between acceptability and prosecution, or even worse. In England in the late 15th century, the work of William Collingborne

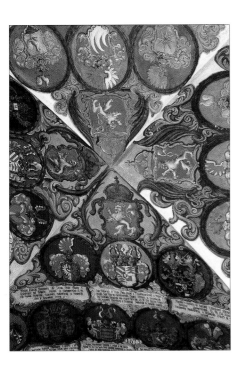

▲ *A magnificent collection of heraldry on the ceiling and walls of the chamber of the land registry court, Prague Castle, in the Czech Republic.*

▲ *Heraldry in miniature is a popular motif in jewellery. This diamond and ruby brooch, c1550, is in the shape of the imperial double eagle, the arms of Austria.*

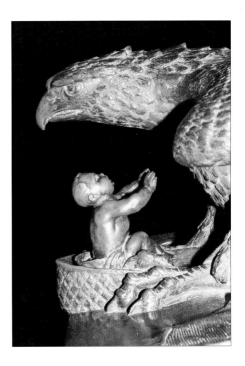

▲ *The eagle and child crest of the Stanleys appears in Liverpool's Anglican Cathedral on the monument to the 16th Earl of Derby, d1906, designed by Sir Giles Gilbert Scott.*

wishing to commemorate the new owner of the chapel, the Prince of Schwarzenberg, he used some of the bones to construct the heraldic achievement of the Prince. The eeriest part of this composition must be the augmentation granted to the family for its part in the Battle of Raab in Hungary, in which the Turkish army had been defeated. In the Sedlec ossuary, the Turk's head of the augmentation, with its eye being pecked out by a crow, is represented by a real human skull.

The Schwarzenberg arms are more traditionally depicted in stained glass in the Cathedral of St Vitus in Prague. This depiction, almost 6m (20ft) high, is kaleidoscopic in its colour, and the viewer needs to know his or her heraldry well to understand the composition.

In nearby Prague Castle, the Schwarzenberg arms also appear with many other shields of the Bohemian nobility. One of the smallest of the castle

▶ *A modern British heraldic standard, for Anthony Ryan of Bath, England. The arms are placed on the hoist (the area nearest the flag pole) and the other segments are charged with the crest (twice) and badge.*

▲ *Heraldry has been adapted to every period of its history. In this design for an IT company, the British royal arms are suggested through computer parts.*

▲ *The crest of the Stanleys, Earls of Derby: the eagle and child in its medieval form.*

chambers contains the finest collection of heraldry. The court of the land registry met here to decide matters relating to the estates of the nobility. Its high officials, the judges and their deputies, all from the aristocracy, are represented by their shields. Each term of the court's life is depicted by arranging the shields of arms of its members in hierarchical order, with the shield of the king at the head of the display, the senior judges below it and the arms of the deputies below them.

Stained glass, murals and human bones: these three examples of the ways in which it has been depicted illustrate the varied appeal of heraldry. Its adaptability and ability to evolve has been its strength.

This book shows how heraldry has used medieval fashion, the paraphernalia of war, animals, imaginary beasts, sputniks, meat hooks, mine workings and musical instruments. All are bound together and held within the world of "belonging", which is what heraldry is all about. In recent years this power to adapt has meant that it has

even taken its place in outer space. In 1992, six copies of the coat of arms of the Canadian Space Agency accompanied Dr Roberta Bondar, the Canadian astronaut, on her voyage in the space shuttle *Discovery*. Back on earth, space travel itself has featured as a motif in the arms of several Russian municipalities, reflecting the pride felt in the USSR over its lead in the 1960s space race.

The use of modern media of all kinds has also helped with heraldry's adaptation into the 21st century. A particularly striking and unusual example was to be found at the former British headquarters of the construction toy company Lego, in Wrexham, North Wales. The building's foyer was dominated by the coat of arms of the Borough of Wrexham Maelor – constructed in Lego, of course.

There was a time, not so very long ago, when the study of heraldry was considered to be the preserve of those who made most use of it – the well-to-do. Now, however, it is open to all, and heraldry societies, both national and local and all less than half a century old, are proliferating. In the age of the internet, genealogical hits on the web are said to be second in number only to pornographic sites.

USING THE FAMILY ARMS

The creativity of modern heraldic artists begs the question, how in the 21st century can one best serve heraldry while using it?

▲ *The heraldic maxim that the charge should fully fit its field was observed by A.W. Pugin when he incorporated the arms of the Talbots in his design for the doors of the Catholic church in Cheadle, England.*

There is a thin line between good and bad taste. Many people of ancient lineage would probably never be seen dead in anything as vulgar as a blazer bearing the family arms or crest; that would be associated with "new money". A discreet signet ring engraved with the family crest might be thought to be acceptable anywhere, yet, confusingly, a recently published guide to job interviews suggested leaving such a ring behind, claiming that it would suggest the wearer was attempting to show their social superiority over the other candidates for the post.

A flag bearing arms would be fine if you had a stately home to fly it from, but is not so appropriate on the average suburban house. But the hard-up owners of British stately homes, who are forced to open their crumbling piles to the public to make a living, may feel that they might as well flaunt the family escutcheon on everything from the guide book to the souvenir china mugs. In view of the declining family fortunes,

▲ *Lego bricks were used to build the local borough's coat of arms, in the foyer of the former Lego offices at Wrexham in North Wales.*

▶ *The heady delights of Amsterdam are advertised in this version of the city arms, with the traditional saltires replaced by objects reflecting the motto.*

▲ *Heraldry can be adapted to suit most needs, and most creeds. Here the coat of arms of the Jewish family of Mocatta makes use of the texts of Hebrew prayers, whose letters make up the entire heraldic design.*

their noble ancestors – victorious commanders at the Battle of Agincourt or, more probably, the owners of a sugar plantation in Barbados – are probably already turning in their crested coffins within the family vault.

▼ *The helm, crest and mantling of medieval times are here adapted to the modern needs of an English football club. Southampton's halo crest reflects the team's nickname – "the Saints".*

BUCKET-SHOP HERALDRY

From the time that heraldry became established in Europe in the Middle Ages there was a constant battle between those who had a right to it and those who had not. There were many complaints from members of the aristocracy about those, such as merchants, who assumed armigerous status for themselves. In every age there have been artists ready to design and execute armorial bearings for any client, or to supply them with coats of arms that really belonged to some other family who happened to have the same surname.

The practice is still alive and well today and is usually known as "bucket-shop" heraldry. It may be as much as some people want. However, "a coat of arms for your name" will almost certainly not have the slightest connection with anyone related to you, and although it might make a pleasant decoration it would certainly be fraudulent to start using the arms on your letter heading, or in any other way that suggests it is your personal property.

For those who have a need to be noticed, there are plenty of institutions that will take their money to help them achieve this, especially bogus orders of chivalry. Such organizations offer their members the chance to take part in curious ceremonies, dress up in cloaks and funny hats and don sparkling badges and stars. They will relieve their credulous clients of even more money as they rise in rank in the "order".

Some of these bodies may be harmless, and some may even contribute to charity. Some may boast a member of an exiled royal family as their "Grand Master". Most are simply money-making enterprises, and the area is a minefield for the innocent subscriber, especially prevalent in those countries that no longer have any legitimate orders of chivalry.

In Britain, there is also the matter of lordships of the manor, which increasingly become available for sale. A lordship of the manor is a feudal title that simply concerns the ownership of land. The property in question may be perhaps no more than a small patch of turf upon which once stood an actual manor house, now long gone. Such a title gives the owner no seat in Parliament, no peerage and no automatic right to a coat of arms (though, like anyone else, he or she can apply to the College of Arms for a grant). If you are the lord of a manor you could put the title on your letter heading, but you would risk derision from those in the know, and to call yourself "Lord…" or "Lady…" would be considered decidedly beyond the pale.

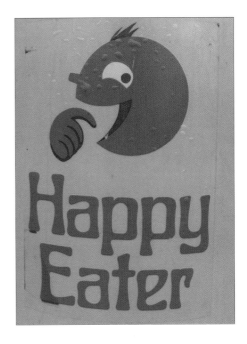

▲ ▼ *In recent years the logo has often replaced the coat of arms as a more apt device, yet it needs to be designed just as carefully. In this logo for a restaurant chain the hand of the little man, seen in the original version (above), was later removed after members of the public pointed out an unfortunate interpretation – it looked as if he was trying to make himself throw up.*

A MODERN GRANT

Few nations today still retain formal heraldic authorities that grant arms to individuals. If they have heraldic institutions at all, these tend to concern themselves with matters relating to the regulation of civic and military heraldry, though those of Canada, the Republic of Ireland and Scotland often grant arms to individuals as well as to corporations. Let us take a look at how the oldest heraldic authority in the world, the English College of Arms, approaches the matter.

THE PETITION

Before an achievement of arms can be granted to an individual, he or she must formally request the right to bear them. If an attempt to prove a right to arms through descent from an earlier grantee has failed – direct male descent from the grantee being necessary in England – or if no claim to existing arms is put forward, an individual of English or Welsh nationality, and (outside Canada) of English descent, must formally petition for a patent of arms from the Crown, which is the "fount of all honour".

Patents creating and conferring the right to display armorial bearings, and to transmit them to one's heirs, are granted by the Crown through its officers, commonly called the heralds (appointed by separate letters patent from the Crown) for the purpose, upon payment of certain fees. This is the system that has existed in England since the late medieval period.

Although anybody of English nationality or descent is entitled to petition the English heralds for arms, it is not an unquestioned right that arms should be granted to them. There are certain criteria that the heralds look for when deciding if the petitioner is worthy of bearing arms. Just what these criteria are is known only to the heralds themselves, although the publicity material issued by the College of Arms makes mention of persons "eminent" in certain fields. The matter of around £3,000 ($4,200), the cost of a patent of arms at the beginning of the 21st century,

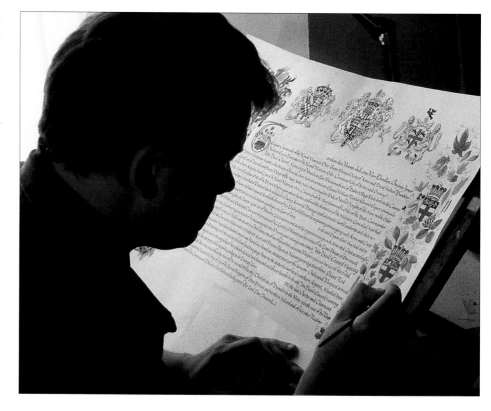

▲ *The heraldic artist Andrew Jamieson works on the patent of Baz Manning.*

▼ *Baz Manning's patent seen in its resplendent finished state.*

▲ *The patent of arms granted by Ireland's Chief Herald to the Irish Genealogical Society in March 2001. The patent is worded in both Gaelic and English.*

may also inhibit some people who might otherwise have considered the possibility of making a petition.

The whole business of payment for the patent can raise the questions, "Can arms really be considered an honour? Are they just a purchasable conceit like any other status symbol?" Whatever the answer to this conundrum, for those who do eventually decide to press forward with their petition, the business will proceed along the following lines.

The petitioner may have a particular Officer of Arms in mind when approaching the College of Arms, but it is more likely that he or she will deal with whoever is the Officer in Waiting at the initial approach. Each of the heralds takes a turn at being duty officer and will meet any casual enquirer during the period of duty. Assuming that the officer believes the petitioner to be of good character and therefore likely to be granted arms, the process can begin in earnest.

THE MEMORIAL

First, the petitioner submits a quaintly worded "memorial" to the Earl Marshal of England, His Grace the Duke of Norfolk,

who on the advice of the officer of arms will officially endorse the petition. The memorial includes the following words:

The Memorial of…showeth, That your Memorialist being desirous of having Armorial Bearings duly established with lawful authority has the honour to request the favour of Your Grace's Warrant to the Kings of Arms for their granting and assigning such Arms and Crest as they may deem suitable to be borne and used by him and his descendants with due and proper difference according to the Law of Arms. And Your Grace's Memorialist will ever pray, etc."

A curriculum vitae (CV) also has to be submitted by the petitioner. All being well, once the petitioner has been found to be of good character and generally an asset to society, the business can proceed. Prompt payment of the fee helps to speed the process up, although it can still be several years before the petitioner has the finished patent in his or her hands.

The reason given by the College of Arms for the time taken from payment to patent is the number and complexity of the stages through which it passes before being signed, sealed and registered. The Officer of Arms (known as the "agent") who is assigned to the petitioner now discusses any ideas that he or she may have for a heraldic design. Before a suitable design can be finalized, the agent is required to check through the College's splendid collection of ordinaries of arms, or armorial rolls, showing all the arms already granted, to make sure the prospective design of the shield is truly unique – not only when it is displayed in full colour, but also in black and white.

The petitioner is kept fully informed about the progress of the patent, and is made welcome at the office of the agent should he or she wish to call personally

▼ *The patent of arms of the late George Messer of Bath, granted in 1992. The designs are unique, but keep to medieval simplicity and clarity.*

▲ *One of the innovative recent heraldic designs from the English College of Arms, sketched by Peter Gwynn-Jones, Garter King of Arms, for Prior's Court Foundation for autistic students. The jigsaw piece is the symbol of autism. The crest reflects the love of cats of the foundation's founder, Dame Stephanie Shirley, and the unicycle is a sport much enjoyed by the pupils.*

(with prior appointment) at the herald's private office in the College of Arms. The agent is always pleased to discuss the client's personal requirements for an armorial design, and once this has been approved, the agent will commission an artist to paint the arms on the patent.

DESIGNING A COAT OF ARMS

Anyone desiring their own coat of arms would do well to have some idea of what is deemed good and not good in heraldic design. It is the duty of heralds (in those countries where they are still to be found), or heraldic designers, to educate their clients, whether they are individuals or district councils. It would be easy to include a multitude of charges representing an armiger's personal cares and conceits, but it is important to remember all the different ways in which the arms might be used after the achievement is approved.

One of the most popular ways of displaying a shield or crest is on a signet ring, and it can be awkward to place a very complex design on an area this size. Charges that point in a particular direction are another problem: usually they point towards the dexter and for a seal or signet application this has to be reversed if the impression is to be correct. A non-directional charge may be preferable.

A LESSON IN DESIGN

The heraldic author and designer, Arnold Rabbow of Brunswick, Germany, is often called upon to design new arms for district or community councils in his own province of Lower Saxony. His approach to the subject of heraldic design – whether civic or individual – offers a lesson to both prospective armiger and herald.

Herr Rabbow first asks for a meeting with the client – usually a town or regional council at one of its regular sittings – during which he asks for details of the history of the community, together with any special points of interest, such as local customs, distinctive geographical features, flora, fauna and dialectic curiosities. The notes he makes on the information he is given may run to many pages, since everyone will want to have their say.

He then takes out three existing armorial designs, usually all shields of German provinces. One might be complex, such as the arms of Rheinland-Pfalz, in which four separate arms are quartered on one shield. He then shows a shield of middling complexity, with several charges, and finally a simple shield, perhaps that of his own province of Lower Saxony, which bears a single charge of a white rearing horse on a red field. Herr Rabbow takes away the three shields and asks the assembly which one they remember. The answer is usually the arms of Lower Saxony – in other words, the simplest shield.

At a subsequent meeting, Herr Rabbow's next step is to show three shields he has designed based on his discussions with the

▲ *A slightly less complex shield for Schleswig-Holstein, combining the lions of Schleswig and the nettle leaf of Holstein.*

▲ *The simplicity of the German state of Lower Saxony's arms makes it the most memorable of these three designs.*

▲ *The arms of the state of Rheinland-Pfalz. A complex design that says a great deal but is difficult to recall.*

assembly. The first includes all the ideas that were suggested as charges, the second features several of the most popular ideas, and the third is a simple design, often using one colour and one metal, and with very few charges, or even a single charge. After the lesson of the previous meeting, the clients choose the third design.

Herr Rabbow does not always hit the right note. Some years ago when he was asked by a community near Wolfsburg to design its arms, he came up with a shield charged with a single red water lily leaf, a design that, for several reasons, he thought appropriate to the place. However, when he showed it to the village elders it was received with a mixture of amusement and embarrassment. When he asked why, he was eventually told that the design bore an unmistakable similarity to the glowing red neon heart that hung over the entrance of the local brothel.

APPROPRIATE CHARGES

Whichever heraldic authority would-be armigers consult, they will be asked to present some form of curriculum vitae, detailing their hobbies, military service, family pedigree (if known), any knowledge of ancestors, professions, tales of bravery or, indeed, infamy. Personal paraphernalia, ranging from pets to puns on a surname – the more the merrier – all help to give the herald or heraldic artist a précis of the individual's life and likes. Yet too much knowledge can be a dangerous thing, especially on a shield of arms. It is good to remember the principle of early heraldry – that a shield of arms should be identifiable across a battlefield. Happily, most people today do not have to worry about being clubbed over the head by a knight on a charger, but the same rule can still be usefully applied. Any

▼ *The arms of the English heraldist Robert Harrison, interpreted in a medieval style by one of the greatest modern heraldic artists, the late Dan Escott.*

▲ *This lily leaf charge designed for Mörse by Arnold Rabbow caused raised eyebrows on the local council.*

▲ *The finalized arms for Mörse, reflecting its name, derived from the phrase meaning "a marshy place".*

art student knows that simplicity is the essence of good design.

Surprisingly, there are still many designs of a simple geometric nature available for a new coat of arms, and heraldic authorities are delighted to see innovations in partition lines, counterchanging and such like, so long as the designs are sufficiently different from other existing arms. Lions, unicorns, and other ancient heraldic beasts can still be made distinct through a variety of attitudes and attributes, especially when combined with other charges.

Counterchanging can lead to a refreshingly simple and unique design. The important thing is to think in medieval terms, and if possible restrict the design to two tinctures – one colour and one metal. This does not mean that modern objects cannot be included, but can a boiler flue, or a computer chip, be represented in a way appropriate to heraldry? Any charge should be recognizable to the layman and easily translated into blazon. If the charge is a creature, its characteristics should be reasonable. It might be able to hold something in its paws or claws, but would not like having another charge, such as a key or a star, pinned on its neck or wings.

A coat of arms does not stop at the shield. The crest needs to be designed in the round. The English heralds are now taught to do so, although some modern crests still appear too much like "paper heraldry" – they could never be worn on a real helmet. Real crests, as depicted in medieval scenes of the *Helmschau* ("display of helmets"), especially that in King René's tournament book, were full of imagination, and were designed to be seen from the back and front, not just from the side as in a standard heraldic painting.

In those nations that possess full heraldic authorities, the heralds are there to guide the would-be armiger in matters of design. The correspondence between herald and client is just one of the delights involved in the making of a new coat of arms. When the whole process is complete it can literally be said to be a splendid achievement, not only for the armigers themselves, but for their descendants, part of a tradition going back many centuries.

CHOOSING AN ARTIST

If you live in a country that has its own heraldic authority, you will have had your arms granted by a herald who will have a wide range of artists and craftsmen to call upon. He may put you in touch with the relevant people, or offer to organize all the work on your behalf. For the patent itself, an English herald might choose one of the herald painters at the College of Arms to execute the painting. These artists have their studios in the attic rooms at the top of the College building, reached by an ancient staircase of many flights. Many a famous name in heraldic artistry has had his studio, as befits a herald painter, in the cramped attics of the College of Arms. Once appointed they tend to stay for many years. Several have died up there, which can pose a problem as few people venture into the venerable chambers (there is no lift).

Often the herald painter is of such renown as to have a backlog of work, and the herald may decide to farm out the work to an out-of-house heraldic artist,

◀ *The arms of the Cornish heraldic artist, Dennis Endean Ivall, painted in Mr Ivall's own characteristic Celtic style.*

▲ *A bookplate by the Dutch artist Daniel de Bruin in which the lozenge of the armiger is portrayed in a surreal style.*

whom he knows to be capable of such a commission. Should the petitioner favour a particular heraldic artist, it is essential to make this preference clear at the outset. They are perfectly entitled to do so, although any delay in declaring such an interest might cause inconvenience and embarrassment if the agent has already approached an artist of his choice.

Part of the pleasure of applying for a new grant of arms, or adapting the re-discovered arms of a direct ancestor, is choosing for yourself ways in which your personal arms can be portrayed. If you live in a country without a heraldic authority you will have no option but to deal directly with an artist.

THE SOCIETY OF HERALDIC ARTS

The organization that exists as a shop window for heraldic artists in England is the Society of Heraldic Arts, based in Reigate, England. Its craft members are expected to meet a particularly high degree of craftsmanship to join, and range from stained glass artists to bookplate designers. Not only do they experiment in different media, they often have very different styles, ranging from the graphic style of the Dutch artist Daniel de Bruin, through the medievalism of Anthony Wood and Andrew Jamieson, to the swirling Celtic creations of Dennis Ivall. Associate membership, which is open to all, enables heraldists to receive the Society's journal and to rub shoulders with the artists. Clients receive a register of members whom they can contact direct, listing the items each produces and showing examples of their work.

There are very few heraldic artists in the world, so it is not surprising that a trawl through the telephone directory will not often produce a result, although a heading does exist for them in the British Yellow Pages. It is more productive to join a heraldry society, as their journals carry advertisements from a wide variety of artists, many of whom do not belong to the SHA and may only otherwise be found by word of mouth.

HERALDIC STYLES

The painting of a coat of arms on the patent is by no means the only way in which it can be portrayed. Heraldry is always open to interpretation, and the re-visualizing of a coat of arms by a number of different artists can be a stimulating and enjoyable experience.

No two artists will draw in the same way. The house style of the English College of Arms differs markedly from that of the Scottish Lyon Court, and the personal styles of British artists can be remarkably varied and often instantly recognizable, while bookplates executed by a Dutch artist and a Canadian one will be refreshingly different from each other. Artists as far apart as Russia, Sweden and Zimbabwe may all be keen to execute private commissions and all will produce distinctive interpretations of arms.

For every occasion a coat of arms is used, it can be rendered in a different way. Slaveish copies of the grant painting do not do justice to the creative skills of heraldic artists, and can look appalling in the wrong situation. A large colour painting to hang on a wall can have a great deal of detail added to it, while a small bookplate should be drawn quite differently. An engraver will want to draw a design suitable for cutting, while monochrome artwork for stationery will be rendered with clarity of line and small-scale printing in mind.

A large number of shield shapes have been used over the last 850 years of heraldry, and each will give a different feel to the arms. The charges and the crest may all have a variety of possible designs, all heraldically accurate yet each distinctive and often unusual.

▼ *The bookplate of the English heraldic author Stephen Friar shows the versatility of the modern artist, Andrew Jamieson.*

GLOSSARY

abatement: heraldic mark of dishonour

accolée: descriptive term for two coats of arms set side by side, to indicate marriage, with the charges on each facing each other

achievement: the complete display of armorial bearings

addorsed: of beasts, back to back

affronty: of a *charge*, facing the viewer

ailettes: "little wings", shoulder plates bearing the arms of the wearer

alwyte: bright steel armour from the late medieval period

Argent: silver

armed: of a human being, clothed in armour; of a beast, having teeth, beak or claws in a separate colour

armiger: a person who is entitled to bear arms

arming cap: a padded cap worn under a helmet

arming doublet: a long-sleeved, hip-length tunic worn as an undergarment for armour

armorial bearings: the symbols borne by an *armiger* to distinguish him or her from others

armorial: a roll or book listing *armorial bearings* arranged alphabetically by the names of the bearers

armory: the study of *coats of arms*, heraldry

at gaze: of deer, looking towards the viewer

attainder: the extinction of civil rights, including the right to bear arms or titles, following conviction for treason or felony

attitude: of a beast or human being, posture

attribute: of a beast or human being, a characteristic with which it is represented

attributed arms: arms devised posthumously for individuals who lived before the age of heraldry

augmentation: an addition to the arms that reflects the gratitude of the donor (usually a sovereign)

aventail: a chain mail neck guard

Azure: blue

bachelor: a knight of the lower order

badge: a heraldic device belonging to an *armiger*, worn by retainers

banner: a square or oblong flag bearing a knight's arms

bar: a narrow horizontal stripe

baron: heraldic term for a husband; also the lowest rank of the peerage

bascinet: a lightweight, close-fitting domed helmet

Bath, Order of the: a British chivalric order

baton: a narrow diagonal band which does not reach the edges of the shield

bedesman: or beadsman, someone who was employed to pray for another person or group of people

bend: a diagonal stripe on a shield, from *dexter* chief to *sinister* base

bend sinister: a diagonal stripe on a shield, from *sinister* chief to *dexter* base, often used as a mark of illegitimacy

bendlet: a narrow *bend*

bezant: a gold *roundel*

billet: a small rectangular *charge*

billetty: covered all over with *billets*

blazon: the verbal description of *armorial bearings*

Bleu celeste: sky blue

bonacon: a mythical heraldic beast

bordure: a narrow band around the edge of the shield

boss: a circular protruding central knob on a shield

brizure: a difference mark used in *cadency*

cadency: a system of small alterations and additions to differentiate the arms of children in a family from those of its head

canting: of arms, with a design that alludes to the name of the bearer, also known as punning arms

canton: a square section, smaller than a *quarter*, in the top *dexter* or *sinister* corner of a shield

chamfron: a horse's head-guard

chapeau: a hat with a turned-up fur lining, symbolizing dignity

charge: a device on a shield or other item

chequey: covered all over with squares of equal size, in two alternating colours

chevron: an inverted V-shaped stripe on a shield

chevronel: a small *chevron*, or bent *bar*, on a shield

chief: the upper third of the shield

cinquefoil: a stylized flower with five petals

cipher: a monogram

coat armour: a quilted linen garment worn over armour and emblazoned with *armorial bearings*

coat of arms: the common term for the heraldic shield

cockatrice: a mythical heraldic monster, part serpent and part cockerel

cognizance: a distinguishing *badge*

compartment: the representation of the ground or other surface on which the *supporters*, shield and motto stand

coronel: blunted, crown-shaped lance tip used in jousting

couchant: of a beast, lying down with head erect

counterchanged: descriptive of a partitioned shield where the disposition of *tinctures* on one side of the partition line is reversed on the other side

counterermine: see *ermines*

couped: of a *charge*, such as an arm or branch, clean cut

couter: armour worn to protect the elbow

crest: a three-dimensional object adorning the top of the helmet

cross crosslet: a cross with the end of each limb itself crossed

cuir-bouilli: leather boiled in oil to make it malleable

cuirass: plate armour for the torso

cuisse: leg armour

cushion: a *charge* in the shape of a cushion with tassels at the corners

dancetty: "dancing", of a *line of partition*, a zigzag with large indentations

degradation: demotion from knighthood

delf: a square geometric *charge*

dexter: right (from the point of view of the shield bearer)

diaper: an all-over pattern resembling designs woven into damask fabric

difference mark: a *charge* added to a shield to differentiate a branch of a family

dimidiated: an early form of *marshalling* arms by halving them

dovetailed: of a *line of partition*, like a joint in carpentry

embattled: of a *line of partition*, like battlements

engrailed: of a *line of partition*, scalloped, with the points facing outwards

ensign: to place a crown, coronet, cap, helmet or cross above, and touching, a *charge*

erased: of a *charge* such as a limb, torn off

ermine: one of the *furs*, white with black tails (the stoat's winter coat)

ermines or counterermine: one of the *furs*, black with white tails

erminites: like *ermine*, with a red spot on each side of the black tail

erminois: one of the *furs*, gold with black tails

escarbuncle: a wheel-like device with spokes radiating from the centre of the shield

escutcheon: a small shield

escutcheon of pretence: a small shield bearing the wife's family arms set in the centre of her husband's shield

estoile: star with wavy points

femme: heraldic term for a wife

fess: a horizontal stripe across the middle of the shield

field: the background *tincture* of the shield

fimbriated: of a *charge*, edged with a narrow band of another *tincture*

fitched: usually of a cross, pointed at the foot

flanches or flaunches: a pair of curved segments on each side of the shield

fleur de lis: a stylized heraldic lily

formy: of a cross, having triangular limbs wide at the ends and narrow at the centre

fountain: a *roundel* bearing blue and white wavy bars

fraise: a white *cinquefoil* representing the strawberry flower

fret: a *voided lozenge* interlaced with a *bendlet* and a *bendlet sinister*

fretty: covered all over with a grid of diagonal lines

fur: a *tincture* representing an animal pelt

fusil: an elongated *lozenge*

gambeson: a quilted undergarment worn with chain mail

gambs: animals' paws

garb: a sheaf (usually of wheat)

Garter King of Arms: the most senior English herald

Garter, Order of the: the senior order of knighthood in England

golpe: a purple *roundel*

gonfalone: a large flag often hung from a cross-beam

gonfalonier: a standard-bearer of the Church

gore: a portion of the shield cut off by a curved line, like a *flanch*, but ending in a point

gouttes: small *roundels* or droplets

goutty: covered all over with *gouttes*

great helm: a helmet made with a

series of hammered plates rising to a gradual point

greaves: leg-guards

griffin or gryphon: a mythical monster with the forepart of an eagle and the hindquarters of a lion

guardant: of a beast or human being, looking out of the shield at the viewer

guidon: a long flag used in battle as a marker or standard

guige: a strap to hold a shield when not in use

Gules: red

gusset: a side portion of the shield, cut off at top and bottom by diagonal lines

gyron: a wedge-shaped *charge*

gyronny: covered with *gyrons*, arranged around the centre of the shield

harness: a suit of armour

hatchment: a diamond-shaped board painted with a *coat of arms* to indicate the death of the bearer

heater shield: shield shaped like the base of a flatiron

heraldic heiress: the daughter of an *armiger*, who inherits his arms in the absence of any sons

hoist: the area at the top of a flag near the pole

honour point: the upper middle point of a shield

hurt: a blue *roundel*

imbrued: bloodied

impalement: the placing of two *coats of arms* side by side on a single shield

impress or impresa: a personal *badge* incorporating a motto

in chase: of deer, running

indented: of a *line of partition*, with small saw-like points

inescutcheon: a small shield borne in the centre of another shield

invected: as *engrailed*, with points facing inwards

jupon: a short, close-fitting quilted coat, usually decorated with the bearer's arms

king of arms: a senior herald

knight banneret: 1 a high-ranking knight in command of a body of

men; 2 a square or oblong banner denoting his presence in battle

label: a difference mark across the *chief* of the shield applied to the arms of a son, usually the heir

langued: of a beast, with a tongue in a separate colour

line of partition: a line delineating a division of the shield

lists: a jousting enclosure at a tournament

livery: the uniform worn by a lord's retainers, made in his colours

livery collar: a chain of office indicating allegiance

lodged: of a deer, lying down

lozenge: 1 a diamond-shaped *charge*; 2 a diamond-shaped device used to display the arms of women

Lyon, Lord: the chief herald in Scotland

mantling: material protecting the back and sides of the helmet and the wearer's neck

marshal: to combine two or more coats of arms on one shield

mascle: a *lozenge* with its centre removed

matriculation of arms: the updating of family arms in Scotland

maunch: a medieval sleeve with a hanging pocket

melée: a battle staged as a tournament event

mullet: a five-pointed star

mural coronet: a circlet of stone with battlements or columns

Murrey: mulberry, a purplish-red

nebuly: of a *line of partition*, shaped like the edges of clouds

nombril or navel point: the lower middle point of a shield

officer of arms: a herald

ogress: a black *roundel*

Or: gold

ordinary: 1 a basic geometric *charge* on a shield; 2 a *roll of arms* in which *coats of arms* are catalogued according to the charges they bear

orle: a narrow band following, but set in from, the edge of the shield

pageant helmet: a helmet with ornamental bars across the face

pairle: a division of the *field* into three sections radiating from the centre

pale: a vertical band down the middle of the shield

pall: a Y-shaped band on a shield

panache: a feathered *crest*

paper heraldry: a derogatory description of accessories, such as *crests*, designed after heraldry ceased to have a practical function, which could not have been used for their ostensible purpose

partition lines: see *lines of partition*

passant: of a beast, walking across the shield

patty: of a cross, having triangular limbs which are wide at the ends and narrow at the centre

pean: one of the *furs*, black with gold tails

pellet: a black *roundel*

pencil: a small *pennon*

pennon: a personal flag, long and tapering, with a rounded or divided end

peytrel: a horse's chest-plate

pheon: an arrowhead

pile: an *ordinary* consisting of a triangular wedge with one side along the top of the shield

plate: a silver *roundel*

point: the base of the shield cut off by a horizontal line

point champain: the base of the shield cut off by a shallow concave line

pomme: a green *roundel*

potent: in the shape of a crutch

proper: shown in natural colours or form

punning arms: see *canting*

Purpure: purple

pursuivant: a junior herald

quarter: 1 a *sub-ordinary* occupying the top *dexter* quarter of the shield; 2 to divide a shield into any number of divisions each bearing a different *coat of arms*

quatrefoil: a stylized four-petalled flower, similar to a clover leaf

queue fourchy: a forked tail

raguly: of a *line of partition*, like battlements but set obliquely

rampant: of a beast, rearing up to fight

recursant: usually of an eagle, displayed with its back towards the viewer

reguardant: looking backwards

respectant: of two beasts or human beings, looking at each other

reversed: upside-down

roll of arms: a herald's catalogue of *coats of arms*

roundel: a circular *charge*

rustre: a *charge* like a *lozenge* with a hole in the middle

Sable: black

saltire: a diagonal cross on a shield

Sanguine: blood red

segreant: of a *griffin*, rearing up to fight

sejant: of a beast, sitting upright facing *dexter*

semy: covered all over with small *charges*

sinister: left (from the point of view of the bearer of the shield)

springing: of a deer, leaping

stain: a heraldic colour that is not one of the primaries

standard: a long tapering flag in *livery* colours bearing the national emblem, usually placed at the commander's tent

statant: of a beast, standing facing *dexter*

sub-ordinary: one of the smaller, less frequently used geometric *charges*

supporters: figures supporting the shield of arms

surcoat: a quilted linen garment worn over armour and emblazoned with *coats of arms*

tabard: a short tunic emblazoned with *coats of arms* and worn by heralds

talbot: a large hunting hound, now extinct

targe: a shield

Tenny: tawny orange

Thistle, Order of the: the senior order of knighthood in Scotland

tierced in pairle: of a shield, divided in three in the form of a Y

tilt: a wooden jousting barrier

tincture: the generic term for heraldic colours, stains, metals and furs

torse: see *wreath*

tourney shield: a small rectangular shield, with a notch for a lance

tourteau: a red *roundel*

trapper: a development of the saddle-cloth which covered the horse entirely, decorated with *armorial bearings*

tressure: a narrow band following, but set in from, the edge of the shield, narrower than the *orle* but often doubled

tricking: a method of noting a *blazon* in shorthand

trippant: of deer, walking or trotting across a shield

vair: one of the *furs*, represented as a pattern of blue and white

Vert: green

visor: the opening front of a helmet

voided: of a *charge*, represented in outline only

vulned: of a beast, wounded and bleeding

wreath, torse: a twisted cord of material around the top of the helmet, below the crest

wyvern: a heraldic winged dragon with two feet and a serpentine tail

yale: a heraldic beast resembling an antelope with tusks and curved horns, always shown parted

BIBLIOGRAPHY

Barber, Richard and Barker, Juliet *Tournaments: Jousts, Chivalry and Regents in the Middle Ages* (Boydell Press, Woodbridge, 1989)

Bascape, G.C. and Del Piazzo, M. *Insegne e simboli* (Ministero per i beni culturali e ambientali, Rome, 1983)

Bedingfield, Henry and Gwynn-Jones, Peter *Heraldry* (Magna Books, Leicester, 1993)

Campbell, Una *Robes of the Realm, 300 years of Ceremonial Dress* (Michael O'Mara, London, 1989)

Carek, Jiri Mestské *Znaky v Cesk'ych Zemich* (Academia, Prague, 1985)

Casas, R. D. *Arte y Etiqueta do los Reyes Catolicos* (Editorial Alpuerto, Madrid, 1993)

Cascante, Ignacio Vincente *Heraldica General y Fuestes de las Armas de Espana* (Barcelona, 1956)

Ceballos-Escalera y Gila de, A *Heraldos y Reyas de Armas en la Corte de España* (Prensa y Ediciones Iberoamericanas, Madrid, 1993)

Collectible Stamps of the Arms of German Districts and Towns (Kaffee Hag, 1900–1930s)

Corswant-Naumburg, Inga von Huvudbaner och anvapen under stormaktstiden (Ödin, Stockholm, 1999)

Coss, Peter *The Knight in Medieval England 1000-1400* (Alan Sutton Ltd, 1993)

Crouch, David William Marshal (Longman, Harlow, 1990)

Csáky, Imre A Magyar királyság vármegyéinek címerei a XVIII–XIX (Corvina, Budapest, 1995)

D'Acosta, Lino Chaparro *Heraldica de los Apellidos Canarios* (Estudios Tecnicos del Blason, 1979)

De-la-Noy, Michael *The Honours System* (Allison & Busby, London, 1985)

Dennis, Mark D. *Scottish Heralds: An Invitation* (Heraldry Society of Scotland, 1999)

Dower, John W. and Kawamoto, Kiyoshi *The Elements of Japanese Design* (Walker/Weatherhill, New York, 1971, revised 1979)

Foppoli, Marco Gli stemmi dei comuni di Valtellina e Valchiavenna (Alpinia Editrice, 1999)

Foss, Michael *Chivalry* (Michael Joseph, London, 1975)

Friar, Stephen *A New Dictionary of Heraldry* (Alphabooks, Sherborne, 1987)

Friar, Stephen and Ferguson, John, *Basic Heraldry* (Herbert Press, London, [1993])

Gittings, Clare *Death, Burial and the Individual in Early Modern England* (Croom Helm, London, 1984)

Given-Wilson, Chris and Curteis, Alice *The Royal Bastards of Medieval England* (Routledge & Kegan Paul, London, 1984)

Godlo i Barwa Polski Samorzadowej (Instytut Wzornictwa Przemyslowego, 1998)

Gonzalez-Doria, Fernando *Diccionario Heraldico y Nobiliaria de los Reinos de España* (Bitacora, Madrid, 1987)

Guerra y Villegas, J. A. de Discurso Histórico Político Sobre el Origen y Preheminencias de el Oficio de Heraldos, Reyes de Armas, Feciales y Caduceadores (Mateo de Llanos y Guzmán, Madrid, 1693)

Heim, Bruno *Heraldry in the Catholic Church* (Van Duren, Gerrards Cross, 1978, revised 1981)

Hildebrandt, Adolf M. Wappenfibel, *Handbuch der Heraldik* (Degener, Berlin, 1967)

Hopkins, Andrea *Knights* (Collins & Brown, London, 1990)

Hupp, Otto *Deutscher Wappenkalender* (1900s–1930s)

Innes of Learney, Sir Thomas *Scots Heraldry* (Oliver & Boyd, Edinburgh, 1934, revised 1956)

Janácek, Josef and Louda, Jiri *Ceské erby* (Albatros, Prague, 1974, revised 1988)

Kissane, Noel, ed. *Treasures from the National Library of Ireland* (Boyne Valley Honey Co, 1994)

Laars, T. van der Wapens, *Vlaggen en Zegels van Nederland* (van Campen, Amsterdam, 1913)

Leaf, William and Purcell, Sally *Heraldic Symbols: Islamic Insignia and Western Heraldry* (Victoria & Albert Museum, London, 1986)

Litten, Julian *The English Way of Death: the Common Funeral since 1450* (Robert Hale, 1991)

Mandich, Donald R. and Placek, Joseph A. *Russian Heraldry and Nobility* (Dramco Publishers, Florida, 1991)

NAF Veibok 2001 (NAF, Oslo, 2001)

Niesobski, Mariusz *Popularny herbarz rodzin i radów polskich* (Tychy, Kadem, [1991])

Nordenvall, Per Kungliga Serafimerorden (*Armorial Plaques of the Knights of the Seraphim*), 1748–1998 (Swedish Royal Orders, Stockholm, 1998)

Nyulásziné Straub, Eva Öt évszázad címerei a Magyar Országos Levéltár címereslevelein (Budapest, Corvina, 1987)

Pastoureau, Michel *Heraldry: An Introduction to a Noble Tradition* (Abrams, New York, 1997)

Pinches, J. H. *European Nobility and Heraldry* (Heraldry Today, Ramsbury, 1994)

Platts, Beryl *Origins of Heraldry* (Procter Press, London, 1980)

Rietstap, J. B. *Armorial General*. Originally published in the 19th century, reprinted several times since, and can be obtained through the services of Heraldry Today, Ramsbury, England.

Rothero, Christopher *Medieval Military Dress, 1066–1500* (Blandford Press, Poole, 1983)

Scheffer, C.G.U. Svensk vapenbok för landskap, län och städer (Generalstabens litografiska anstalt, Stockholm, 1967)

Uden, Grant *A Dictionary of Chivalry* Kestrel, (Harmondsworth, 1977)

Urquhart, R.M. *Scottish Burgh and County Heraldry* (Heraldry Today, Ramsbury, 1973)

Urquhart, R.M. *Scottish Civic Heraldry* (Heraldry Today, Ramsbury, 1979)

Woodcock, Thomas and Robinson, John Martin *The Oxford Guide to Heraldry* (OUP, Oxford, 1988)

Zieber, Eugene *Heraldry in America, 1895* (Greenwich House, New York, 1984)

AUTHOR'S ACKNOWLEDGEMENTS

For making this book possible and for the hospitality always shown to me, Steve and Kate Friar. For the inspiration to follow the project through, Arnold Rabbow of Braunschweig. To Arnaud Bunel, Sebastian Nelson and Peter Taylor for help with parts of the text. Thanks to William and Mrs Sybil O'Neill for the kindness in allowing me at all times to make use of Terry's library. Joan Robertson, Karen and John Say, and Margaret Smith for their companionship in the many hours I have bored them silly over escutcheons and hatchments. Baz Manning, without whose help and kindness I would have been unable to complete such a project. Mikhail Medvedev of St. Petersburg for his answering my many questions on Russian heraldry. Alice Hall for her translating letters to foreign locations. Roland Symons for his delightful and unfailing assistance.

Sr Marco and Sra Lia Foppoli for their long and happy friendship. James and Mrs Cathy Constant for the refuge they so often afford me. Robert Harrison for his unstinting encouragement. Sebastian Nelson, a true friend of heraldry from the United States. The Officers of Arms, College of Arms, London for their kindness and expertise in answering many a curious and obscure question. David Hubber with many thanks for his kindness and his artwork. The staff at QinetiQ Larkhill, most especially Andy Pike for his patience and understanding. Joanne Rippin of Anness Publishing, whose patience and tenacity have largely been responsible for making sure this work became a reality and Beverley Jollands for her excellent copy editing. Russ Fletcher for the use of his library. Mrs Manning for her excellent deciphering of my scatty notes. Daniel de Bruin for his

kindness in giving me access to his splendid collection of grants/patents of arms. Veneta Bullen for finding some of the more obscure pictures.

Thanks also to the following people and organizations for help with information or images: Peter Trier of Warpool Court Hotel, St David's; Lt Colonel Herbert A. Lippert (Retd); Mrs Malina Sieczkowska; Michael Messer; Anthony Ryan; the Staff of HM Security Service; The Central Intelligence Agency of the United States, John Uncles; HH the Prince of Oettingen; Herr Willem Jorg; Herr Gunter Mattern; Anthony Jones; Colonel Carnero, Military Attache, Spanish Embassy, London; Risto Pyykko; Keith Lovell; Gordon and Jean Ashton; Bruce Patterson, Saguenay Herald and the Canadian Heraldic Authority; Micheal O'Comain, Consulting Herald, Office of the Chief Herald of

Ireland; Fergus Gillespie, Deputy Chief Herald of Ireland; Elisabeth Roads, Lyon Clerk and the staff of the Court of Lord Lyon, Edinburgh; Andrew Martin Garvey; Jennifer Marin, Curator, The Jewish Museum, London; Dr Adrian Ailes; Mrs Marian Miles OBE; Distributed Technology Ltd, Robin Lumsden; Dame Stephanie Shirley DBE, and the staff of the Prior's Court Foundation; Adjutant Luc Binet and the staff of the Service Historique de l'Armée de Terre, Vincennes; Dr. Jan Erik Schulte, Kultur/Kreismuseum, Buren; Bruce Purvis; Martin Davies; David Phillips; Dr Malcolm Golin; The staff of the Haermuseet, Oslo; Lt. Colonel Nick Bird OBE, RA (Retd) and staff of the Royal School of Artillery; Kevin Fielding; Per Nordenval, Riddarhuset, Stockholm; Anna Lilliehöök, KMO.

And finally, to all bonacons, wherever they may be.

PICTURE ACKNOWLEDGEMENTS

While every attempt has been made by the publishers to credit sources correctly, any further information would be welcome.

AKG London: pp51t; 55b; 57tr; 101t; 112t; 125t&br; 137. **Ancient Art & Architecture Collection:** pp56t; 111t. **Anness Publishing Ltd,** courtesy Daniel de Bruin, photography Jos Janssen: pp15b; 22tr&bl; 30tl; 53b. King René's Tourney Book; 8&27tl; 12tr; 26bl; 28ml; 29tl; 30tr; 42b; 43; 44; 47b; 48bl; 50bl&bm; 61t; 66tl,tm&tr; 67tr,mr&br; 68t; 69t&b; 72m&t; 74bl; 75mr; 76b; 100t&b; 110br; 118bl&br; 119t; 122 all; 123ml; 125bl; 128b; 136br; 138 all; 143tr. Archive of Stato di Massa, Ministero peri Beni le Attivita Culturali, photograph Progra Immagini, Massa: p29br. **Art Archive:** pp45t; 60t; 61b; 62b; 92t; 108br. **Associated Press:** p139t. **Bridgeman Art Library:** pp62t; 64b; 77t, courtesy St Bride's Church; 78tr. **British Association of Urological Surgeons, London:** pp58; 82tl. **Camera Press:** p46 all. **Collections:** pp82t; 93br, Oliver Benn. **Corbis:** pp65b.**Sylvia**

Cordaiy: p70tl. **DERA,** Boscombe Down: p73br. **Ede & Ravenscroft Ltd:** p47t. **Edifice:** p121tl, Sarah Jackson. **Tim Graham:** p63b. **Sonia Halliday Photography:** pp36t, Laura Lushington; 54t; 109t, F.H.C. Birch. **Hulton/Getty:** pp116t; 143br, Stone. **Irish Heraldic and Genealogical Office, Dublin:** pp97; 98 all. **The Jewish Museum, London:** p147tl. **Leixlip Town Clerk:** p99t. **Gordon Lockie:** p91b. **Lothian & Borders Police photographic unit:** p75tl. **Maltese Tourist Board:** p57b. **Maryland Office of Tourism:** p127b. **Det Nationalhis-toriske Museum på Frederiksborg:** p128t. **Peter Newark's Pictures:** pp40br, from Froissart manuscript; 52t; 70tr; 102t; 127t. **Novosti** (London): pp118t; 119m; 120tl; 121tr. **Orlogsmuseet/ Copenhagen:** p70b. **University of Padua:** p80bl&br. **Press Association:** pp45b; 64t. **Resianische Militara-kademie, Wiener Neustadt,** Austria: p114tr. **Photo RMN,** Paris, France: p101b, Arnaudet. **Royal Palace of Stockholm/**Alexis Daflos: p129b. **Scala:** pp84bl; 104 all; 106tr; 111bl;

114bl. **Scottish Viewpoint:** pp88b; 90b. **Mick Sharp:** p93t. **Stephen Slater:** pp11bm; 25bl, Salisbury Cathedral, England; 28bl; 29bl, Abbey of St Denis, Paris; 32tm; 37m&bl, West Lavington Church; 38; 40t; 41bl; 48t&br; 49; 50r; 51b; 52b; 53t; 55tl; 66b; 68bl,bm&br; 71bl&bm; 74tr&br; 75tr&br; 76t; 77b; 78bl&br; 79 all; 80t; 81tl&tr; 82b; 83br; 84br; 85br; 86&134tr; 88tr; 89tr,mr,br; 90t; 92b; 94bl&bm; 99b; 106bl; 107b; 109b; 110bl; 111br; 112b; 123 all; 115 all; 123tl,tr&b; 129tl; 133 br; 139bl&br; 143tl&bl; 144 all; 145tl,tr,mr; 146 all; 147 mr,bl&br. **Stockczech:** p25bm, Karla Koruna. **Zeiner, Josef:** p24br. **Private Collections:** pp117tr & 153t, Daniel de Bruin; 108t, Mr Jim Constant; 81br, Eton College; 27bl, Marco Foppoli; 153b, Stephen Friar; 150t, Peter Gwynn-Jones; 130t, 131bl & 151br, Robert Harrison; 152 Denis E. Ivall; 93bl, Tony Jones; 133tr, Mike Mailes; 72b, 73t&bl, 148 all, 149 all, Baz Manning; 91t, William Naesmyth of Posso; 129tr, Mr Naumberg; 85br, Les Pearson; 119br, Risto Pÿykko; 110t, 145b, Tony Ryan;

124t, Malina Sczieskowska; 83br, Peter Taylor; 12bl, Derek Walkden.

Unattributable: pp11br; 17bl&br; 24tr, Zurich Roll; 24bl; 26tl, Ripon Cathedral, Yorks, England; 30bl; 31tl&tr; 33br; 34bl; 40ml&bl; 42t; 54bl; 63t; 65t; 70bl; 75bl; 83m; 89bl; 94t; 96bl&bm; 105bl; 108bl; 114br; 116bl; 117m&bl; 124b; 134 all; 135t&b; 136t&bl; 142t; 145tm&m.

Artworks: Antony Duke: p96tr,m&mr. Dan Escott: pp140, 151br. David Hubber: p142b. Marco Foppoli: pp17tl; 23 all; 25tl&br; 31br; 41tl, tm,tr&m; 56bl&br; 57tl; 102b all; 103 all; 105tm,tr&br; 106tl; 107t; 119mr; 120b; 126 all; 150bl,bm&br. Alfred Znamierowski: pp10 all; 11t&m; 13 all; 14 all; 15t; 16; 18 all; 19 all; 20 all; 21 all; 24tl&m; 26bm&br; 27tr,mr&br; 28tr&br; 29tr; 30mr&br; 32tl,tr,bl,bm &br; 33ml,bl,tr,&tm; 34tl, tr&br; 35 all; 36bl,bm&br; 37tl,tm,tr &br; 55tr; 60bl&bm; 67tl; 71tm&tr; 85tl; 95 all; 116tr &br; 121b; 130b; 131t,m&br; 132 all; 133tl&mr; 135mr; 151ml&mb.

INDEX